Ram Dass

He was born Richard Alpert. Like many people, Ram Dass discovered that success—or making it in our society—is not enough to make a person happy. And he wasn't sure the therapeutic couch was the answer. Some people seek fulfillment in revolution, some in "dropping out," and others in trying to milk more and more gratification out of our environment. Still others seek a solution to the problem in different cultures, philosophies, religions.

For Alpert, that search took him from being a psychology professor at Harvard through experimentation with LSD, to the Himalayas in India where he met his spiritual teacher and was named Ram Dass (Servant of God). And there, as Ram Dass, he came to understand that through meditation one can reach his inner being and learn a lasting answer. In *Journey of Awakening* he shows, in practical terms, how you, too, can share the journey.

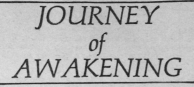

JOURNEY
of
AWAKENING

A Meditator's Guidebook

by

Ram Dass

Edited by Daniel Goleman
with
Dwarkanath Bonner
and Ram Dev (Dale Borglum)
Illustrated by Vincent Piazza

BANTAM BOOKS
NEW YORK • TORONTO • LONDON • SYDNEY • AUCKLAND

JOURNEY OF AWAKENING: A MEDITATOR'S GUIDEBOOK
A Bantam Book / June 1978
8 printings through December 1985

Photograph on back cover by Peter Simon.

ACKNOWLEDGMENTS

We gratefully acknowledge the following people for quotations published here: Marie Idol, pp. 55, 56; Ram Tirth, p. 61; Surya Singer, pp. 62, 63; Soma Krishna, pp. 63, 64; K. K. Sah, pp. 68, 69; Maharaji, p. 69; K. K. Sah, p. 73; Soma Krishna, pp. 74-76; Father Ed Lavin pp. 76, 77; Saraswati Ransom, pp. 83, 84; Tara Bennett, pp. 85, 86; Saraswati, p. 181; and, Anjani, p. 217.

Grateful acknowledgment is made to the following publishers for permission to reprint copyrighted material: HARPER & ROW, PUBLISHERS, INC., for "Roshi Taft" in The Wheel of Death, edited by Philip Kapleau; copyright © 1971 by Philip Kapleau. MACMILLAN PUBLISHING CO., INC., as well as the Trustees of the Tagore Estate and Macmillan London and Basingstoke, for poems XXIV, XXII, and XLI as they appear in One Hundred Poems of Kabir (originally published as Songs of Kabir), translated by Rabindranath Tagore; copyright 1915 by Macmillan Publishing Co., Inc., renewed 1943 by Rathindranath Tagore. NEW DIRECTIONS PUBLISHING CORPORATION for portions of "The True Man," "The Man of Tao," "Symphony for a Sea Bird," and "When the Shore Fits" as they appear in The Way of Chuang Tzu by Thomas Merton; copyright © 1965 by The Abbey of Gethsemani. PRINCETON UNIVERSITY PRESS and ROUTLEDGE & KEGAN PAUL LTD. for a poem by Ryokwan as it appears in Zen and Japanese Culture by Daisetz T. Suzuki, Bollingen Series LXIV; copyright © 1959 by Princeton University Press. RAMAKRISHNA-VIVEKANANDA CENTER for quotations from The Gospel of Sri Ramakrishna, Complete Edition, by Swami Nikhilananda, published by Ramakrishna-Vivekananda Center of New York, Inc., 1942. SHAMBHALA PUBLICATIONS, INC., for quotations from The Jewel Ornament of Liberation by sGam.po.pa, translated by Herbert V. Guenther; copyright © 1971 by Shambhala Publications, Inc.; The Myth of Freedom by Chogyam Trungpa; copyright © 1976 by Chogyam Trungpa; and Visual Dharma by Chogyam Trungpa, Rinpoche; copyright © 1975 by Chogyam Trungpa, Rinpoche. UNITY PRESS, INC., for quotations from The Experience of Insight, A Natural Unfolding by Joseph Goldstein; copyright © 1976 by Joseph Goldstein. UNIVERSITY BOOKS, INC. for a portion of "The Song of Mahamudra" by Tilop as it appears in Teachings of Tibetan Yoga by Garma C.C. Chang, and for quotations from The Hundred Thousand Songs of Milarepa by Garma C.C. Chang; both copyright © 1962 by Oriental Studies Foundation. Every reasonable effort has been made to obtain appropriate permission to reproduce those copyrighted materials included in this volume. If notified of omissions, the editor and publisher will make the necessary corrections in future editions.

ISBN 0-553-25845-1

Published simultaneously in the United States and Canada

TEXT PRINTED IN CANADA

COVER PRINTED IN U.S.A.

U   17 16 15 14 13 12

ACKNOWLEDGMENTS

In 1974 the Hanuman Foundation was formed to further the spiritual awakening in our society. One of its original projects was to promote the development of a broad base for meditation in the West. We began with a list of meditation facilities. As time went on we felt it would be more useful if we added explanations and advice by Ram Dass, and helpful quotations from a wide variety of teachers. The material mushroomed, and we found we had a book.

We approached Bantam for help in producing and distributing a full-sized book at the cheapest possible price. In the spirit of service and right livelihood the royalties from the sale of this book are being divided equally between the Hanuman Foundation and the author-editors. Thus in part the returns from this project will help to support further work of the foundation.

Four of us collaborated on this book, Ram Dass providing inspiration and text, Daniel Goleman organizing and editing, Ram Dev (Dale Borglum) nursing the project from the start and collating the directory, and Dwarkanath Bonner administering, designing, and helping edit.

The many other people who helped include:

The artists—Vincent Piazza, who with his ingenious pen gave birth to our concept of the little meditator; and Jay Bonner, who designed and drew the mandala dividers.

Laura Huxley, Soma Krishna, K.K. Sah, Father Ed Lavin, Tara Bennett, Saraswati Ransom, Surya Singer, Marie Idol, and Ram Tirth whose articles or portions thereof we are very pleased to be able to include.

Bill Alpert, Mirabai Bush, Richard Clark, Polly Constantine, David Graves, Willow Norris, Acharya Anagarika Munindra, Betsey Serafin, Swaha Smith, Brother David Steindl-Rast, and Robert Thomson, whose energy and assistance have been invaluable.

Lakshmi (Gael Malloy), who did several stages of typing with great patience and good cheer.

And Cecilia (Ceci) Hunt, our editor at Bantam, who helped us focus the book and gave us plenty of space in which to play.

And the many people who have permitted quotations to be used throughout the book, including Richard Clark and Whitall N. Perry. (A few of the quotations have come from secondary sources. The original sources were unknown to us so we left them out. We hope that you will pardon any lack of scriptural scholarship and appreciate, nevertheless, the transmission or transmutation.)

For us the preparation of this book has itself been a meditation. It has been permeated from the outset with the love and spiritual purpose that we have come to know and treasure through our guru, Neem Karoli Baba.

We offer it to you as an invitation to join in the feast.

Ram Dass
Daniel Goleman
Ram Dev
Dwarkanath Bonner

Contents

THE DIRECTORY

INTRODUCTION

When we make it in our society and then don't feel good inside—happy, at peace with ourselves—we are confused. As we strive for external security and success we anticipate that the pot of gold at the end of the rainbow will not only look good, but make us feel good. If it doesn't, we conclude that there is something wrong with us, that we need to "adjust." The assumption is that an adjusted being would be happy with success. But success usually turns out not to be enough to make us happy, and the therapeutic couch isn't necessarily appropriate for what ails us.

Disillusioned by the hollowness of success, some of us have sought fulfillment in revolution, others in "dropping out," and others in trying to milk more and more gratification from our environment—and some of us have sought a solution to our problems in other cultures, philosophies, or religions.

For me this search took me from being a psychology professor at Harvard University, through experimentation with LSD and other psychedelics, and finally to the Himalayas in India. There I came to understand that I would have to approach my inner being directly to find a lasting answer. Meditation has been the best way to do this.

There are innumerable meditative techniques deriving from many philosophies and religions. Over the past years I have sought training in and practiced a variety of these—and have profited greatly from each. The inner experiences of these past years have changed the perception and meaning of the daily events of my life: achievement, sexual desire, anger, boredom, pleasure, money, relationships, work, and play. I no longer feel that one part of me is fighting another. I experience an integrity in my being that includes the deepest as well as the most superficial. More of the time, the moment—no matter what I am doing—is permeated with space, peace, equanimity, joy, and lightness.

In this book, as in my others, I have attempted to share what I have found. In the final analysis what has been found is simple. The challenge is to say it simply. I hope you will find this book to be of use.

Ram Dass

JOURNEY
of
AWAKENING

1

GETTING YOUR BEARINGS

The Flow

There have been moments in your life when you were pure awareness. No concepts, no thoughts like "I am aware" or "That is a tree" or "Now I am meditating." Just pure awareness. Openness. A spacious quality in your existence. Perhaps it happened as you sat on a river bank and the sound of the river flowed through you. Or as you walked on the beach when the sound of the ocean washed away your thinking mind until all that remained was the walking, the feeling of your feet on the sand, the sound of the surf, the warmth of the sun on your head and shoulders, the breeze on your cheek, the sound of the seagull in the distance.

For that moment your image of yourself was lost in the gestalt, in the totality of the moment. You were not clinging to anything. You were not holding on to the experience. It was flowing—through you, around you, by you, in you. At that moment you were the experience. You were the flow. There was no demarcation between you-sun-ocean-sand. You had transcended the separation that thought creates. You were the moment in all its fullness.

Everyone has had such experiences. These moments are ones in which we have "lost ourselves," or been "taken out of ourselves," or "forgotten ourselves." They are moments in flow.

It is in these moments of your life that there is no longer separation. There is peace, harmony, tranquillity, the joy of being part of the process. In these moments the universe appears fresh; it is seen through innocent eyes. It all begins anew.

> *The past has flown away.*
> *The coming month and year do not exist;*
> *Ours only is the present's tiny point.*

> *—Shabistari*

> The Secret Rose Garden of
> Sa'd Ud Din
> Mahmud Shabistari

We try so hard to overcome the separateness. More intimacy. More rubbing of bodies. More exchanging of ideas. But always it's as if you are yelling out of your room and I am yelling out of mine. Even trying to get out of the room invests the room with a reality. Who am I? The room that the mind built.

We spend so much effort to get out of something that didn't exist until we created it. Something that is gone in a moment. We've all had moments when there was no room. But we freaked. Or explained it away, ignored it, or let it pass by.

A moment. The moment of orgasm. The moment by the ocean when there is just the wave. The moment of being in love. The moment of crisis when we forget ourselves and do just what is needed.

We each come out again and again. We turn and look and realize we're out—and panic. We run back in the room, close the door, panting heavily. Now I know where I am. I'm back home. Safe. No matter how squalid the room is, no matter how unmade the bed, no matter how many bugs are crawling around the kitchen. Safe.

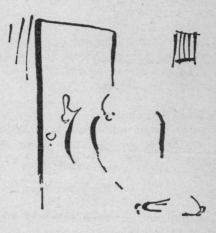

These moments appear again and again in our lives. For many people it first comes as a glimpse into other states of consciousness brought about by emotional trauma, drugs, sex, nature, or a love affair. This glimpse reveals to the person that there is something more. That he or she isn't exactly who he or she thought.

You may link these moments with the conditions out of which they arose. Perhaps it's the moment of sexual orgasm when you transcend self-consciousness. Perhaps it's a moment of trauma, of extreme danger when you "forget yourself." Perhaps it's when you are out in the woods away from people and you let down your defenses, loosen the boundaries of your self-consciousness. Perhaps when you are lazing by a stream. Perhaps when you are sitting quietly with friends you trust and love.

For surfers it is the moment when they come into equilibrium with the incredible force of the wave. For skiers it is when the balance is perfect. When our skills fit the demand perfectly, then there is no anxiety. Then we have proved ourselves. There is nothing left to do. In that moment our awareness expands.

These moments bring a sense of rightness, of total perfection, of being at-one-ment, of clarity, of feeling intimately involved with everything around you, of being free of the tension self-conscious thought brings. But you mistakenly identify the moment with the vehicle. You cling to these situations; you keep going back to them to recreate those moments. But you needn't cling to the situations that have triggered them in the past. These moments of flow can happen anywhere, anytime. Throughout life, each of us has had many of these moments. They are ephemeral. But such moments are the essence of meditation.

What concerns us in this book are the practices, that increase these meditative moments in your life, until ultimately your entire life is meditation-in-action. Then all of your acts are part of the flow of the universe. Why meditate? To live in the moment. To dwell in the harmony of things. To awaken.

IF I HAD MY LIFE TO LIVE OVER

I'd like to make more mistakes next time. I'd relax. I would limber up. I would be sillier than I have been this trip. I would take fewer things seriously. I would take more chances. I would climb more mountains and swim more rivers. I would eat more ice cream and less beans. I would perhaps have more actual troubles, but I'd have fewer imaginary ones.

You see, I'm one of those people who live sensibly and sanely hour after hour, day after day. Oh, I've had my moments, and if I had it to do over again, I'd have more of them. In fact, I'd try to have nothing else. Just moments, one after another, instead of living so many years ahead of each day. I've been one of those persons who never goes anywhere without a thermometer, a hot water bottle, a raincoat, and a parachute. If I had to do it again, I would travel lighter than I have.

If I had my life to live over, I would start barefoot earlier in the spring and stay that way later in the fall. I would go to more dances. I would ride more merry-go-rounds. I would pick more daisies.

—*Nadine Stair,*
85 years old,
Louisville, Kentucky

Relax

Thought Prison

Your ego is a set of thoughts that define your universe. It's like a familiar room built of thoughts; you see the universe through its windows. You are secure in it, but to the extent that you are afraid to venture outside, it has become a prison. Your ego has you conned. You believe you need its specific thoughts to survive. The ego controls you through your fear of loss of identity. To give up these thoughts, it seems, would annihilate you, and so you cling to them.

There is an alternative. You needn't destroy the ego to escape its tyranny. You can keep this familiar room to use as you wish, and you can be free to come and go. First you need to know that you are infinitely more than the ego room by which you define yourself. Once you know this, you have the power to change the ego from prison to home base.

All that we are is a result of what we have thought.

—The Dhammapada

The epitome of the human realm is to be stuck in a huge traffic jam of discursive thought.

—Chogyam Trungpa

The Myth of Freedom

Consider awakening on a usual morning. The alarm clock rings, you come out of sleep, focus enough to think "Alarm clock," and reach over to turn it off. Your thoughts might go something like this:

"It's time to get up. I have to go to the toilet. It's warm in here. Do I smell coffee perking? I could still sleep for ten more minutes. Oh, I forgot to do the dishes last night. I need to go to the toilet. Gee, my mouth tastes awful. I could still sleep for ten more minutes. What was I dreaming about? Who was that person in my dream? Wonder if it's warm outside. Boy, I'm hungry. What's that sound in the other room? I really need to go to the toilet. God, I wish I could stay in bed all day."

Thought after thought with the rapidity of a triphammer. Thoughts about what you hear, what you taste, what you smell, what you see, what you feel, what you remember, what you plan. On and on they go. A raging roaring river of thoughts pouring through you: "Think of me, think of me, think of me, me, me, me, me first, think of me." And so it goes all day, until you go to sleep.

You are totally in the control of your senses and thoughts. The alarm sounds and captures your attention, draws your awareness to it. But "you" are not your ears hearing the clock. You are awareness attending to your ears hearing. It's like when you're reading something so absorbing that you fail to hear someone enter the room. The sound of their steps triggers the processes of hearing, yet you do not "hear." For you are busy reading and thinking. Just as you are not your ears hearing, you are not your other senses either. You are not the eyes seeing, nose smelling, tongue tasting, or skin feeling. Only your thoughts are left. Here is where most people cannot escape. For they identify totally with their thoughts. They are unable to separate pure awareness from the thoughts that are its objects. Meditation allows you to break this identification between awareness and the objects of awareness. Your awareness is different from both your thoughts and your senses. You can be free to put your awareness where you will, instead of it being grabbed, pushed, and pulled by each sense impression and thought. Meditation frees your awareness.

A being whose awareness is totally free, who does not cling to anything, is liberated.

> *Wherever there is attachment*
> *Association with it*
> *Brings endless misery.*

> —*Gampopa*
>
> The Jewel Ornament
> of Liberation

We need the matrix of thoughts, feelings, and sensations we call the ego for our physical and psychological survival. The ego tells us what leads to what, what to avoid, how to satisfy our desires, and what to do in each situation. It does this by labeling everything we sense or think. These labels put order in our world and give us a sense of security and well-being. With these labels, we know our world and our place in it.

TV's Archie Bunker shows us an ego made public. He has definite labels for who everybody else is. As long as he stays within the labels, he seems content. When the world refuses to fit his labels—when the black turns out to be a corporation vice-president or his doctor a woman—Archie's world collapses.

Our ego renders safe an unruly world. Uncountable sense impressions and thoughts crowd in on us, so that without the ego to filter out irrelevant information, we would be inundated, overwhelmed, and ultimately destroyed by the overload. Or so it seems.

The ego has convinced us that we need it—not only that we need it, but that we are it. I am my body. I am my personality. I am my neuroses. I am angry. I am depressed. I'm a good person. I'm sincere. I seek truth. I'm a lazy slob. Definition after definition. Room after room. Some are in high-rise apartments—I'm very important. Some are on the fringe of the city—just hanging out.

Meditation raises the question: Who are we really? If we are the same as our ego, then if we open up the ego's filters and overwhelm it, we shall be drowned. If, on the other hand, we are not exclusively what the ego defines us to be, then the removal of the ego's filters may not be such a great threat. It may actually mean our liberation. But as long as the ego calls the shots, we can never become other than what it says. Like a dictator, it offers us paternalistic security at the expense of our freedom.

We may ask how we could survive without our ego. Don't worry—it doesn't disappear. We can learn to venture beyond it, though. The ego is there, as our servant. Our room is there. We can always go in and use it like an office when we need to be efficient. But the door can be left open so that we can always walk out.

Outside there is flow, no definition. We don't have to be thinking all the time about who we are. The tree is not saying, "I'm a tree, I'm a tree; I'm an elm, I'm not an oak, I'm an elm." It's just being an elm. Why couldn't we have the same harmonious relationship to the universe that the elm does? The elm is harmonious whether it's a seed, or a little sapling, or a huge elm, or a rotting dead tree. Not us. We fight the flow. We think. "I gotta stay young." Or, "It's horrible." Or, "I don't dare." That stops the flow.

> *The intelligent man who is proud of his intelligence is like the condemned man who is proud of his large cell.*
>
> —*Simone Weil*
>
> Simone Weil: A Life

If your mind is empty, it is always ready for anything; it is open to everything. In the beginner's mind there are many possibilities; in the expert's mind there are few.

—*Shunryu Suzuki*

Zen Mind, Beginner's Mind

Initially most people choose to meditate out of curiosity or to relieve psychological pain, increase pleasure, or enhance power. The goal of all these motives is to strengthen the ego. For as the ego gets more comfortable, happy, and powerful, its prison walls thicken. The ego's motives do not allow examination of the ego itself, nor allow insight that the ego is your prison. These motives paradoxically contain the seeds of freedom, because they lead you to meditate more. Meditation makes you more calm and quiet, and in this new stillness other motives, deeper motives, arise for going further into meditation. As your meditation develops beyond the level of ego payoffs, the prison walls begin to crack.

You might think of these deeper motives in many ways:

to answer the question, "Who am I?"
to awaken cosmic consciousness
to see things just as they are
to rend the veils of illusion
to know God
to tune to the harmony of the universe
to gain more compassion
to reach a higher consciousness
to become liberated
to be born again
to know the truth which lies beyond dualism
to transcend the wheel of birth and death
to abandon desire
to be free

These motives all describe the same peak from different points at its base. They all express a single desire: to escape the prison of ego.

> *From the moment you came into the world of*
> *   being,*
> *A ladder was placed before you that you might*
> *   escape.*

> —*Divani Shamsi Tabriz*

> Selected Poems from the
> Divani Shamsi Tabriz

In the process of pursuing my own deeper motives, the ego neuroses that once preoccupied me, my obsessions wih sexuality, achievement, love, and dependency, haven't all gone away. What has gone is my preoccupation and my identification with them. Now they are merely quaint and fascinating, an interesting room or passing show rather than the huge mountains and crevices and devastating potential disasters which once seemed to surround me on every side. Though I may get angry, I let go of the anger more quickly. And more important, I let go of the guilt connected with the anger. These feelings now simply arise and pass away, without my resisting or clinging to them. More and more I am just awareness.

The explanation is involvement without clinging. Not grabbing at anything. You may be attached to your lover: you say "my woman" or "my man." There's the clinging. It can be part of the flow of the moment to be with a man or woman, but if he or she disappears tomorrow, that's a new moment. No clinging. Your life just lives itself.

You're not sitting around saying, "How am I doing? Am I a failure in life? Am I a success?" You're not judging. Your life is just a process unfolding.

I'm a Ram Dass. I do whatever it is I do. I see people, teach, and write my books. I eat, sleep, and travel, get tired and irritable, go to the bathroom, touch, and taste, and think. A continuous stream of events. A flow. I am involved with it all, yet I cling to none of it. It is what it is. No big deal.

The man in whom Tao
Acts without impediment
Does not bother with his own interests
And does not despise
Others who do.
He does not struggle to make money
And does not make a virtue of poverty.

He goes his way
Without relying on others
And does not pride himself
On walking alone.
While he does not follow the crowd
He won't complain of those who do.
Rank and reward
Make no appeal to him;
Disgrace and shame
Do not deter him.
He is not always looking
For right and wrong
Always deciding "Yes" or "No."

—Thomas Merton

The Way of Chuang Tzu

The mind of a yogi is under his control; he is not under the control of his mind.

—Sri Ramakrishna

The Gospel of
Sri Ramakrishna

Your duty is to be; and not to be this or that.

—Sri Ramana Maharshi

Talks with Sri
Ramana Maharshi

The Game of Awakening

We have built up a set of ego habits for gaining satisfaction. For some it involves pleasure; for others, more neurotic, it involves pain. As you look at many people's lives you see that their suffering is in a way gratifying, for they are comfortable in it. They make their lives a living hell, but a familiar one.

This network of thoughts has been your home since you can remember. Your home is safe and familiar. It may be sad and painful sometimes, but it's home. And besides, you've never known any other. Because this structure has always been your home, you assume that it is what reality is—that your thoughts are Reality with a capital R.

If you start to use a method that makes gaps in this web of thoughts of who you are and what reality is, and if it lets the sunlight in and you peek out for a moment, might you not get frightened as the comforting walls of ego start to crumble? Might you not prefer the security of this familiar prison, grim though it sometimes may be, to the uncertainty of the unknown? You might at that point pull back toward the familiarity of your pain.

That is the criticial point. For here is your choice: whether you truly wish to escape from the prison or are just fooling yourself. For your ego includes both the suffering and the desire to be free of the suffering. Sometimes we use cures halfheartedly, with the secret hope that the cures will not work. Then we can hold on to our suffering while protesting we want to get free. But meditation does work. It gives you moments of sunlight—of clarity and detachment. Sooner or later you must either stop meditation, do it in a dishonest way, or confront your resistance to change.

When you begin meditation you may approach it as you would a new course in school, a new method to learn, a new goal to achieve. In the past when you took a new course you studied the rules of the game so you'd do well. You wanted to receive a high grade from the teacher, to get approval, or to be more powerful. As you advance in meditation, these external motives fall away. You begin to feel a spiritual pull from within. It is profound and it is scary.

Most people start to meditate for psychological reasons. It's not that they feel a great yearning for God. They're just kind of miserable. Or they feel they'd be a lot more efficient if they had a quieter mind. Or that life would be more beautiful if their hearts were more open. Or that they would be more powerful if their minds were focused. Because this is all true, the mass movements in the spiritual community market their product to play on these ego motives. If there were nobody buying, they wouldn't be selling.

For example, I recently got a magazine on meditation. On the back page it shows a couple, both very gentle-looking people. He is putting his hand on her breast, and she's looking down sort of pleased-shy. The blurb says, "Very often the meditator is attracting more potential partners than ever before." And it's true. It's not a hustle, it's true. When everybody's light is veiled, as though they had dark clouds over them, even a little flicker of light makes the meditator seem special or attractive.

The game of awakening is very subtle. At first you may buy the package of meditation because you're nervous, anxious, uptight. You want to get rid of all your pain and and have a little pleasure out of life. But you really don't know what you're buying. They say, meditate and you can have a Cadillac, but they don't tell you that when you get the Cadillac it's liable to feel a little empty. By the time you get to the Cadillac, who it was that wanted it isn't around any more. See the predicament? Meditation changes your desires in the course of fulfilling them.

You may meditate in order to get rid of your pain and increase your pleasure. When you have moments where you see your suffering as just a set of thoughts that come and go, you begin to develop a new perspective. But as you see that pain and suffering come and go, you also see that pleasure passes. If you use meditation to avoid pain and to have more pleasure, in the bargain you also come to see the transitory nature of pleasure.

While at first you were motivated only to maximize your pleasure, you are now faced with what lies beyond pleasure and pain. Enlightened beings have always said that clinging to any experience or possession that is in time causes suffering, for everything changes. Both pleasure and pain are in time. To fully escape suffering, you must seek what lies beyond the polarities of pleasure and pain, beyond time.

Time is the grim reaper of it all, of all forms. Form is always changing. Time, change, flow. Going to hold on? Where? Remember Shelley's poem about Ozymandias? He had been king of a long-forgotten desert empire. All that remained to tell his story was a broken statue half-buried in sand. And on its pedestal it bore the inscription:

My name is Ozymandias, King of kings:
Look on my works, ye Mighty, and despair!

The great sages have warned again and again about things in time. Buddha said, "Cling not to that which changes," and Christ said, "Lay not up your treasures where moth and rust doth corrupt." Both are saying the same thing, though they use different images to talk to different people. The truth is one and the same.

There are many ways the message is transmitted. If you're ready, one Zen story can change your whole life. I've met people whose lives were transformed by some simple little story. *The Way of the Pilgrim. The Little Flowers of St. Francis.*

Everyone needn't go through the big public routes at all. The spiritual journey is individual, highly personal. It can't be organized or regulated. It isn't true that everybody should follow any one path.

Listen to your own truth.

It's characteristic of the ego that it takes all that is unimportant as important and all that is important as unimportant.

—*Meher Baba*

Discourses

All worldly pursuits have but the one unavoidable and inevitable end, which is sorrow: acquisitions end in dispersion; buildings, in destruction; meetings, in separation; births, in death.

—*Milarepa*

Tibet's Great Yogi Milarepa

There once was a king who was going to put to death many people, but before doing so he offered a challenge. If any of them could come up with something which would make him happy when he was sad, and sad when he was happy, he would spare their lives.

All night the wise men meditated on the matter.

In the morning they brought the king a ring. The king said that he did not see how the ring would serve to make him happy when he was sad and sad when he was happy.

The wise men pointed to the inscription. When the king read it, he was so delighted that he spared them all.

And the inscription? "This too shall pass."

The world is so constructed, that if you wish to enjoy its pleasures, you must also endure its pains. Whether you like it or not, you cannot have one without the other.

—*Swami Brahmananda*

Discipline Monastique

Relative Realities

You have at this moment many constellations of thought, each composing an identity: sexual, social, cultural, educational, economic, intellectual, historical, philosophical, spiritual, among others. One or another of these identities takes over as the situation demands. Usually you are lost into that identity when it dominates your thoughts. At the moment of being a mother, a father, a student, or a lover, the rest are lost.

If you go to a good movie, you are drawn into the story line. When the house lights go up at the end of the film, you are slightly disoriented. It takes a while to find your way back to being the person sitting in the theater. But if the film is not very good and it does not capture you, then you notice the popcorn, the technical quality of the movie, and the people in the theater. Your mind pulls back from involvement with the movie.

The quietness meditation brings your life is like pulling back from the movie. Your own life is the movie, its plot melodramatic: Will I learn to meditate? Will I become enlightened? Will I marry, will I have children, will I get a better job? Will I get a new car? These are the story lines.

The autobiographical part of the book *Be Here Now* was initially called His-Story. Each of us has his story. History. To see your life as His-Story or Her-Story is to break the attachment to the melodrama of your story line. But be careful. This doesn't mean to push it away, to reject or deny it or consider it trivial. It merely means to surround the events of your life with quiet spacious awareness.

It is not that you erase all of your individuality, for even an enlightened being has a personality marked by all sorts of idiosyncrasies. An enlightened being doesn't necessarily have beautiful hair, sparkling teeth, a young body, or a nice disposition. His or her body has its blemishes; it ages and dies. The difference is that such a being no longer identifies with that body and personality.

Another way to understand the space you approach through meditation is to consider dreams. Perhaps you have never experienced awakening from a dream within a dream. But when you awaken every morning, you awaken from a dream into what? Reality? Or perhaps another dream? The word "dream" suggests unreality. A more sophisticated way of saying it is that you awaken from one relative reality into another.

We grow up with one plane of existence we call real. We identify totally with that reality as absolute, and we discount experiences that are inconsistent with it as being dreams, hallucinations, insanity, or fantasy. What Einstein demonstrated in physics is equally true of all other aspects of the cosmos: all reality is relative. Each reality is true only within given limits. It is only one possible version of the way things are. There are always multiple versions of reality. To awaken from any single reality is to recognize its relative nature. Meditation is a device to do just that.

Normal waking consciousness, dream states, emotional states, and other states of consciousness are different realities, somewhat like channels of the TV receiver. As you walk down the street you can tune your "receiver" into the world on any number of channels. Each way of tuning creates a very different street. But the street doesn't change. You do.

You see what you look for. If you are primarily preoccupied or tuned to the physical body, as you look at people you see them as man or woman, fat or thin, tall or short, attractive or unattractive. If, on the other hand, you are busy looking at personalities you might see them as introverted or extroverted, hysterical or paranoid, happy or sad. If you were tuned to astral identities you'd see a Leo or a Taurus, an angel or a demon. It's all in the eyes of the beholder.

Christ could walk up to you and you might see him as a pleasant carpenter, dressed plainly. You might think: interesting teacher, he has a nice vibe. If you were looking beyond that, you might see Him as Living Spirit.

Meditative awareness is a vantage point from which you can focus on any event from various levels of reality. Take, for example, your relationship with your parents, spouse, or children. Most relationships are very reactive. Your parent comes along and says something to which you immediately react and the parent in turn reacts to you. These are habitual reactions, almost collages, in which nobody really listens; there is merely a mechanical run-off between people.

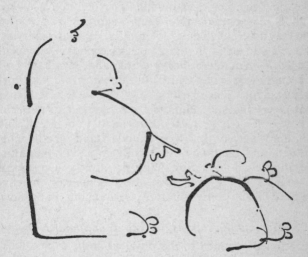

If you are rooted quietly in your awareness, there is space. In the moment, after your mother or father speaks to you, you see the reaction you would usually make. But you also see the situation in a variety of other ways. You might see that your parent is in fact your parent only in this incarnation; from another level, like you, your parent is just another soul running off karma, living out the results of his or her past actions. You are part of each other's karma. To appreciate this allows you to understand your dialogue in terms of cause and effect. Or you might understand it from other vantage points: in Freudian terms or as a power struggle, or as a symptom of the generation gap, or perhaps your parent simply has a stomach ache. Or you might see this dialogue as God talking to God.

Every event in your life is incredibly significant on level upon level upon level. Were you to attempt to think of each of these levels at the moment someone says something, you would be swamped by an overwhelming number of thoughts. The meditative awareness is not one of intellectual analysis nor one of labeling different "takes" of reality. It allows all ways of seeing to exist in the space surrounding an event. Meditative awareness has a clarity that lays bare both the workings of your mind and the other forces at work in a situation. This clarity allows you to see the factors that determine your choices from moment to moment. Yet you don't have to think about it to grasp all this. You find that you know, you understand. In this inner stillness and clarity you are fully aware of the entire gestalt, the whole picture. With no effort your response is optimal on all levels, not just mechanically reactive on one. The response is in tune, harmonious, in the flow.

> *The manifestations of mind outnumber the*
> *myriads of dust-motes*
> *In the infinite rays of sunlight.*
>
> —*Milarepa*
>
> The Hundred Thousand
> Songs of Milarepa

> *You carry heaven and hell with you.*
>
> —*Sri Ramana Maharshi*
>
> Talks with Sri
> Ramana Maharshi

What am I doing at a level of consciousness where this is real?

—*Thaddeus Golas*

The Lazy Man's Guide
to Enlightenment

2

SETTING OUT

What to Expect

When you begin to meditate you may notice changes right away. You may feel less anxious or more alert. You may be better able to concentrate, have more energy, be more at ease socially, or be more powerful intellectually. Or nothing much may seem to change. Don't count on anything dramatic. Most changes happen slowly.

There is a wide variety of experiences you will have during meditation itself, such as feelings of a pleasant calmness, a slight exhilaration, or, if you're fatigued, strong drowsiness. A common report is the feeling of the mind speeding up. Actually, this is not what is happening, but rather your awareness is standing back a bit so that for the first time you notice the normal speediness of your thoughts. Other kinds of experiences can include seeing images with your eyes closed, hearing inner sounds, or having inner smells, tastes, or new sensations in the body; these are less common. Outside meditation, you may find a sense of spaciousness in your life, a new peace.

All of these experiences, because of their novelty, have a great fascination. But they are best seen as markers along the way, signposts to be noticed, read, perhaps enjoyed, and then left behind as you go on.

There is no "best" or "right" kind of experience in meditation; each session is as different and unique as each day of your life. If you have ideas of what should happen, you can become needlessly disappointed if your meditation doesn't conform to these expectations. At first meditation is likely to be novel, and it's easy to feel you are changing. After a while, there may be fewer dramatically novel experiences, and you may feel you're not making any progress. In fact, you may be making the most "progress" when you don't feel anything particularly significant is going on—the changes you undergo in meditation are often too subtle to detect accurately. Suspend judgment and let whatever comes come and go.

Some people find meditation boring. They feel as if nothing is happening. This is another way in which the old you holds on tight; and it is important to be able to persist even through the experiences of boredom. Set yourself a period of time to seriously try meditation, perhaps a period of two weeks or a month in which you say to yourself, "No matter what I experience in meditation I will continue to do it regularly." This will give you a chance to get through discouraging experiences in meditation such as boredom.

On the other hand, the initial reaction to meditation may be just the opposite of boredom—ecstasy.

Many people find things happening after their first few meditative experiences that give them incredible enthusiasm and truly ecstatic states. This may lead them to proselytize, to want to tell others. I suggest that in the early stages you move gently and slowly. Don't overreact.

Positive experiences may well be followed shortly after by indifference. If you don't keep your experiences to yourself you may find yourself caught in a social situation in which you have created a monster of enthusiasm which you must pump up in a false way in order to be consistent. It is wise in all stages of meditation to be calm and not to make too much of any of your experiences, positive or negative. Merely notice them and keep on with your meditation.

Some people overreact to their experiences and go around saying that they're enlightened—they're the Buddha, they're the Christ. This is a self-deception. Others go to the other extreme and say they are nothing, they are unworthy. Both these positive and negative attitudes have to go.

Be open to whatever experiences come in your meditation. Don't get fixed on a model of what meditation is supposed to feel like. Set aside judging, being critical, having opinions. Meditation is giving up models and labels.

The less you expect, the less you judge, the less you cling to this or that experience as significant, the further you will progress. For what you're seeking is a transformation of your being far beyond that which any specific experience can give you. It is important to expect nothing, to take every experience, including the negative ones, as merely steps on the path, and to proceed.

When you practice zazen, just practice zazen. If enlightenment comes, it just comes.

—*Shunryu Suzuki*

Zen Mind, Beginner's Mind

Your Body

Body, posture, and health determine, in part, the quality of meditation. Until your meditation becomes deep it will be difficult, for example, to override physical pain. In a sitting meditation your neck may hurt, your spine feel tense, you may be restless and unable to find a comfortable position. If so, you should work on your body. Hatha yoga is designed to prepare your body to sit still. The series of stretching positions and movements (called asanas) help your body become straight, clear, and at rest for sitting. (There is a sample of hatha yoga in the section on movement in the next chapter.)

When you first start to do a sitting meditation, find any comfortable position with your back straight. If you sit on the floor, raise your bottom with a pillow. A straight back keeps you alert. Sit so you can stay still for a long time without moving or having to think about your body. If you're not used to sitting on the ground with crossed legs, don't try it right away.

A straight-backed chair is fine for beginners. Later, as your meditation gets stronger, you can gradually try sitting crosslegged, in a half lotus or full lotus. It doesn't really matter whether you sit on a straight-backed chair or crosslegged or lie flat on your back. It is important that your back and head be straight. If this is difficult, just be as alert as you can.

When I sit in meditation, first I find a comfortable position. If my body bothers me because of discomfort or pain, meditation is more difficult. I sit either in the half lotus on a firm pillow or in a chair. To sit half lotus (crosslegged with one foot resting on the opposite thigh), you may need to do hatha yoga postures daily to loosen up your ankle, calf, knee, and thigh. The advantage in sitting half lotus is that it is a very stable position. This physical stability makes it easier for you to enter meditative states. Then your body becomes a meditation temple.

> *I have visited in my wanderings shrines and other places of pilgrimage. But I have not seen another shrine blissful like my own body.*
>
> —*Saraha*
>
> Buddhist Texts

Food for Thought

Diet is important to your practice. Within certain limits the food you eat affects the quietness of your mind. Let your diet change gently and naturally; be honest with yourself. Don't force changes: to try to give up a food too soon merely makes you focus on it all the more. If you think of nothing else but juicy steaks while eating your soya burger, you're going too fast. The point is to let go of the thoughts as well as the food—your attachments are more important than whether you eat or abstain from certain foods.

Some foods make you more agitated and stimulated, so it's hard for you to sit quietly. Your sensitivity to such foods will change. As you come to feel lighter, for example, red meats may seem too heavy for you. Slowly your diet may shift away from meat, toward chicken, fish, eggs, and finally perhaps just fruits, grains, and vegetables. In the same way, you may drift away from sugar, alcohol, and cigarettes. Remember: there are no specific rules to this game. Beings have become enlightened eating anything and everything.

Be sure to honor your dietary needs of the moment. Be careful as you shift your diet not to upset your protein balance. If you are moving toward a vegetarian diet, use protein supplements if necessary. Keep up your vitamin intake as well, particularly B and C, minerals, and perhaps E. Flagging energy and anemia are obstacles to deep meditation.

Fasting is also useful to purify and cleanse your body. But be moderate. You should do extensive fasting only with the guidance of a teacher.

Along with growing awareness about your food, it is well to become more sensitive to what you feed your mind. Some spiritual systems, like macrobiotics, are built around diet. Very often, however, people focus on food with little attention to what they put in their minds. To eat sprouts, grains, and fruit and then watch sadistic violence and greed-ridden games on television is hardly feeding your spirit in a balanced way. Be conscious of both kinds of food.

As you progress you become less excited about collecting the melodrama of the daily news; for as you delve within yourself, you want less and less to feed your mind unnecessary images and thoughts that agitate it. You simplify what you talk about, what you watch, and what you read. You find yourself drawn to new kinds of books, perhaps books written by those who speak from the quiet of meditation. They are invaluable in creating a space in which your mind can become quiet also.

We stuff our minds with trivia just to fill the emptiness we feel. When I sit in a New York subway train and watch people read the *Daily News*, I see how much unnecessary information they are collecting. I once spent six months in a temple in India. I had no communication with the rest of the world. It was during an election period, and I did not know who was the new president of the United States. This was ironic, for as a psychologist one of the questions on tests I had given to mental patients was, Who is the president of the United States? When I returned from India, I found that in about one day of reading back issues of magazines, I caught up with the significant events of the last half-year. At the same time I escaped being preoccupied with the personalities, events, and drama of the news. One can be a responsible citizen without allowing one's mind to be captured by the media and their need to create news. There is a saying: "When you sweep out the temple courtyard, don't stop to read the old newspapers."

We act as if the human intellect were a runaway monster which must be fed continuously at all costs. I myself am becoming less of an information addict. Now I sit on the subway doing mantra or following my breath and end the trip tranquil and ready for the next mo-

ment. Meanwhile others, immersed in collecting information to feed their minds, end the trip more tense, fragmented, and speedy than when they started.

> *Do not therefore ascribe blame or praise to the eating (or not eating) of foods, or to the drinking (or not drinking) of wine, but ascribe praise, or woe, unto those who make use properly or improperly of meat and drink.*
>
> —*Palladius*
>
> Stories of the Holy Fathers

> *What need of so much news from abroad, when all that concerns either life or death is at work within us?*
>
> —*William Law*
>
> The Perennial Philosophy

The teaching which is written on paper is not the true teaching. Written teaching is a kind of food for your brain. Of course it is necessary to take some food for your brain, but it is more important to be yourself by practicing the right way of life.

—*Shunryu Suzuki*
Zen Mind, Beginner's Mind

Where to Meditate

Meditation is work. It helps to have a physical space to work in—a room or corner set aside for meditation. All you do there is meditate, study holy books, or chant. Do nothing there that's not part of your spiritual practice. If you have the choice, you may want to keep this corner of the room simple, just bare white walls. Or you may decorate it in keeping with its unique part in your daily routine. A candle or stick of incense may do. Or maybe add a few pictures of beings who inspire you—Christ, Buddha, or Ramakrishna. You might also keep a few helpful books there such as the Bible or the Bhagavad Gita.

When you sit down in that corner or go into that room, make sure that all you do there is meditate or study. Don't use it for any other purpose. Dedicate it to the awakening of your spiritual self. Such a space becomes invested with the effects of your every attempt at meditation. You consecrate it. If you keep its use

pure, the space fills with a vibration that smooths your way for meditation.

Find a quiet place, free of distractions. A beginning meditator is easily distracted. In deeper meditation it won't matter what your surroundings are, but in the beginning the outer quiet helps you find an inner silence. Familiar places, where there are few things that catch your attention, are best.

While it is desirable to have a specific space or a private corner for your meditation, it is not necessary. Once you have a meditative practice that suits you, you can do it most anywhere. You will find many ordinary moments in your life are perfect for meditation: when you are waiting in the dentist's office, or for the bus, or sitting on a subway. Moments which usually were times for boredom or wandering thoughts become a gift—a chance to meditate.

Often I have had my deepest meditations when I least expected them: not when I was sitting on my meditation cushion surrounded by other meditators, but while driving my car, or sitting in an airplane, or waiting in the Internal Revenue Service office, or standing in line in the New Delhi railway station. Even standing in a crowded subway you can go within. The stronger your meditation, the less your surroundings distract you. Eventually, you will be able to meditate anywhere, anytime.

> When a monk goes into a tavern, the tavern becomes his cell, and when a haunter of taverns goes into a cell, that cell becomes his tavern.
>
> —Hujwiri
>
> Kashf al-Mahjub

> The happiness of solitude is not found in retreats. It may be had even in busy centres. Happiness is not to be sought in solitude or in busy centres. It is in the Self.
>
> —Sri Ramana Maharshi
>
> Talks with Sri Ramana Maharshi

When to Meditate

When should you meditate? Timing, like place, is important in the early stages. Just as you should find a comfortable place to sit, you should find a convenient time of day for your meditation. If you've just eaten a large meal, you may become drowsy. If you're hungry, that too may interfere with your meditation. Most serious meditators practice at least twice a day, in the morning after awakening, and some time during the evening. The first sitting puts your mind in a relaxed state before your day begins. The second sitting refreshes you for the evening.

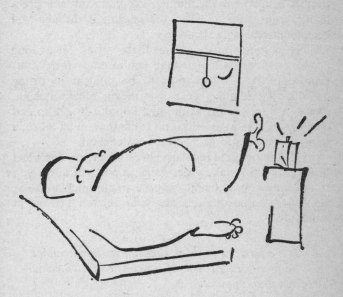

It's best to meditate each day at the same time in your daily rhythm—for example, before leaving the house each morning and before dinner each evening. Find or make times when you can be free of concerns and responsibilities for a while. Let someone else answer the phone or mind the children. The habit of meditating daily provides an outer framework for the inner process of meditation. So be regular.

In the beginning, twenty or thirty minutes is a good length for each meditation session. You can gradually extend the length of your sitting by increments of five minutes or so up to forty-five minutes to an hour, as your schedule and inclinations allow.

You can keep track of the time with a kitchen timer or with a watch, opening your eyes briefly to see if the time is up. These quick glimpses to check on time won't disrupt your meditation. As you continue practicing, your sense of when the session is through will become increasingly accurate.

How long you should meditate varies. Sit as long as you can, but no longer than you're ready for. Whatever time you set for yourself, be diligent in sitting out the allotted time, even if it means clockwatching. Don't stop meditating at the first impulse to get up and do something else—meditation is the time to let all such thoughts come and go, without attachment.

If you meditate regularly, even when you don't feel like it, you will make great gains, for it will allow you to see how your thoughts impose limits on you. Your resistances to meditation are your mental prisons in miniature.

> *It is a mistake to think that the sadhana cannot be practiced for lack of time. The real cause is agitation of mind.*
>
> —*Swami Brahmananda*
>
> Discipline Monastique

With Whom to Meditate

Find other people with whom you can share your interest in meditation. They can become your support system. The nineteenth-century Indian saint Ramakrishna remarked that a beginner in spiritual life is like a young tree that needs to be circled with a fence for protection. This is the seeker's need for satsang, a group of fellow aspirants who strengthen one another's sometimes shaky faith on the journey. In sharing your experiences with other meditators you benefit from their feedback. You get a broader view of what's possible in meditation than you would have if you meditated alone.

To meditate with a group will certainly strengthen your practice. Your mind will create ruses to disrupt your practice. At those moments when you feel bored or agitated, if you were alone you might be inclined to stop and get up. An agreement to meditate with another person for a set time keeps you in place. When you sit with others, the pretexts that arise in your mind for quitting meditation are more often simply observed, rather than acted upon.

At a more profound level, meditating with sat-sang creates a group vibration that often intensifies your meditation. It's as if there is a summation of quieting thoughts that pass from one person to another. I have often come into meditation halls in Japan and in the United States where the hall itself would seem thick with these vibrations. Many churches and temples provide this peaceful space.

Your group could meet in someone's living room, light a candle and perhaps some incense, and sit quietly for an agreed period of time. Gradually you might add other activities done in a meditative spirit. For example, eat together afterward, or take turns reading aloud from books about meditation, or chant together.

Finding such a group may be as simple as checking bulletin boards or putting up a note in the laundromat, health-food store, or bookstore, asking if anyone would like to meditate with you one or two evenings a week. Maybe a friend would like to meditate with you. Or you might sit in at a Quaker meeting, for their form is itself meditative in nature. There may already be a neighborhood group that meets informally in someone's home, or in an adult-education evening course, or perhaps regular sittings of some meditation group.

The directory at the back of this book may help you find people with whom you can sit. There are listings for nationwide meditation organizations and for smaller meditation groups—perhaps there is one in your community. Each group has its own style and view, and in the long run, any one of them may or may not be attractive to you. Initially it makes little difference so long as you feel comfortable with the group. Later, with more experience, you may find you prefer to drop out of one group or join another. But don't waste too much time in the beginning by trying to judge this group or that, this individual or that. The important thing is to start meditating.

For where two or three are gathered together in My Name, there am I in the midst of them.

—*Matthew 18:20*

The New Testament

3

PICKING
A
PATH

Which Method is for Me?

Most people don't realize what a wide variety of possibilities there are among meditative practices. Perhaps because of mass advertising, they've come to identify meditation with a specific practice, like sitting with your eyes closed to repeat mantra, as in the TM technique, or facing a blank wall to empty your mind, as in zazen. The choice of methods available to help you gain inner freedom is actually quite diverse. There are many, many methods and groups to choose from, besides the few well-known names.

People sometimes are turned off by meditation when they begin with a method that is too hard for them. It helps to use a method which uses your natural tendencies, and so reinforces a positive attitude. At the outset choose a method that harmonizes with what you are already good at, a method that interests you. Follow it until you feel a strengthened connection to a quietness of mind, to a meditative awareness, to God.

Look at your life and see what has really turned you on. Perhaps you are very athletic. To sit motionless for an hour would be to fight your body. Instead you might begin with karate or kung fu and then go on to t'ai chi or some other moving meditation. If you are more sedentary or scholarly you might start by reading Krishnamurti or Buddhist doctrine and practicing vipassana meditation. An emotional person might find these practices too dry and be drawn instead to Sufi dancing or to singing or chanting. These are also forms of meditation.

As your meditation develops, you may find yourself drawn back to the methods you avoided when you began. You may get frustrated because the fire is not hot enough and you want to move faster than easier methods permit. So you work with one method after the next until all aspects—heart, mind, and body—are balanced. If you begin with one of them, sooner or later you will probably want to integrate the others as well. It makes no difference which technique you start with. Try to sense what you're ready for and what you need. Above all, be honest with yourself.

A useful tactic is to pick a method that feels right and do it for two weeks. During this trial run, agree with yourself, "I will treat all my negative reactions to this form of meditation as merely thought forms prompted by my ego to keep me from taking it seriously.

I will suspend judgment, criticism, and doubt." At the end of two weeks, you're free to evaluate the method. Or, give yourself three months or six months.

Plunge in. Eventually you have to stop trying to figure out where you are if you want to get somewhere else. Imagine Lindbergh flying from New York to Paris with only his little periscope sticking out of the *Spirit of St. Louis* to guide him. He can calculate his position from the stars, but all he sees is that there's a lot of ocean below. He doesn't really know whether he's miscalculated or not until he arrives. He's going on the faith that he's getting there and that it will all work out. That's what the spiritual journey is like. You need discipline to persist when the going gets rough or uncertain, faith to stick it out—to the end.

> *Does one really have to fret*
> *About enlightenment?*
> *No matter what road I travel,*
> *I'm going home.*
>
> *—Shinsho*

A Trial Run

If you've never done any meditation before, you can try one right now. First of all, quiet down a bit and find a comfortable seat. Your favorite armchair will do, or, if you want to sit crosslegged, try that.

Sit up as straight as you can without making yourself uncomfortable. Sooner or later you'll have to learn to sit with your back straight and your head, neck, and chest in a line. For the moment just get really comfortable. Stop reading for a few moments and get comfortable.

Now as you sit comfortably, your mind wanders. It turns to fantasies, memories. You think, what is this about, this meditation? What am I doing? If you don't hold on to any of these thoughts, but just let them keep flowing by, you are already in the act of meditation. This is it. You're doing it. But one of these thoughts may grab at you and lead you off into plans, fantasies, memories, or problem solving. Then you're just thinking, not meditating.

Here's a way you can keep from getting too lost in your thoughts. See your thoughts go by as if they were autumn leaves floating down a stream. But focus on the stream. The leaves drift by, being moved this way and that by the eddying water. On some there are drops of water that glisten in the sunlight. Let the leaves, the thoughts, float by, but keep your attention on the water itself. Your mind may dwell on a sound, a memory, a plan, or any of a thousand things. When you notice your mind clinging to any of these, these leaves, very gently bring it back to the stream, back to the water flowing. Let the leaves float by. Don't get angry because your attention got caught, for that anger is just another leaf. Don't get frustrated, because your attention will get caught thousands of times. Each time, very gently but firmly bring it back to the flowing water. Now try this meditation for a few minutes.

This is the beginning of the quiet mind.

Many Paths

Sitting quietly with eyes closed is only one of many ways to meditate. People can meditate while dancing and chanting the names of God, while making a cup of tea, or during practically any activity. And for those who meditate with eyes closed, there is a wide variety of inner practices. It is not what you do with your body but what you do with your mind that counts in meditation.

Sampling the variety of meditative practices in the sections that follow, you will come to appreciate that there is a wide range of possibilities. While all of the practices described here lead ultimately to the same result, each emphasizes different qualities of the meditative state. Thus, for example, one type of meditation will emphasize quietness of mind, another tuning to the forces of the universe, another compassion. I think of this difference as merely a matter of timing, for although each of these practices starts with one quality or another, ultimately all the qualities come into play in the course of the seeker's path.

To pursue any method brings you to more subtle considerations and more advanced levels of practice. What initially may have been irrelevant takes on significance later. For example, take mantra. When you begin to work with mantra, any one will do. Later, however, you become aware of nuances, such as the subtle differences between mantras and the states to which they bring you.

Each method reveals subtleties as you advance in it. Experiment until you find one that seems right for you. Then focus on it wholeheartedly, either on your own or with a teacher.

Concentration

Concentration is the root skill in all meditation practices. The meditator must be able to keep the mind fixed on a specific task or object, and let distractions go by, no matter which technique is used. This skill is simple in definition, but takes great patience to develop in practice. To begin developing concentration you need simply pick some object, thought, or part of the body and fix your mind on it for a fixed length of time. When your mind wanders, return your focus gently but firmly to the object of your meditation. Once you develop even a little concentration—which happens after a relatively short period of meditation—you will find it enhances all other methods of spiritual practice.

One simple exercise for bringing your awareness to a single object is concentrating on a candle flame. Place a candle in front of you a foot or so away and focus on the flame. As you look at the flame, countless thoughts will float by about the candle, the flame, meditation, sounds you hear, feelings in your body, and so forth. In each case you notice the thought, let it go, and merely come back to an awareness of the candle flame. By gently but firmly trying to keep your attention focused on the candle flame, you begin to see your thoughts and senses grabbing at your awareness. You become aware of the process of attachment.

This training in one-pointedness of mind is the first step in learning not to cling. The goal of meditation is to free your awareness from its identification with your senses and thoughts. So freed, your awareness permeates everything but clings to nothing.

> *The attainment of the one-pointedness of the mind*
> *and the senses is the best of austerities.*
>
> —*Sri Sankaracharya*
>
> A Thousand Teachings

> *The very essence of meditation is one-pointedness*
> *and the exclusion of all other considerations,*
> *even when these considerations happen to be*
> *enticing.*
>
> —*Meher Baba*
>
> Discourses

Try these directions for mindfulness of breathing, a basic concentration practice: When you're ready to meditate, close your eyes and bring your attention to the motion of your breath as it enters and leaves your nostrils. Keep your focus at the nostrils, noting the full passage of each in-breath and out-breath, from beginning to end. Don't follow the breath into your lungs or out into the air; just watch its flow in and out of the nostrils. If you can, notice the subtle sensations of the breath as it comes and goes. Be aware of each in-breath and out-breath as it passes by the nostrils, just as a doorman watches each person who comes and goes through a door.

Attend to the feeling of the breath. Don't try to imagine it or visualize it. Note the sensation of the breath just as it is, exactly as you feel it. You may feel the breath at the rim of the nostrils, or just inside the nose, or on the upper lip beneath the nose. The sensations you feel will change—you may sometimes feel the breath like the light touch of a feather, like a dull throb, or as an intense point of pressure on your lip, or in countless other ways. There is no "right" way for the breath to feel; just be aware of what is. Each time you notice your mind has wandered to other thoughts, or is caught by background noises, bring your attention back to the easy, natural rhythm of your breathing.

Don't try to control your breath. Simply watch it. Fast or slow, shallow or deep, the nature of the breath does not matter. Your full attention to it is what counts. If you have trouble keeping your mind on the breath, count each one up to ten, then start over again at one. Or, to anchor your mind on your breath, you can occasionally make a strong, deliberate inhalation and exhalation. Then let your breath return to its normal rate.

Whenever you realize you're thinking about something else, return your awareness to your breath. Don't try to fight off thoughts. Just let them go.

If sounds distract you, do the same: Let them be and simply start watching your breath again. If aches or itches bother you, slowly move or shift to ease them if you must. But keep your mind on breathing while you do it.

Your mind will wander, and when you first start to meditate you may be acutely aware of how active it is. Don't worry about it. Just keep returning your attention to your breath, letting go of whatever the mind wanders to. This is the essence of meditation: letting go of your thoughts.

Mantra

A word, a name of God, or a spiritual phrase that is repeated over and over again is known as a mantra. The practice of mantra is an effective way to concentrate your mind. But as important as concentrating your mind is what you concentrate on. Although the mind can focus on anything, only certain words can qualify as mantra. A mantra must connect you with the sacred. Most of them focus you on God through repetition of a divine name. A mantra provides a boat with which you can float through your thoughts unattached, entering subtler and subtler realms. It is a boat that steers itself—to the threshold of God.

The use of mantra sets up one thought, one wave, that repeats over and over again, dislodging your attachment to all other thoughts, until they are like birds gliding by. For example, you can quietly or silently repeat the Sanskrit mantra "Ram," a name of God. Just repeat "Ram, Ram, Ram, Ram." A billboard goes by and disappears into "Ram, Ram, Ram." If a passenger in your car asked what you were doing, you might tell him, "I'm saying 'Ram, Ram, Ram' " instead of, "I'm taking my foot off the accelerator." All you're thinking of consciously is the mantra, while the driving is taken care of automatically. In the same way you begin to see your life from the detached vantage point of the mantra.

Although groups like TM recommend that beginners not meditate more than twenty minutes twice daily, I have found it useful to sit quietly and do nothing else but practice mantra for longer periods. You can work concentratedly with mantra for an extended time, three or four hours, or even longer. In this way you will become intimate with the sound of the mantra and you will begin to surrender into it, to merge.

Offer all your thoughts as a sacrifice to the mantra. If you think, "This isn't going to work," take that thought and imagine yourself offering it to the mantra on a golden tray with a silk handkerchief, incense, and a candle. Offer it as you continue to repeat the mantra undisturbed. Keep offering your thoughts, your doubts, discomforts, boredom, even your sore throat.

Later, when you have gotten up to go about the business of the day, keep remembering the mantra; invite it to stay with you. You can coordinate the mantra with your steps as you walk or with any rhythmic activity. No matter what else you do, keep doing the mantra. If you are typing, each time you hit the carriage return, "Ram"; if you are talking, each time there is a pause, "Ram."

One very effective and widely used method of remembering a mantra is the "counting" of beads with a rosary or mala. Any easily handled beads will do. You pass the beads across your fingers, bead by bead, with

each repetition of the mantra. If your mind wanders, the activity of the hand or the touch of a bead will remind you of the mantra. The rhythm becomes more compelling, the experience more total as your body works in harmony with the mind. Also, you can use the beads to keep track of how many times you have repeated the mantra as part of your daily meditation routine.

As you practice you will notice that when your mind is calm the mantra will be delicate and subtle. When your mind is agitated the mantra will be as strong and gross as is needed. Just keep bringing your mind back to the mantra and let it make you more and more still.

Some examples of mantra besides "Ram" are "Aum," the one basic sound or totality of all sound; "Aum Mani Padme Hum" (pronounced AH-OWM MAH-NAY PAHD-MAY HOOM), the Tibetan mantra meaning "The All is a precious jewel in the lotus flower which blooms in my heart"; and the Buddhist mantra "Gate Gate Paragate, Parasamgate, Bodhi Svaha" (pronounced GAH-TAY GAH-TAY PAH-RAH GAH-TAY PAH-RAH-SAHM GAH-TAY BOW-DEE SWAH-HAH), which means "Beyond, Beyond, the Great Beyond, Beyond that Beyond, to Thee Homage." As far as you can think, as far in as you can go, these mantras keep going beyond, drawing you on until finally you go beyond any need of the mantra into the source of all thought.

There are various stages as your practice of a mantra deepens. An exquisite description of this process is found in *The Way of a Pilgrim*, written by an unknown Russian whose practice was to repeat the Jesus Prayer.

After no great lapse of time I had the feeling that the prayer had, so to speak, by its own action passed from my lips to my heart. Further there came into my heart a precious warmth. None of these things made me feel at all cast down.

It was as though they were happening to someone else and I merely watched them. The prayer brought sweetness into my heart and made me unaware of everything else.

How fast this takes place depends on how wide open and ready you are. But before too long, if practiced continually, a mantra becomes somewhat autonomous, like a top spinning inside which every now and then needs just a flick to keep it going. Eventually, it will go on with no need of encouragement, as in the case of the saint Kabir who said, "Ram practices my japa [repetition of God's name] while I sit relaxed." It's a blissful moment when you notice that happening: Instead of doing mantra, the mantra is doing you.

If your spirit is ripe for it, you might only have to hear a mantra or see it in a book to sense that it is the right vehicle for you. Or you might try a particular mantra and find, when you begin to use it, that nothing happens. It may feel foreign and irrelevant as you repeat it. Don't worry about your pronunciation. In the course of time it will take care of itself. Give a mantra a chance. Then, if it still feels strange and uncomfortable, perhaps it is not the right mantra for you. No harm done. Just try another.

Mantras can range from a simple word or phrase which you might want to work with, to the Sanskrit and Tibetan mantras designed so that each syllable activates a particular chakra or a particular type of consciousness. A powerful English mantra comes from Herman Rednick: "I am a point of sacrificial fire held within the fiery Will of God." Do this mantra while keeping your attention focused on the point between the eyebrows. As you bring your energy to this point with mantra, day after day after day, you gradually become a channel of God's will.

The Hindu mantra "Aditya Hridayam Punyam, Sarva Shatru Bina Shanam" (pronounced AH-DIT-EYA HRI-DAEE-AHM POON-YAHM SAHRVA

SHAH-TROO BEE-NA SHA-NAM) means "When the sun is kept in the heart all evil vanishes from life." If you wish to practice this mantra, as you repeat it visualize the sun. Consider how the sun sends light and warmth on everything, good and evil alike. It doesn't say, "I won't shine on you because you aren't playing the game." It just keeps sending out light and warmth. Do this in the morning. Contemplate the sun, Aditya, and bring it slowly down into your heart. Feel its warmth and radiance in your heart. To send this warmth and love out you don't have to do anything; the sun is the emission of light. Let it shine. As you repeat this mantra and follow the visualization, you are tuning to the Self residing in your spiritual heart, or Hridayam. When the sun is kept in your heart, all evil vanishes from your life.

In the Bible is a natural mantra as simple as its name—the "Jesus Prayer" or "Prayer of the Heart." In Luke 18:13, it says: " . . . but the publican standing afar off, would not so much as lift up his eyes to heaven, but kept striking his breast, saying: 'O God, be merciful to me the sinner.' " This mantra has come to read: "Lord

Jesus Christ, son of God, have mercy on me a sinner." It may be reduced to as few as three words depending on the one who prays:

"Lord Jesus Christ, son of God, have mercy on me, a sinner."

"Lord Jesus Christ, have mercy on me, a sinner."

"Jesus Christ, have mercy on me, a sinner."

"Jesus Christ, have mercy on me."

"Christ have mercy."

If you discipline yourself to learn this mantra and repeat it constantly, it will sink down into your heart and after awhile it will go on by itself.

—Marie Idol

In the beginning was the Word, and the Word was with God, and the Word was God.

—John 1:1

The New Testament

It is in pronouncing Thy Name that I must die and live.

—Muhammad

Introduction aux Doctrines esotériques de l'Islam

*Thus abide constantly with the name of our Lord
Jesus Christ, so that the heart swallows the Lord
and the Lord the heart, and the two become one.*

—*St. John Chrysostom*

Writings from the Philokalia
on Prayer of the Heart

*Blessed is the person who utterly surrenders his
soul for the name of YHWH to dwell therein
and to establish therein its throne of glory.*

—*Zohar*

Major Trends in
Jewish Mysticism

*I am a happy man, indeed!
I visit the Pure Land as often as I like:
I'm there and I'm back,
I'm there and I'm back,
I'm there and I'm back,
"Namu-amida-butsu! Namu-amida-butsu!"*

—*Saichi*

Mysticism Christian and
Buddhist

Contemplation

Reading scripture, praying, and communing with nature are all forms of contemplation.

You should read enough of the thought underlying your spiritual practices to understand fully what you are doing. Use this study as seeds for contemplation. Collect a series of books written or spoken by beings who are liberated or attuned to higher states of consciousness. Quotations from some of these books are sprinkled throughout this one. Each day in the morning or evening open a book at random or read until you find a paragraph or a sentence with which to work. Reflect on it throughout the day. See your own life through the lens of the passage. Through this practice, in time, comes a transformation of your perception, your ways of understanding the nature of reality.

Contemplation can also be free-form. Thoreau wrote:

> *Sometimes, I sat in my sunny doorway from sunrise till noon, rapt in a revery, amidst the pines and hickories and sumacs, in undisturbed solitude and stillness, while the birds sang around*

*or flitted noiseless through the house, until by
the sun falling in at my west window, or the
noise of some traveller's wagon on the distant
highway, I was reminded of the pass of time. I
grew in those seasons like corn in the night,
and they were far better than any work of the
hands would have been. They were not time sub-
tracted from my life, but so much over and above
my usual allowance. I realized what the
Orientals mean by contemplation and the
forsaking of work.*

*To some extent, and at rare intervals, even
I am a yogi.*

The revery of which Thoreau speaks just happens
to us. To let your mind float around an idea or image
in a relaxed but focused way is the most familiar kind
of contemplation. It is not so different from the almost
formless prayer described by St. John of the Cross.
Prayer can range from a simple silent openness to a
very personal dialogue with God.

*When you go apart to be alone for prayer, put
from your mind everything you have been doing
or plan to do. Reject all thoughts, be they good or
be they evil. Do not pray with words unless you
are really drawn to this; or if you do pray with
words, pay no attention to whether they are many
or few. Do not weigh them or their meaning. Do
not be concerned about what kind of prayers you
use, or whether you formulate them interiorly,
by thoughts, or express them aloud, in words.
See that nothing remains in your conscious mind
save a naked intent stretching out toward God.
Leave it stripped of every particular idea about
God (what he is like in himself or in his works)
and keep only the simple awareness that he is as
he is. Let him be thus, I pray you, and force*

*him not to be otherwise. Search into him no
further, but rest in this faith as on solid ground.
This awareness, stripped of ideas and deliberately
bound and anchored in faith, shall leave your
thought and affection in emptiness except for a
naked thought and blind feeling of your own
being. It will feel as if your whole desire cried out
to God and said:*

> *That which I am I offer to you, O Lord,
> without looking to any quality of your
> being but only to the fact that you are
> as you are; this, and nothing more.*

*Let that quiet darkness be your whole mind
and like a mirror to you. For I want your
thought of self to be as naked and as simple as
your thought of God, so that you may be
spiritually united to him without any fragmentation
and scattering of your mind. He is your being
and in him, you are what you are, not only
because he is the cause and being of all that exists,
but because he is your cause and the deep center
of your being. Therefore, in this contemplative
work think of your self and of him in the same
way: this is, with the simple awareness that he is
as he is, and that you are as you are. In this way
your thought will not be fragmented or scattered,
but unified in him who is all.*

*Leave your thought quite naked, your
affection uninvolved and your self simply as you
are, so that grace may touch and nourish you
with the experimental knowledge of God as he
really is. Look up joyfully, and say to your Lord,
in words or desire:*

> *That which I am, I offer to you,
> O Lord, for you are it entirely.*

*Go no further, but rest in this naked, stark,
elemental awareness that you are as you are.*

—*St. John of the Cross*

The Ascent of Mount Carmel

*Hear, O Israel: The Lord our God, the Lord is
One! And thou shalt love the Lord thy God
with all thy heart, and with all thy soul, and with
all thy might. And these words, which I command
thee this day, shall be upon thy heart, and thou
shalt teach them diligently unto thy children,
and thou shalt talk of them when thou sittest in
thy house, and when thou walkest by the way,
and when thou liest down, and when thou risest
up. And thou shalt bind them for a sign upon
thy hand, and they shall be for frontlets between
thine eyes. And thou shalt write them upon the
door-posts of thy house and upon thy gates.*

—*Deuteronomy 6:4–7*

The Old Testament

*Everywhere, wherever you may find yourself,
you can set up an altar to God in your mind by
means of prayer.*

—The Way of a Pilgrim

Prayers are answered in the way they're asked.

—*Ram Tirth*

I felt it better to speak to God than about him.

—*St. Therese of Lisieux*

You pray to what you love; for true, whole prayer is nothing but love!

—*St. Augustine*

Nature is the easiest object of contemplation for our surroundings can inspire and lead us into the quiet unity of all creation. Surya Singer and Soma Krishna suggest these ways to open to nature:

As children, the play of the sun on rippling water brought us before God's throne. Did you ever see an infant gaze at a lightbulb or the moon? Spiritual techniques are discovered naturally by infants and little children: holding their breath, staring unblinking, standing on their heads, imitating animals, turning in circles, sitting unmoving, and repeating phrases over and over until all else ceases to exist. Stop thinking that meditation is anything special. Stop thinking all together. Look at the world around you as if you had just arrived on Planet Earth. Observe the rocks in their natural formations, the trees rooted

*in the ground, their branches reaching to the sky,
the plants, animals and the interrelationships
of each to the other. See yourself through the eyes
of a dog in a park. See a flower through its
essence. See a mountain through its massiveness.
When the mind allows its objects to remain
unmolested, there may be no mind and no object
—just breathless unity.*

—Surya Singer.

*To see the world in a grain of sand
And Heaven in a wild flower
Hold infinity in the palm of your hand
And eternity in an hour.*

—William Blake

Auguries of Innocence

*Devise meditations in which you draw nature into
your own being through your senses. You can
experiment with some of these:*

*Sit with your back pressed against the
trunk of the mightiest tree you can find and pull*

*its strength into your spine with each breath.
Lose awareness of where the tree trunk and your
back become one. Thank the tree.*

*Rest an evergreen branch on the top of your
head and let its power pour into you as though
to fill an empty vessel. The overflow bathes you
in green mist and you are renewed.*

*Hold a rock in your hand. Feel its texture,
weight, and reconstruct its geological history.
How old is it? Did it travel from deep within the
earth or from space as a meteorite before it
reached your hand? Become that rock.*

*Feed on the smell of fresh-cut grass, even
the lawn, drawing the odor into your nose and
mouth. Let it nourish body and spirit.*

*Taste the wind. What does it carry? Salt
from the sea, perhaps? Or clean pine essence
from the mountains, or parched desert air? Lick
snow and rain from the wind's fingers.*

*Lie on the sun-warmed ground and share its
gratitude as the generous rays kindle the soil's
own latent life. Imagine that you are a seed. Watch
yourself sprout and grow.*

*Listen to the ocean pound on the beach.
Close your eyes and let the intensity of the sound
fill your head, then your whole body, until you
vibrate with it. Try to hear beyond the ocean to the
roar of the raw primal energy in the universe.*

*Watch the flow of a river. Throw your
burden of worry and negative emotions to the
passing water to carry off. Breathe deeply to
dislodge old crystallized tensions from around
your heart, as the current sweeps away layer after
layer of ancient woes on its way to the ocean.
Visualize the ocean waiting, neutralizing all,
and converting it back into pure energy once
more.*

—Soma Krishna

There is a sadhu in Hrishikesh who gets up early
in the morning and stands near a great waterfall.
He looks at it the whole day and says to God:
"Ah, You have done well! Well done! How
amazing!" He doesn't practice any other form of
japa or austerity. At night he returns to his hut.

—*Sri Ramakrishna*

The Gospel of
Sri Ramakrishna

At Kugami
In front of the Otono,
There stands a solitary pine tree,
Surely of many a generation;
How divinely dignified
It stands there!
In the morning
I pass by it;
In the evening
I stand underneath it,
And standing I gaze,
Never tired
Of this solitary pine!

—*Ryokwan*

Zen and Japanese Culture

*The voice of the mountain torrent is from one
    great tongue;*
*The lines of the hills, are they not the pure body
    of the Buddha?*

—Zenrin

The Gospel According to Zen

Devotion

Prayer, sitting with a picture of a holy being, singing
to the Beloved—all of these are devotional meditative
practices, the way of the heart. Devotion balances the
more impersonal wisdom that comes from most kinds
of meditation. It allows us to cultivate our humanity
while we transform our consciousness. This outflowing
of the heart toward the object of our devotion facilitates
most other methods as well, through the flow of loving
energy.

    As an example, imagine a being standing before
you, someone to whom you feel particularly tuned,
such as Abraham, Christ, Mary, or Hanuman. This
being is radiant, luminous, a being whose eyes are
filled with compassion, a being in whom you feel the
wisdom that comes from an intimate harmony with
the universe.

    Despite all of the impurities to which you cling,
despite all your feelings of unworthiness, such a being
loves you unconditionally. To sit before such a being,
or to imagine such a being sitting in your heart, to be

with that being and return the love, to see yourself reflected in such compassionate, unjudging eyes, to open more and more, as if to a beloved, to carry on imaginary conversations with such a being, opens you to compassion, tranquility, warmth, patience, to all the qualities of a free being.

This interpersonal quality of devotional meditation allows you to start from your psychological needs, to love, to be loved, to be in the presence of wisdom, compassion, and peace. When you are with a being who embodies these qualities, they rub off, and you feel more evolved, even to the point of recognizing the radiant light within yourself. This acknowledgment of your own beauty allows you to open even more to the beloved, until finally the lover and the beloved merge and you find out that what you had seen outwardly as perfection is a mirror of your own true being.

There are lower and higher stages of devotion. In the lower you romanticize the journey. You merely shift the focus of your melodrama from marketplace to temple. The images in the temple, the temple itself, your participation in worship, the love, say, of Christ, of Krishna, of Buddha, become preoccupations. You want to think about, talk to, play with, and open your heart to them. This level is romantic; you have fallen in love with your vehicle for going to God. But your love grows and your beloved becomes the whole object of your life, you tune to a deeper place within yourself. Then the emotional, romantic qualities of devotion give way to a new kind of love where finally you see all people as the beloved.

> *O Sadhu! the simple union is the best.*
> *Since the day when I met with my Lord,*
>   *there has been no end to the sport of our love.*
> *I shut not my eyes, I close not my ears,*
>   *I do not mortify my body;*
> *I see with eyes open and smile, and*
>   *behold His beauty everywhere;*

I utter His Name, and whatever I see,
it reminds me of Him; whatever I do, it
becomes His worship.
The rising and the setting are one to
me; all contradictions are solved.
Wherever I go, I move around Him,
All I achieve is His service:
When I lie down, I lie prostrate at His feet.
. . . I am immersed in that one great bliss which
transcends all pleasure and pain.

—Kabir

One Hundred Poems of
Kabir

Devotion is easy and natural and has no hard and
fast rules regarding how one should meditate.
By devotion one can realize the secret of love
itself. On this path the aspirant sees the universe
as the very expression of his Beloved.

The only thing it requires is faith—implicit
faith. There is nothing to argue, it is beyond
logic. It is like learning to swim: a person cannot
enter the water unless he can swim, and swimming
is impossible without entering the water.

There are various attitudes or feelings with
which one may approach the Beloved. You
might feel as though God were your child, like
the feeling of Yashoda (Krishna's mother) toward
her baby Krishna, or the feeling of Mary for the
infant Jesus. Or you could see God as a friend.
Again there is the attitude of the servant toward

his Master, where you serve the Lord as Hanuman serves Lord Rama in the Ramayana. Then there is the attitude of lover, where you see your Beloved with the love of husband or wife. . . . becoming the bride of God, like the gopis sporting with Lord Krishna, or St. Therese the Little Flower married to her beloved Jesus. Finally there is the attitude of peaceful contemplation of the great saints and sages, the ancient yogis of India.

There are many ways to open yourself, to make oneself more receptive to this love for God. One way is through satsang, the company of saints, contact with the living spirit of Truth and Love in other beings. Delighting in the stories and incidents of God in His many forms and incarnations—like the life of Christ, or Rama or Krishna— can also bring this love. Or by humbly serving at the feet of the Guru, the devotee can efface the ego in surrender to God. And constantly singing His Name and His praises further centers the mind and heart on Him. For the devotee the mere repetition of the Name of God brings His Presence. Then, with firm faith, one crosses the ocean of desire in the boat of the Name.

—*K.K. Sah*

Christ was lost in love.

—*Maharaj-ji (Neem Karoli Baba)*

True devotion is for itself; not to desire heaven or to fear hell.

—Rabia el-Adawia

And thou shalt love the Lord thy God with all thy heart, and with all thy soul, and with all thy mind, and with all thy strength: this is the first commandment.

—Mark 12:30

The New Testament

The Names of God or praises of God can be sung as well as spoken. Often when your heart wells up, singing alone expresses the fullness of your love for God. As you sing the Name repeatedly, the rhythm and melody fan your emotions. If this ecstasy is heightened, distinctions begin to fall away until only love, only the beloved, remain.

Kirtan, the singing of mantra, is an old and revered technique used in India and other parts of Asia. While kirtan uses music as a vehicle, aesthetics or musical ability are not the main concern. The ability to sing beautifully is enjoyable but not necessary. What matters is singing from the heart. In India often it is the old man who sings last, with no teeth, a raspy voice, and hacking cough, who blows everyone away because he knows to whom he is singing, and the beauty of his contact with God is moving and powerful.

Kirtan, like any other devotional practice, can be done from any state of mind or level of evolution.

By mere persistence it leads to deeper levels of opening and understanding. Whatever space you start from, if you persist in kirtan the space will change. You may want to get high, but find yourself getting bored. You may want to "feel devotional." If you allow each experience to arise and pass, making space for new experiences to come from within, you will open to the power that comes from singing the Names of God.

If you are blissful, be blissful and sing. If you are bored, be bored and sing. Just keep offering your experiences into the fire of the Name and it will guide you through them all.

When you are in love with God, the very sound of the Name brings great joy. It is said that "in its highest aspect, Divine Love is nothing less than the immortal bliss of liberation." To open fully to kirtan, to the singing of the divine Name, is to know this sweetest form of bliss.

What follows is the musical scoring for two mantras. The first of them, Sri Ram Jai Ram Jai Jai Ram, is a mantra often sung at the request of my guru. The second is a beautiful and simple prayer. Any devotional verse or song can be repeated as a meditation.

SRI RAM

Pronounced: SHREE RAHM JAY RAHM JAY JAY RAHM

TWAMEVA MATA

Thou art my Mother and my Father art Thou
Thou art my Friend and my Companion art Thou
Thou art my Learning, my Wealth art Thou
Thou art my All in All, My Lord of Lords.

Pronounced:

TWAH-MEY-VA MAH-TAH CHA PEE-TAH
  TWAH-MEY-VA
TWAH-MEY-VA BAN-DHU SCHA SA-KAH
  TWAH-MEY-VA
TWAH-MEY-VA VI-DHYA DRA-VEE-NAHM
  TWAH-MEY-VA
TWAH-MEY-VA SAHR-VAM MA-MA DEY-VA
  DEY-VA

*The more pure, true, and penetrating is the song
or chant, the nearer and clearer it is to His ears.
This permeates the atmosphere of the gathering
with purity, peace, love, and bliss, and all feel the
great joy of that Essence. As one becomes
absorbed and submerged in it, the chanting itself
becomes the meditation.*

—*K.K. Sah*

Visualization

In directed visualizations you bring to mind a mental image on which you meditate. Visualization resembles our familiar habits of fantasies, daydreams, and imaginings but brings discipline to them. Unlike ordinary daydreams, spiritual visualization exercises focus your mind on a holy image. The power of this method is that it enables you to find the qualities of the imaged beings within yourself.

You can try the following visualizations. Either read them through and then do them, or have a friend read them to you.

Sit with a straight back, eyes closed.

As if it had a nose, breathe deeply in and out of your heart center (located in the middle of your chest) for a few minutes until this area of your body feels warm and expanded. Rise up to your throat center and breathe in and out of this chakra until it feels alive. Come up to your third eye area and breathe in and out. Rise into your crown chakra on the top of your head, breathing in and out vertically. Then return your awareness and breath into your heart center. Feel the connection between your heart and your head centers. Be conscious of the energy flow that unites them.

Again, breathe into your heart, and visualize a tiny Buddha seated there, radiant, perfect. He embodies all virtues, all strengths. He radiates equanimity, compassion, all-enduring love. With each breath, the tiny Buddha glows brighter and begins to expand. Follow this expansion with your breath and flow of attention, feeding the figure until it fills your entire heart center. Keep breathing life into this Buddha-self until it overflows your heart center and slowly fills every part of your being, every cell of your body, until you and the Buddha are one. As the Buddha, there is no more striving. You are there. Just pause before the next stage.

As the Buddha, now begin to breathe into your Buddha-heart, drawing in light with each breath, converting it into love in your heart,

*and sending it out Buddha's third eye to the
world. With each breath your heart glows brighter.
Feel the love stream out of Buddha's forehead.
Keep breathing in light and sending out love as
the love-emanation from your third eye becomes
a continuous river that flows out to cover the
whole universe. Let body awareness fade and
become the mighty channel for this blessing.
There is no you—only a vast Buddha-heart and
a spiritual eye.*

*Buddha's work is finished for now. Slowly,
slowly start to draw into your heart center once
more, until the luminous figure fills it. As the
Buddha-body contracts, it becomes even more
brilliant, leaving you with a fiery radiance in your
heart for the rest of the day. In your dealings with
the world this day, remember that part of you is
still the Buddha.*

—*Soma Krishna*

*When you are composed and feel yourself in
the presence of the Spirit, try this meditation. Do
it slowly and with intensity.*

*Imagine yourself on a hilly plain. It is spring.
The grass is fresh and green. The sun is warm on
your skin. Feel the breath of the gentle breeze.
Smell the sweet air and the new grass. A wonderful
feeling of well-being flows over your body.*

*You are surrounded by people who are silent
and waiting in prayer. Try to feel the vibrations
of their devotion.*

Now look to a slightly elevated hill some yards in front of you. A number of people on top of the hill surround a figure whose presence you feel immediately. Look carefully with your mind and your ear. It is Jesus, enveloped in a beautiful white light. An intense light shines from each of His wounds. Gaze upon Him and feel the warmth of His love. Whisper His name.

From the heart of Jesus, a ray of light bursts forth and enters into your heart. See Him looking at you, white light joining you heart to heart. He approaches you and slowly enters the center of your heart. See Him there. Feel Him, feel your heart, warm with His love and brilliant with His light. Your mind stops, overwhelmed with God's love. Stay there awhile. Surrender to the presence of God.

Now, imagine that you are going up with Jesus. Cast up your awareness to the center of your head. Concentrate and go through the top of your head, you and Jesus, going up and up through the sky.

Above you is a vast ball of pulsating intense light. Go into this light with Jesus. Let it penetrate each cell of your body. Again, surrender yourself. Open to your true being. Rest in the heart of God.

At any time during a meditation you may be taken over by God. Everything stops. The mind stops, the body seems to stop and you enter into an ineffable quiet—an intense quiet of love. Just rest in it. Be bathed in God.

The peace and love of Jesus be with you always.

—*Father Ed Luvin*

At times you will think of your Guru.
Whenever such yearning arises
Visualize him upon your head
And for his blessing pray.
Visualize him sitting in the center of your heart
And forget him never.
But you should know that even your Guru
Is delusory and dreamlike;
That all things are unreal and magical.

—Milarepa

The Hundred Thousand
Songs of Milarepa

Worship me in the symbols and images which re-mind thee of me.

—Srimad Bhagavatam

The Wisdom of God

Movement

Every move is a prayer.

—Man of the Crow Dog
Family

Akwesasne Notes

Though most meditation is done sitting still, you can also meditate as you move. The flow of energy in your body, its stance and positions, the way you walk, all can be meditation. In hatha yoga, for example, there is a set of postures, called asanas, each of which embodies a specific attitude and relationship to the universe. It's as if you're changing the receiving channel of your body by changing positions. If at this moment you put your hands together in prayer, you can feel as you hold them there the quality of a prayerful attitude. Or on the other hand, if you make a fist and hold it out menacingly, you can feel the way the fist accentuates a threatening attitude. So it is that each body position makes a statement of one kind or another. Just in the arching of your back, you change the movements of energy throughout the body. Hatha yoga postures open the energies of the body; each position becomes a meditative posture that allows you to tune in to a different space.

There are also hand positions, called mudras, that reflect various states of consciousness. If you study statues of the Buddha you will notice that his hands take various positions. Each of these is a mudra. In t'ai chi a flow of mudras develops into a moving meditation. While t'ai chi appears to be a continuous movement, it is actually a series of tiny stops—like a movie in slow motion.

T'ai chi, like all Oriental martial arts, is a spiritual path in itself. Indeed, Bodhidharma, who brought Buddhism to China from India, is credited with inventing karate (kung fu in Chinese). When the way of the martial arts is pursued to its highest point, the practitioner loses all trace of his ego in the perfection of his movements. To reach this point requires as intense a self-discipline as any sitting meditation.

Still another tradition that uses movement to develop a meditative awareness is Sufi dancing. The Dervishes are fabled for their whirls, but there are many other kinds of dances and walks the Sufis use. In most of these the movement is keyed to a chant, the combination of motion and prayer focusing the dancer's mind and body on God.

For a master of hatha yoga, t'ai chi, or Sufi dancing, movement is stillness.

Asanas should preferably be done in the morning or afternoon before sitting for meditation. Do not hurry through the postures. It is better to do just a few asanas in a relaxed manner than to speed through them all. Use a flat surface—a mat or a well-padded rug—and wear comfortable, loose clothing. Do not do asanas if you are sick or during menstruation unless you are being instructed by a teacher. Wait for two or three hours after eating before doing asanas and do not eat for at least twenty minutes afterwards.

If asanas are not practiced too fast, the breath will remain even. Always breathe through the nose. As you bend forward, let the breath be exhaled. As you bend backward, let the breath be inhaled. As you stretch farther into an asana, take a little breath. Inhale if you stretch backward, exhale if you bend forward. Hold the breath for a few seconds when exerting force to balance the body. By practice your body gradually will become loose. Again, go easy; do not use much force in stretching.

Each asana may be done two or three times if possible. But always take at least a fifteen- to twenty-second rest lying flat on your back (corpse pose) after each asana—letting your breath come back to normal. Or after a standing asana you may rest standing.

The following asana, Surya Namaskar— the salute to the sun—integrates several yoga positions into a flow of movement that balances and tones the body. It is in itself a meditation as well as a good prelude to sitting. As you do this asana you can concentrate on the morning sun. Let yourself become one with it. Begin by doing this exercise three times and gradually build up to six or so.

1. Stand relaxed, feet together, hands held palms together, fingers upward, at the middle of the chest. Exhale.

2. Lock thumbs and raise arms over head. Keep arms close to ears. Bend backward looking up at hands, inhaling.

3. Bend forward, head between arms, and place palms on the floor on either side of feet. Keep knees straight and try to touch head to knees, exhaling.

4. Stretch left leg back, knee to floor. Keep right foot between hands, knee to chest. Arch back, looking up, inhaling.

5. Throw right leg back to meet left foot. Raise buttocks to form a triangle with the feet, heels to floor, and the hands on floor (arms extended, head between arms), exhaling.

6. *Bring knees, chest, and chin to floor, in that order. Keep pelvis raised and palms beneath shoulders. Inhale and hold.*

7. *Bring pelvis to floor and stretch head, neck, and chest up, looking toward the ceiling, elbows alongside body, slightly bent. Hold breath.*

8. *Push up and raise the body back into the triangle in one movement, exhaling.*

9. *Thrust left leg up between hands, knee to chest. Leave right leg extended, knee to floor. Arch back, looking up, inhaling.*

10. *Bring right leg up, back into position number three, exhaling.*

11. *Stretch up and back into position number two, inhaling.*

12. *Return to beginning position, exhaling.*

—*Adapted from* Inside/Out

Learn to experience the chi, or breath energy, flowing through and moving your body. On the beach accompanied by the crash of the surf and the call of the seagull; in your own yard lit with the symphony of the rising sun, glistening dew and chirping birds; or in your room where you have the privacy and peace of familiarity— experience the chi for yourself. Try just standing quietly, arms at sides and feet at shoulder width. Let your knees be flexed. Just

*stand there relaxing your mind of all thoughts;
let yourself flow into the rhythm of your
surroundings. Your breath will become deep
and regular as you relax. Sense the energy flowing
up from the ground into your feet and through
your body. Sink into that energy. Let your arms
ride up before you on the wave of that rising
energy, slowly, effortlessly. Let them slide off the
energy wave, and slowly sink back down to your
sides. Play with this flow awhile. Perhaps at some
point you will feel the need to turn gently to one
side, your arms floating outwards. Maybe you will
need to take a step in some direction to maintain
your balance. Take your time and move slowly. Be
loose; allow the energy from within you to move
your body, instead of imposing movement through
will and muscles.*

*In t'ai chi all movements are generated
from the center of gravity within the body—the
tant'ien, just below the navel. Body and earth
and air are still one, flowing through and within
each other. Experiment with this, as a further
refinement of the earlier exercise. Again, standing
quietly, arms at side, feet at shoulder width,
knees lightly flexed, rest until your breath
becomes deep and regular. Experience the energy
flowing through your body, but instead of
moving your arms, try turning to one side from
your tant'ien. Step into the direction of that
turn. Let your shoulders follow, but don't force
them. Just experiment walking around in various
directions. Let each turn originate from your
tant'ien. Let your arms be loose, and your knees
flexed. After some time, keeping the awareness of
your tant'ien, let your arms slowly rise and
move to the flow of energy. Expanding and
contracting, rising and falling, circular flowing
nowhere going.*

—*Saraswati Ransom*

*The following Sufi walks were developed by
Murshid Samuel Lewis.*

*Begin by walking naturally, relaxed but
alert, with back straight. Concentrate on your
breath. Let your walking and breathing
coordinate naturally. Count rhythmically with
each two steps: 1–2. Take two steps as you inhale,
then two steps as you exhale.*

*To create a balance of the elements earth,
air, fire and water in yourself, you can develop
whichever element is weak through specific walks.
For example, if you are feeling flighty or
unstable the earth walk would ground you.*

*Or you may try the walks that express the
qualities of love or of strength and courage.
Continue each of these walks until you feel as
if you have become its essence.*

*Earth: Good for stabilizing emotions and
grounding, balance energy. Walk with a simple
drumbeat if possible. Bend your knees slightly
and walk with hands at sides, palms facing the
earth. Look down; feel gravity pulling your
palms and weighing down your body. Feel
your connection with the earth. Breathe in
heavily and exhale lightly. Coordinate your
steps and breath to the drumbeat 2 counts
in and 2 counts out.*

*Air: Light, good for a free joyful mind. Not
grounded, no rhythm. Flow as you walk in
erratic directions. Feel light and airy. Move
in a manner that expresses what you imagine*

this quality to be. The breath is refined and light.

Water: Sensitive, flowing, emotional, imbalanced. Walk like dancing to a waltz—Step 2–3, Step 2–3. Sway from side to side. Without holding the nose breathe in the right nostril and out the left.

Fire: Inspirational, courageous, great desire to reach one's goal. Unstable. Walk quickly and every few steps hop on your right foot stretching your body as you reach up and clap your hands like a spark. Breathe heavily through the right nostril (without holding nose). Feel the energy of fire filling you.

The Quality of Loving: Step gracefully and lightly. The breath is refined. Slightly bow your head in reverence and cup your hands over your heart. Feel love pour into your hands, then offer the love to your Beloved with head and hands held upward. Do this several times until you feel love flowing. If you like you can softly repeat the Arabic phrase "ya wadood" which means "O thou loving."

The Quality of Strength and Courage: Walk proud with forceful steps, shoulders back, arms swinging, fists closed. You can chant the phrase "ya Malik"—"O King of Kings."

—*Tara Bennett*

Mindfulness

Perhaps at some time you have sat quietly by the side of an ocean or river. At first there is one big rush of sound. Listening quietly, you begin to hear a multitude of subtle sounds: the waves hitting the shore, the rushing current of the river. In that peacefulness and silence of mind you experience precisely what is happening. It is the same when you listen to yourself. At first all you can hear is one "self" or "I," but slowly this self is revealed as a mass of changing elements, thoughts, feelings, emotions, and images, all illuminated simply by listening, by paying attention.

In mindfulness you are aware of what happens in each moment. You remain alert, not allowing yourself to become forgetful. When you develop mindfulness and concentration together, you achieve a balance of mind. As this penetrating awareness develops it reveals many aspects of the world and of who you are. You see with a clear and direct vision that everything, including yourself, is flowing, in flux, in transformation. There is not a single element of your mind or body that is stable. This wisdom comes not from any particular state, but from close observation of your own mind.

Joseph Goldstein gives the following instructions for developing mindfulness by meditating on one's thoughts, on eating, and on walking.

MEDITATION ON THE MIND

*To meditate upon thoughts is simply to be aware,
as thoughts arise, that the mind is thinking,
without getting involved in the content: not going
off on a train of association, not analyzing the
thought and why it came, but merely to be aware
that at the particular moment "thinking" is happening. It is helpful to make a mental note of
"thinking, thinking" every time a thought arises;
observe the thought without judgment, without
reaction to the content, without identifying with
it, without taking the thought to be I, or self, or
mine. The thought is the thinker. There is no
one behind it. The thought is thinking itself. It
comes uninvited. You will see that when there is
a strong detachment from the thought process,
thoughts don't last long. As soon as you are
mindful of a thought, it disappears. Some people
may find it helpful to label the thinking process
in a more precise way, to note different kinds of
thoughts, whether "planning" or "imagining" or
"remembering." This sharpens the focus of
attention. Otherwise, the simple note of "thinking,
thinking" will serve the purpose. Try to be
aware of the thought as soon as it arises, rather
than some minutes afterward. When they are
noticed with precision and balance they have
no power to disturb the mind.*

*Thoughts should not be treated as obstacles
or hindrances. They are just another object of
mindfulness, another object of meditation. Don't
let the mind become lazy and drift along. Make
the effort for a great deal of clarity with respect
to what's happening in the moment.*

Suzuki Roshi in Zen Mind, Beginner's Mind
writes: "When you are practicing Zazen
meditation do not try to stop your thinking. Let
it stop by itself. If something comes into your
mind, let it come in and let it go out. It will not

*stay long. When you try to stop your thinking,
it means you are bothered by it. Do not be
bothered by anything. It appears that the
something comes from outside your mind,
but actually it is only the waves of your mind and
if you are not bothered by the waves, gradually
they will become calmer and calmer. . . . Many
sensations come, many thoughts or images
arise but they are just waves from your own
mind. Nothing comes from outside your mind.
. . . If you leave your mind as it is, it will
become calm. This mind is called big mind."*

Just let things happen as they do. Let all
images and thoughts and sensations arise and
pass away without being bothered, without
reacting, without judging, without clinging,
without identifying with them. Become one with
the big mind, observing carefully,
microscopically, all the waves coming and going.
This attitude will quickly bring about a state of
balance and calm. Don't let the mind get out
of focus. Keep the mind sharply aware, moment
to moment, of what is happening, whether the
in-out breath, sensations, or thoughts. In each
instant be focused on the object with a balanced
and relaxed mind.

MINDFUL EATING

There are many different processes of mind and
body which go on while we eat. It is important
to become mindful of the sequence of the

*processes; otherwise, there is a great likelihood
of greed and desire arising with regard to food.
And when we are not aware, we do not fully
enjoy the experience. We take a bite or two and
our thoughts wander.*

*The first process involved when you have
your food is that you see it. Notice "seeing,
seeing." Then there is an intention to take the
food, a mental process. That intention should be
noticed. "Intending, intending." The mental
intention becomes the cause of the arm moving.
"Moving, moving." When the hand or spoon
touches the food there is the sensation of touch,
contact. Feel the sensations. Then the intention
to lift the arm, and the lifting. Notice carefully
all these processes.*

*Opening the mouth. Putting in the food.
Closing the mouth. The intention to lower the
arm, and then the movement. One thing at a
time. Feeling the food in the mouth, the texture.
Chewing. Experience the movement. As you
begin chewing, there will be taste sensation
arising. Be mindful of the tasting. As you keep on
chewing, the taste disappears. Swallowing. Be
aware of the whole sequence involved. There
is no one behind it, no one who is eating. It's
merely the sequence of intentions, movements,
tastes, touch sensations. That's what we are—a
sequence of happenings, of processes, and by
being very mindful of the sequence, of the flow,
we get free of the concept of self.*

MINDFUL WALKING

*The walking meditation is done by noticing the
lifting, forward and placing movement of the
foot in each step. It is helpful to finish one step
completely before lifting the other foot. "Lifting,
moving, placing, lifting, moving, placing." It is
very simple. Again it is not an exercise in
movement. It is an exercise in mindfulness. Use
the movement to develop a careful awareness. In
the course of the day, you can expect many
changes. Sometimes you may feel like walking
more quickly, sometimes very slowly. You can
take the steps as a single unit, "stepping,
stepping." Or you may start out walking quickly
and, in that same walking meditation, slow down
until you are dividing it again into the three
parts. Experiment. The essential thing is to be
mindful, to be aware of what's happening.*

*In walking, the hands should remain
stationary either behind the back, at the sides, or
in front. It's better to look a little ahead, and
not at your feet, in order to avoid being involved
in the concept of "foot" arising from the visual
contact. All of the attention should be on
experiencing the movement, feeling the sensations
of the lifting, forward, placing motions.*

—Joseph Goldstein

The Experience of Insight

Meditation in Action

The final step in integrating meditation into your awareness is to use the stuff of daily life as part of meditation. There are ways of perceiving the world and the way you live in it such that each experience brings you more deeply into the meditative space. At the same time, however, this kind of meditation requires firm grounding: you must continue to function effectively in the world as you meditate on it. This is meditation in action. It finally becomes the core of a consciously lived life, a meditative space within you. This space stands between each thing you notice and each response you make, allowing a peaceful, quiet, and spacious view of the universe.

I find that even an act as stimulating as walking through New York City can be a profound meditative experience. For as I walk down the street, if I stay quiet inside—either through mantra or watching my breath—I can see my consciousness being pulled this way and that by the things along the street. Each time my consciousness is pulled, it reflects some desire system, such as desires for power or sex, to which I am still attached. Each time I notice this, I let it be, let it stay or leave as it chooses. As I do, I remain in the meditative space, not getting lost in the desire. In this way I can walk through the city, staying quiet inside, despite the incredible panoply of stimuli that impinge upon my every sense.

There are techniques that help you see moment-to-moment experiences in such a way that everything serves to awaken you. The Bhagavad Gita describes karma yoga as the path of awakening through ordinary activities. You see every action, be it eating, sleeping, marrying, or earning a living, as an act offered to God. Your every act becomes a meditation on your relation to God. If your path is through the guru, then you see each daily life experience as part of a dialogue in which the guru keeps facing you with experience after experience, each one designed for your awakening.

When you finally develop the capacity to meditate from the moment of awakening to the moment of sleep, and yet stay perfectly at ease in the world, moment to moment living becomes a totally delightful and freeing experience.

Zen is not some kind of excitement, but concentration on our usual everyday routine.

—*Shunryu Suzuki*

Zen Mind, Beginner's Mind

Let me explain to you the function of Kavvanah. Kavvanah means intention. Our intention is always free. There is nothing that can obstruct your intending. Even if the whole world coerces

*you into a pattern of actions, you can always
"intend" whatever you want. For instance, you sit
in the dentist's chair. He drills and you feel a
sting of pain, but you can "intend" this pain as
an offering of love. You offer to God the moment
of pain, intending to suffer it for Him. You might
put it somewhat in this way: "Ribbono Shel
Olam!—You are good and Your universe is
good. The all is filled with Your mercy and
goodness, as is the pain I feel. I cannot bring You
any other sacrifice. Please accept this moment
of pain as a love offering from me." Or you
work in your day by day endeavor. You do
whatever you must do, and you intend: "God
of Law and Order, You have ordained work for
man. In doing . . . I intend to do Your Will. I
wish to cleave to You in this action." Or you
travel and time is taken up by it. You lean back
and wink at Him in your mind as if to say,
"Sweet Father, I enjoy Your presence: the rhythm
of the wheels, the fleeting scenery, are all nothing
but You. You contain me and my vehicle. I will
be careful in travel, for this is Your Will.
Guard my going out and my coming back. I am
secure in You."*

*You see these "arrows of awareness" are
rather simple to practice. You will soon find that
placing yourself in His Presence will come with
some practice.*

—Rabbi Zalman Schachter

The First Step

*It is easier for me to tell you about non-meditation
than about meditation. I sit or walk looking at
myself non-meditating—absorbed in dramas
and melodramas, heart-gripping tragedies,
loneliness, shabbiness, delights. As from another
planet I look at them, through a telescope. Then
there is a little space between me and my
all-pervasive feelings. Nevertheless, I still feel
I am my feelings, as well as whatever it is that
elicits them, plus a third entity looking at the
drama of separation between subject and object.
Is that the Eternal Triangle? After a short while
of looking at the show I take off to a more distant
planet and with a more powerful telescope I
look at myself diligently looking at myself.
Surely this self-fascination is not meditation. I
get up and do something pleasant, useful or
beautiful.*

*Then once again the voyeuse, I go back to
peering at my consciousness. It is garbage!
Garbage!? The word inspires me because I use
my kitchen garbage aesthetically and usefully by
putting peelings of fruits and vegetables in tall
colorless glass containers, semi-filled with water.
Floating in it these organic elements become
very lively, their ever-changing essence creating
forms and colors at times vivid and defined—
other times extraordinarily ethereal—a
fascinating, on-going transformation. In a week
or two when the exotic submarine bouquet
becomes too alive I put it in the compost heap
where nature's cycle continues. What about
applying the same principle to the content of my
consciousness? I decide to recycle every bit of
it into a thought of goodwill for anyone or
anything which presents itself.*

*It becomes a fun game to look at a
thought-feeling and convert it into a blessing for
the subject (person, animal, thing—whatever) of*

the thought-feeling. Even science agrees now that "thoughts are things." Surely if random thoughts are consciously converted into a message of goodwill, only something worthwhile can result.

But wait a moment! At times it also happens that when we decide to do something constructive, all the destructive devils within arise and form a powerful coalition. They hurl at us the most toxic feelings and thoughts imaginable —events bearing sadness, resentment and injustice, a sense of uselessness, years of physical pain and mental anguish—all of it parading, mocking us with a challenge to be converted to "choiceless goodwill." Ah ah ah! If this should happen, be sure to salute all little and big devils and acknowledge their irrefutable logic, their astounding skill. Then either say, "We will wrestle later," and give them a definite rendezvous which you will keep (they will, too!) or if devils or toxic feelings are adamant in asking now for attention, then now is the time to exorcise by exercise. Run, shout, breathe fast and deeply, dance naked to music, push with all your might against the wall, swim, jump, write a letter not to be mailed, walk on all fours, etc. Whatever you do, go back to the garbage recycling game afterwards.

I understand that meditation is to be undertaken in purity of intention and not for results. If viewed as an utilitarian project like the one I propose, then meditation becomes but another, although higher, achievement of that ego about which so many seem to be so worried. The garbage recycling game, then, is not meditation because it is ambitious and it has goals and results: the improvement of relationships, ambience, digestion, wrinkles, etc. It is not meditation but, by playing it lightly and constantly, and if "as luck would have it that God is on our side," it could happen (why not?) that one day garbage, recycling, thought, thinker, devils, blessings—all of it becomes one, all separation vanishing in a moment.

> *Then there is Silence.*
> *Luminous Silence.*
> *Silence.*

> *—Laura Huxley*

Ch'ui the draftsman
Could draw more perfect circles freehand
Than with a compass.

His fingers brought forth
Spontaneous forms from nowhere. His mind
Was meanwhile free and without concern
With what he was doing.

No application was needed
His mind was perfectly simple
And knew no obstacle . . .

No drives, no compulsions,
No needs, no attractions:
Then your affairs
Are under control.
You are a free man.

> *—Thomas Merton*
> The Way of Chuang Tzu

If you know how to do one thing well, you can do everything.

—Gurdjieff
Our Life with Mr. Gurdjieff

Meditation Without Form

Most meditative practices give very specific instructions as to what to focus on, what to think, or what to do. But in the last analysis, the meditative state goes beyond practices. Such methods are but stepping off points to this state, but they aren't always needed. There are ways to perceive yourself and the world, right from the outset, that catapult you into the meditative state without the necessity of practices. These ways of perceiving allow you to be keenly alert, to be choiceless awareness, to have clarity. These methodless methods are found in the writings of all traditions. The following writings reflect this pathless path. One of the most beautiful statements of this non-technique is found in the Song of Mahamudra by Tilopa.

excerpts from
THE SONG OF MAHAMUDRA

Mahamudra is beyond all words
And symbols, but for you, Naropa,
Earnest and loyal, must this be said.

The Void needs no reliance,
Mahamudra rests on nought.
Without making an effort,
But remaining loose and natural,
One can break the yoke
Thus gaining Liberation.

If one sees nought when staring into space,
If with the mind one then observes the mind,
One destroys distinctions
And reaches Buddhahood.

The clouds that wander through the sky
Have no roots, no home; nor do the distinctive
Thoughts floating through the mind.
Once the Self-mind is seen,
Discrimination stops.

Do nought with the body but relax,
Shut firm the mouth and silent remain,
Empty your mind and think of nought.
Like a hollow bamboo

Rest at ease your body.
Giving not nor taking,
Put your mind at rest.
Mahamudra is like a mind that clings to nought.
Thus practicing, in time you will reach
  Buddhahood.

Cease all activity, abandon
All desire, let thoughts rise and fall
As they will like the ocean waves.

He who abandons craving
And clings not to this or that,
Perceives the real meaning
Given in the Scriptures.

Transient is this world;
Like phantoms and dreams,
Substance it has none.
Renounce it and forsake your kin,
Cut the strings of lust and hatred,
Meditate in woods and mountains.
If without effort you remain
Loosely in the "natural state,"
Soon Mahamudra you will win
And attain the Non-attainment.

Cut the root of a tree
And the leaves will wither;
Cut the root of your mind
And Samsara falls.

Whoever clings to mind sees not
The truth of what's Beyond the mind.
Whoever strives to practice Dharma
Finds not the truth of Beyond-practice.
To know what is Beyond both mind and practice,
One should cut cleanly through the root of mind
And stare naked. One should thus break away
From all distinctions and remain at ease.

One should not give or take
But remain natural,
For Mahamudra is beyond
All acceptance and rejection.

The supreme Understanding transcends
All this and that. The supreme Action
Embraces great resourcefulness
Without attachment. The supreme
Accomplishment is to realize
Immanence without hope.

At first a yogi feels his mind
Is tumbling like a waterfall;
In mid-course, like the Ganges
It flows on slow and gentle;
In the end, it is a great
Vast ocean, where the Lights
Of Son and Mother merge in one.

—*Tilopa*
Teachings of Tibetan Yoga

Meditation is a never-ending movement. You can
never say that you are meditating or set aside
a period for meditation. It isn't at your
command. Its benediction doesn't come to you
because you lead a systematized life or follow
a particular routine or morality. It comes only
when your heart is really open. Not opened by
the key of thought, not made safe by the intellect,
but when it is as open as the skies without a
cloud; then it comes without your knowing,
without your invitation. But you can never guard
it, keep it, worship it. If you try, it will never
come again: do what you will, it will avoid you.
In meditation, you are not important, you have
no place in it; the beauty of it is not you, but in
itself. And to this you can add nothing. Don't
look out of the window hoping to catch it
unawares, or sit in a darkened room waiting for
it; it comes only when you are not there at all,
and its bliss has no continuity.

—*Krishnamurti*
The Second Penguin
Krishnamurti Reader

And look that nothing remain in thy working mind but a naked intent stretching unto God— not clothed in any special thought of God in himself or any of his works, but only that He is as He is. . . .

—The Cloud of Unknowing

In its true state, mind is naked, immaculate; not made of anything, being of the Voidness; clear, vacuous, without duality, transparent; timeless, uncompounded, unimpeded, colourless; not realizable as a separate thing, but as the unity of all things, yet not composed of them; of one taste, and transcendent over differentiation.

—*Padmasambhava*

The Tibetan Book of
the Great Liberation

*There is no place to seek the mind;
It is like the footprints of the birds in the sky.*

—*Zenrin*

The Gospel According to Zen

All is calm. How can we describe the indescrible? Can we say like this, like that? Things are or are not. There is an unreality, an emptiness, a Maya of everything that is, like the sky that covers all. Past, present and future are the same, beyond thought. How can we explain? Is or is not? Not like this nor like anything else. Away even from transcendency. Emptiness and the Dharma nature are not different. Beyond all signs whatsoever. Beyond communication. Different. Nameless. Sudden like lightning. With a meaning beyond thought. Therefore there is no meaning. Now it's all finished. Words are liars.

—The Fifteenth Gyalwa
Karmapa
Samata Magazine

Words!
The Way is beyond language,
for in it there is

> *no yesterday*
> *no tomorrow*
> *no today,*

—*Sengstan*

Hsin Hsin Ming

4

FINDING
YOUR
WAY

Let It Change

Though you can start meditation any time, it's harder if your life is chaotic, if you're feeling paranoid, if you're overwhelmed with responsibilities, or if you're sick. But even starting under these conditions, meditation will help you to clear things up a bit. Slowly you reorganize your life to support your spiritual journey. At each stage there will be something you can do to create a supportive space. It may mean changing your diet, who you're with, how you spend your time, what's on your walls, what books you read, what you fill your consciousness with, how you care for your body, or where and how you sit to meditate. All these factors contribute to the depth and freedom that you can know through meditation.

You are under no pressure to rush these changes. You need not fear that because of meditation you are going to lose control and get swept away by a new way of life. As you gradually develop a quiet and clear awareness, your living habits will naturally come into harmony with your total environment, with your past involvements, present interests, and future concerns. There need be no sudden ending of relationships in order to prove your holiness. Such frantic changes only show your own lack of faith. When you are one in truth, in the flow, the changes in your life will come naturally.

> *After you have practiced for a while, you will realize that it is not possible to make rapid, extraordinary progress. Even though you try very hard, the progress you make is always little by little.*

> —*Shunryu Suzuki*
> Zen Mind, Beginner's Mind

By the late sixties and early seventies many Americans had seen the limitations of seeking finite pleasures, and began looking for ways to break the cycle of wants. Western models no longer held; Eastern models very quickly became the fashion. But the Eastern systems weren't entirely harmonious. We in the West were used to an education that imposed systems of belief from the outside rather than letting them grow from within. We adopted the outer forms, but not the inner teachings. Wearing beads and white clothes gave the semblance of the East, but was hollow.

There are hundreds of thousands of beings for whom spiritual awakening is a reality. I can go to Omaha, Idaho City, Seattle, Buffalo, or Tuscaloosa, and everywhere thousands of people are ready to hear. They are growing spiritually in their own daily lives, without putting on far-out clothes and wearing beads around their necks. Their spiritual awakening grows from within.

Mention is made of two classes of yogis: the hidden and the known. Those who have renounced the world are "known" yogis: all recognize them. But the "hidden" yogis live in the world. They are not known.

—Sri Ramakrishna

The Gospel of
Sri Ramakrishna

It would be a mistake to think that any Tibetan would see any incongruity or harm in going from a service in Lhasa Temple to the nearest house where there was a chang-drinking party being given. Nor would it be unusual to see a pleasure-seeker in a boatful of revelers, quietly counting the beads on his rosary. . . . Religious activity is as much a part of our life as any other activity, and religious belief and thought is as much a part of our thinking as is our concern for where our next meal is coming from.

—Thubten Jigme Norbu

Tibet

*It is not to be learned by world-flight, running
away from things, turning solitary and going
apart from the world. Rather, one must learn an
inner solitude, wherever or with whomsoever
he may be.*

—*Eckhart*

Meister Eckhart: A
Modern Translation

You start cleaning up your life when you feel that
you can't go on until you do. Cleaning up your life
means extricating yourself from those things which are
obstacles to your liberation. But keep in mind that
nothing in and of itself is an obstacle; it's your attachment to it or your motive for doing it that is the obstacle. It's not an issue of eating meat or not eating
meat; it's who's eating it and why.

If your senses can be caught and held by something, you are still chained to the world. It's your attachment to the objects of your senses that imprisons
you. Failing to break off the attachment of the senses
ultimately holds you back. The minute you aren't preoccupied with what's out there, then that pull is lost.
You are free to go deep in meditation.

It's not easy. It's a stinker to get to that level of
purity. You start out with things like what you eat,
who you sleep with, what you watch on TV, what you
do with your time. Many people fool themselves and
imitate someone else's purity. They do it in an imita-
tive way, one of fear of being unholy. Abstaining from
something for the wrong reasons is no better than

doing it. You can't pretend to be pure; you can only go at your own speed.

As changes occur through meditation you find yourself attracted to things that are inconsistent with your old model of who you are. Usually, for example, after having meditated in a rigorous (and somewhat righteous) fashion, I have then taken time off to wallow in television, go to movies, take baths and relax. Then, to my surprise, I have found myself not being attracted as much as before to these diversions, but being pulled toward just sitting quietly. This new way of being didn't fit with my model of who I was. It was as if I were living with somebody I didn't know very well. My models of myself hadn't changed fast enough to keep up with who I was becoming.

> *Inside yourself or outside, you never have to change what you see, only the way you see it.*
>
> —*Thaddeus Golas*
>
> The Lazy Man's Guide to Enlightenment

The Buddhists see the meditative path as the balanced intensification of three mental traits: punya, sila, and samadhi. Punya is wisdom, or understanding. Sila is purification, or simplifying your life. Samadhi is concentration or one-pointedness. As you meditate and start to calm your mind a bit, that's the beginning of samadhi. This taste of clarity shows you how agitated your mind and body are, and how complicated your life is. So you start to simplify your life, clean up your game—the beginning of sila. The more you simplify your life, the better your meditations become. More samadhi. Stronger samadhi tunes you into more profound wisdom—more sila. More sila, more samadhi; more samadhi, more punya; more punya, more sila. Each feeds and balances the others.

Make It Simple

Meditation helps other parts of your life become more simple. As you enter quieter spaces you will see how clinging to desires has made your life complicated. Your clinging drags you from desire to desire, whim to whim, creating more and more complex entanglements. Meditation helps you cut through this clinging.

If, for example, you run around filling your mind with this and that, you will discover that your entire meditation is spent in letting go of the stuff you just finished collecting in the past few hours. You also notice that your meditations are clearer when you come into them from a simpler space. This encourages you to simplify your life.

As you observe the patterns of your thoughts during meditation, notice which areas of your life keep cropping up as distracting thoughts and pulling on you. You will easily see what you must clean out of your closet in order to proceed more smoothly. For example, if you have heavy debts, and thoughts about these debts intrude when you meditate, rather than accrue more and more debts as our society urges, you will find yourself wanting to lessen them. As you simplify things like your finances, you see more clearly the way the laws of cause and effect work in your life. You will want to get your life lighter and clearer, so that there are fewer expectations upon you from all quarters. Later, when your meditative center is strong, you can carry many responsibilities without clinging to thoughts about them.

Each time you lighten your life, you are less at the whim of thought forms, both your own and others'. It's as if you have built a world based on the thoughts of who you seem to be. As you meditate you become aware that these models are merely thoughts, not really who you are at all. With each attachment to a thought form you give up, your world becomes that much lighter and clearer.

Meditation affects your life and your life shapes your meditation. It goes both ways. Less busyness in life brings greater richness in meditation. This richness makes you content with less of the trimmings of outer life. As this process continues, less is more.

Silence is the garden of meditation.

—*Ali*

Maxims of Ali

I recall that as a Harvard professor I had FM in my car and stereo in my office and home; I was constantly surrounded by music—even with a speaker in my bathroom. In addition there were paintings on all the walls and decorations in my car.

Slowly, as meditation changed my perception of the universe, I started to crave simplicity. I placed objects on the walls that reminded me of higher possibilities: pictures of beings who were in higher consciousness, symbols of this consciousness, and art that represented it. I found that I was beginning to appreciate the silence and was content to enjoy a few pieces of music or art thoroughly rather than fill every space with sound and with imagery.

At times, I even felt the total contentment that comes from sitting in silence in a purely white room.

He who with little is well content is rich indeed as a king; and a king, in his greatness, is poor as the pedlar, when his kingdom sufficeth him not.

—*Shekel Hakodesh*

The Holy Shekel

He who knows that enough is enough will always have enough.

—*Lao Tze*

Tao Te Ching

When my guru Maharaji instructed Hari Dass Baba to train me, Hari Dass had been silent for many years. He communicated with a chalk board on which he wrote simple phrases. He instructed me to be silent also and prepared a chalk board for me.

At first it seemed like a game, but its depth and beauty became apparent in time. First of all I got tired writing long answers, so I started to find simpler ways of saying things, which in turn simplified my thoughts. A dialogue via chalk boards slows down communication sufficiently to see individual thought forms and the space that surrounds them. This space between statement and reaction considerably deepened the quietness within me. There is a great loss of energy in our normal chatter. Silence brought me great energy and clarity. As Hari Dass wrote, "Nothing is better than something."

Unless a man is simple, he cannot recognize God, the Simple One.

—*Bengali Song*

The Gospel of
Sri Ramakrishna

*Stop talking, stop thinking, and there is nothing
 you will not understand.*
Return to the Root and you will find the Meaning;
Pursue the Light, and you will lose its source. . . .
*There is no need to seek Truth; only stop having
 views.*

—*Sengstan*

Buddhist Texts

To Everything There Is a Season

The transformation that comes through meditation is not a straight-line progression. It's a spiral, a cycle. My own life is very much a series of spirals in which at times I am pulled toward some particular form of sadhana or lifestyle and make a commitment to it for maybe six months or a year. After this time I assess its effects. At times I work with external methods such as service. At other times the pull is inward, and I retreat from society to spend more time alone.

The timing for these phases in the spiral must be in tune with your inner voice and your outer life. Don't get too rigidly attached to any one method—turn to others when their time comes, when you are ripe for them.

I first became involved in the journey through study, intellectual analysis and service. I found it difficult to work with methods of the heart. I would try to open my heart, but the methods seemed absurd. I recall going to the Avalon Ballroom in the early 1960s to hear Allen Ginsberg introduce Swami Bhaktivedanta, who led a Hare Krishna chant. This chant seemed weird to me. It left me cold and cynical. I recall thinking, "It's too bad—Allen's really gone over the edge. This chant just doesn't make it." In the years since, I've had moments of ecstasy with the Hare Krishna chant. My heart has opened wide to the beauty of the blue Krishna and the radiant Ram, and I've laughed at my own changes and growth.

A student once came to me and told me that he felt turned off by devotional practices. His practice was Buddhist; his meditation was on the dharma, the laws of the universe. Yet he felt troubled that his heart was closed. So I started him on the practice of the mantra "I love you dharma," breathing in and out of the heart saying, "I love you dharma." He loved it.

It's not an all-or-nothing game. You're not totally out of one phase before you start the next—there's a gradual shift.

> To everything there is a season,
> and a time to every purpose
> under the heaven:
> A time to be born, and a time to die;
> a time to plant, and a time to pluck up that
> which is planted;
>
> A time to kill, and a time to heal;
> a time to break down, and a time to build up;

A time to weep, and a time to laugh;
a time to mourn, and a time to dance;

A time to cast away stones, and
a time to gather stones together; a time to
embrace, and a time to refrain from embracing;

A time to get, and a time to lose;
a time to keep, and a time to cast away;

A time to rend, and a time to sew;
a time to keep silence, and a time to speak;

A time to love, and a time to hate;
a time of war, and a time of peace.

—*Ecclesiastes 3:1–8*

The Old Testament

To a sincere student, every day is a fortunate
day.

—*Zengetso*

Friends

As your meditation practice deepens, your attitudes toward other people change. The desires for gratification that make you turn to others out of need fall away. You may increasingly prefer to be alone—or with only a few people who share your interest in meditation. Let these changes happen gently.

As you grow, your friends change. Unlike your family, to whom you stay connected despite changing interests, you no longer need continue a friendship when the reasons for it no longer exist. At first it may bother you if close friends do not share your pull toward meditation. But leave judgment aside, for people develop in different ways and at their own rate. Your old friends cannot convince you meditation is wrong, nor can you convince them it is right. Simply respect the different paths that you are taking. Above all, do not proselytize. Your own quiet changes are the most convincing statement.

Minimize the drama that you attach to spiritual practices. When your faith is weak, you reinforce the weakness by trying to convince your friends to meditate also. Such efforts are only an attempt to reassure yourself. The fanaticism of large, popular movements often springs from this lack of faith on the part of its followers. The need to proselytize, the need to cling to and talk about your experiences, the need to dramatize them by turning simple acts of meditation into spiritual melodrama, all will fall away in time, leaving meditation a normal daily affair—nothing special.

This sort of melodrama is a form of spiritual materialism: you make spiritual life into something else to acquire, like a new car or television set. Just do your practices; don't make a big deal of them. The less you dramatize, the fewer obstacles you create. Romanticism on the spiritual path is just another attachment that will have to go sooner or later.

If you meditate alone and maintain your old social relationships, you often find yourself among people who don't understand what's happening to you. If so, be discrete. Keep your thoughts about meditation and its effect on your life to yourself unless others ask. Other people's doubts weaken your faith before it has had the opportunity to mature. This is one reason a mantra is often given secretly. It is not that a mantra requires secrecy to be effective, but rather it is important to concentrate singlemindedly on a mantra without entertaining the doubts or ridicule of others.

As meditation affects your life more completely, your desire for satsang, other beings who share similar spiritual interests, may lead you to seek out other spiritual aspirants to live with, either in a community or in a communal arrangement in a single house. Just because a community or commune is "spiritual" does not guarantee any less of the intense psychological melodramas usually found in group living situations. The fact that you meditate together, have a more or less shared outlook, and perhaps have the same teacher will all help you cut through some of the drama. But given human propensities, these factors will not likely cut through all of it. Living in satsang does not change the attachments with which you must work, but it changes your perspective on them. This new perspective brings a newfound sense of joy to daily activities that before seemed tedious and repetitive.

The point of satsang is not to become a meditation freak or cultist, but rather to let a new sense of things permeate your life. The more advanced your meditative practice becomes, the less it matters whether you meditate with others or alone—you need fewer supports. Satsang finally takes you beyond the need for satsang. When your life is fully inner-directed you need nobody's reassurance or help; then you can help others. Until that day, it's useful to have people around to point or share the way.

Who are these by whom you wish to be admired? Are not these the men whom you generally describe as mad? What do you want then? Do you want to be admired by madmen?

—*Epictetus*

Arrian's Discourses of Epictetus

Your kinsmen are often farther from you than strangers.

—*Ali*

Maxims of Ali

Let (the student of our Art) carry on his operations with great secrecy in order that no scornful or scurrilous person may know of them; for nothing discourages the beginner so much as the mockery, taunts, and well-meant advice of foolish outsiders.

—*Philalethes*

The Hermetic Museum

Groups

Come, come, whoever you are,
Wanderer, worshipper, lover of leaving—it
    doesn't matter.
Ours is not a caravan of despair.
Come, even if you have broken your vow
    a hundred times
Come, come again, come.

—Jelal-ud Din Rumi

Perhaps you are concerned about which of the many meditative programs to join. You may wonder about the purity or validity of the numerous kinds of meditation flourishing on the American scene these days. Here are some points to consider.

The first is that you get what you want. You progress at the rate you are ready to. Your true desires will draw from any of these programs what you seek. Be open to groups that teach meditation and sense whether their practices feel harmonious to you. If so, go ahead, learn from them. The drawback is that their goals may be far short of liberation and you may end up despairing at their limited vision.

Some programs are purer than others. Most are sincere efforts to teach meditation; only a very few are cynical exploitations of the marketplace. In general, their impurities will primarily affect them and only incidentally affect you. If you are pure in your desire greed will not touch you.

Most people act out of very strong attachments and clingings, and the mass movements cater to their disillusionments or enthusiasms. The large, public programs make their appeal to many different motives. The best-known, the TM program, has set as its goal initiating one percent of the world's population. I share with them the feeling that if more people would meditate, social decisions would be more harmonious. And certainly, to meditate using a mantra can take you very far along the path. TM gives many people their first taste of stillness, but some eventually find it is not enough and they move on. The TM technique is a pleasant experience, and most certainly will give you some self-control and calm. For those who would go deeper, it is not that the mantra would not take them, but that the TM organization itself is limited. The people who teach the method, except perhaps at its very top levels, like Maharishi Mahesh, do not seem to be the most advanced spiritual beings.

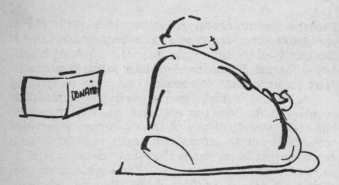

Many people complain about paying for a mantra. There is really nothing wrong with an organization asking people to pay to support its efforts, if its wish to spread meditation is purely motivated. But the going rates of some groups seem excessive. The temptations of wealth are great; gold has been the downfall of many yogis. My guru often warned me against "women and gold," the lures of sex and money. Meditation is a very precious vehicle. It is sad that some teachers—who could know better—seek only wealth or power. They reap what they sow. For example, if you pay to learn meditation and the teacher charges unfairly, he or she is left with the money and you with the vehicle for liberation. If you use the method well, you end up free, your teacher trapped.

In general I find the large meditation organizations offensive, for they tend to attract people who want power. There are many slots in these large organizations for power players who become overbearing in their fraudulent holiness. If your desire is pure—if it is not power you're after—you can reach toward the source of these organizations. Drink from that source and let the impurities pass you by.

Suppose, for example, a group's initiation offers sound traditional techniques, but the organization itself is an obstacle in the long run. If your motive is to be part of a group of like-minded seekers, then you may be attracted to such an organization. Use such a group until your inner discipline is strong enough, then go it alone.

Many meditation groups seek to avoid any spiritual identity. TM, for example, has shed its spiritual side as fast as it can so that it will be more acceptable to the American masses, including the military and the public schools. Some programs—not at all spiritual in outlook—offer only therapeutic changes. They do a lot of good by offering mass psychotherapy that gives people a new feeling of self-worth. For that they're worth the money. They're useful, not a rip-off. Their limit is that they touch on methods that offer people much more than psychological betterment, but define their goals only in psychological terms, and thereby mislead people about the greater possibilities. For some who go these routes it will be enough, for others it won't. Those who want something more will move on. Such movements talk about higher states but actually teach ordinary effectiveness and stay within the bounds of the realities of this world. It is one thing to keep one's ground when one has never flown and quite another to fly and then return to the ground. My criticism of most mass spiritual movements is that they are not directed by people who have first flown and are now living on the ground. Someone who is lost in illusion, no matter how nice his or her words, cannot free another. The lack of freedom in those who guide others creates the most subtle suffering for everyone.

When you are just beginning your journey, almost any method will help. As you get to the more advanced stages you will find that certain guides have aspirations lower than your own. Then you must seek elsewhere for the proper teaching, one that will free you rather than entrap you.

The mass programs offer useful psychological housecleaning. They probably will make you more effective in the world. But for me the most attractive training programs are those which aim for the highest aspirations of humanity. Toward the Living Spirit. Toward knowing, or becoming God. These programs with higher aspirations are also serving humanity. In fact they serve humanity even more, for they create a space of liberation from which you can pursue your involvement in the world with inner freedom. It takes a free being to free another.

There is a story that as God and Satan were walking down the street one day, the Lord bent down and picked something up. He gazed at it glowing radiantly in His hand. Satan, curious, asked, "What's that?" "This," answered the Lord, "is Truth." "Here," replied Satan as he reached for it, "let me have that—I'll organize it for you."

> *Beware of false prophets, which come to you in sheep's clothing, but inwardly they are ravening wolves.*
>
> —*Matthew* 7:15
>
> The New Testament

Benares is to the East, Mecca to the West; but explore your own heart, for there are both Rama and Allah.

—Kabir

One Hundred Poems of Kabir

Teachers

If several teachers are available in your area, how do you select one? I say in your area, because you needn't go far afield to begin meditation. To travel all over looking for the perfect teacher adds more to your melodrama than to your liberation. Virtually any teacher is suitable simply to begin, and if no teacher is available, you can do much on your own. In the end, you are your own best teacher.

Later on you may feel drawn to a specific teacher. As you look about for teachers, be open. Listen, tune, feel. Sense whether the teacher, teachings, and practices are harmonious with your needs.

You may meet a teacher whom everyone else respects, loves, and honors, but in your heart nothing happens. There's no reason to judge this person, nor to persuade or argue with others. Simply decide what's right for you at the moment. Move on if you must. This does not deny the possibility that at some later date the same teacher may be perfect for you, or that he may be perfect for others. It's tempting to sit around and judge teachers rather than use their teachings and get on with it. There's no need for spiritual gossip.

When you take teachings you have certain obligations to your teacher and the lineage from which the teachings come. Surrender. Open yourself to the instructions. Don't hold back, saying, "I'll take just a little teaching from you, but no more." To get the most from a teacher you must dive in and immerse yourself fully. Risk getting wet. Trust that you will be able to get out of the water when you've had enough.

In one meditation course I took, on the first day the teacher said, "During these ten days you must take a vow to surrender to me, to do just as I tell you." This was a limited contract and I had no trouble with it. I understood that this surrender was necessary for the proper transmission of his teaching.

When the teaching is over, what are your obligations? Sometimes a teacher says, "Now that you have taken teachings from me, you must serve me and proselytize on my behalf." Or, "You can't leave now, you're not ready: you need more teachings." Yet you know in your heart that your business together is finished. When you have finished with a teacher, your only debt to that teacher is your own liberation. As Shakespeare said, "This above all—to thine own self be true, . . . Thou canst not then be false to any man."

All a teacher offers really is his or her own being. For example, there are many stories of enlightened teachers who by merely repeating a mantra once could change a devotee's entire life. The devotee might have been very worldly, but the spirit with which the mantra was invested evoked a deep response. Beyond the mantra, what the teacher transmitted was not only the mantra, but the ability to use it properly. If a teacher is trying to transmit what he or she has not fully received, the spirit will be lacking and the transmission will be incomplete. The student's disillusionment upon finding out that the teacher was not qualified to invest the mantra, unfortunately, may make the student averse to continuing the use of a perfectly good mantra.

Some people fear becoming involved with a teacher. They fear the possible impurities in the teacher, fear being exploited, used, or entrapped. In truth we are only ever entrapped by our own desires and clingings. If you want only liberation, then all teachers will be useful vehicles for you. They cannot hurt you at all. If, on the other hand, you want power, a teacher may come along who talks about liberation but subtly attracts you by your desire for power. If you get caught and become a disciple of such a teacher, you may feel angry when this teacher turns out to be on a power trip, not leading you to enlightenment. But remember: At some level inside yourself you already knew. Your attraction to this teacher was your desire for power. Your anger is nothing more than anger toward yourself.

Some say that you should do nothing without the help of a teacher, that to do anything without guidance is dangerous. Others say that a teacher is not necessary, that you can only do it yourself. Of course, people have awakened and come to full realization without any teacher. On the other hand, most people at some point along the path need teachers. For example, if you seek to quiet your mind, at first learning to meditate is enough. Later you might need a teacher to show you how you have misused even the simplest meditation in the service of your ego rather than having used it for your liberation.

Whether teachings experienced along the way are beautiful and pleasant, or unpleasant and harsh, or even bland, all are grist for the mill of awakening. The slightest reaction reflects the subtlest clinging. It is a meaningful clue to where you are still holding on. Simply watching your reaction makes anything a teaching.

Teachers and teachings are forms, and ultimately you must go beyond forms. If you are true to your own inner voice, as it gets subtler and subtler it brings you to the moment beyond separateness of seeker and guide. Then you have served your teacher well.

When Mrs. Albert Einstein was asked if she understood her husband's Theory of Relativity, she replied, "No . . . But I know my husband and he can be trusted."

If you wish to know the road
*   up the mountain,*
Ask the man who goes back and
*   forth on it.*

—*Zenrin*

The Gospel According to Zen

A man does not seek to see himself in running
water, but in still water. For only what is itself
still can impart stillness into others.

—*Chuang-tse*

The Wisdom of China
and India

When you forget all your dualistic ideas,
everything becomes your teacher, and everything
can be the object of worship.

—*Shunryu Suzuki*

Zen Mind, Beginner's Mind

Retreats

There is an ancient and unbroken tradition of people who withdraw from the marketplace for meditation. This withdrawal can range from a day of solitude to the dedication of one's entire life as a recluse or a member of a religious order. You will benefit by devoting at least a few days or weeks to intense inner work. You needn't become a monk, but an occasional retreat accelerates your progress.

I often tell my students to take one day a month or set aside a weekend for solitude. Should you try it, the directions are simple. Go into an empty room, if you have one, or a large closet, if it gets enough fresh air. Don't see or speak to anyone. Don't read or study. Simply sit quietly, aware of yourself and the world around you. Do some formal meditation practices if you wish. Solitude shows you the way your mind creates your universe.

For longer retreats you can go to one of the centers listed in the back of this book, or go out in a tent or a cabin. Go anywhere you can be completely alone for a week, a few weeks, a month or more. During this time, follow your own schedule of methods, such as formal meditation, hatha yoga, chanting and mantra. But also spend time just sitting quietly. Sit near a tree, a brook, a rock. Set aside your intellect. Let the natural flow of the universe course through your being and harmonize your soul. Let it draw you into an eternal sense of time, of flow. While sitting quietly you may get depressed from rerunning the old movies of your life. Your fantasies and plans may plague you. But eventually a deep quietness will pervade your being, connecting you with profound aspects of yourself and of the universe. It will open you to deeper guidance from within, guidance that brings you closer to God.

There is a pleasure in the pathless woods,
There is a rapture on the lonely shore,

There is society, where none intrudes
By the deep sea, and music in its roar.

—Lord Byron

Childe Harold's Pilgrimage

The homes of householders who have
well-governed minds and have banished their
sense of egoism are as good as solitary forests,
cool caves or peaceful woods.

—*Yoga-Vasishtha*

The World Within the Mind

The mind is all. If the mind is active even solitude
becomes like a market place.

—*Sri Ramana Maharshi*

Talks with Sri
Ramana Maharshi

I've spent time every year or so in many types of retreat facilities—Buddhist, Hindu, Christian—and have received much sustenance from doing so. A few years ago I stayed in a Benedictine monastery in New York State. I was given a cell, attended the daily offices and services, and joined in the monks' silent round of meditation, study and work. I vividly recall a moment that affected me profoundly. We dwelt in silence. We had taken our modest meal on our tin-plated plates and cups, and we stood in line to wash our dishes. There was a large tub for soaping and another one for rinsing. The soaping dish had a sponge in it on a stick.

It was the rare moment when some kind of social relationship was acceptable. As we stood in line we were allowed to whisper to one another. I was standing behind a healthy, powerful man in his forties—very radiant. I was watching the sponge go around on the plate he was washing as I asked, "How long have you been at this monastery?" His answer came back—"Sixteen years."

The image of that sponge going around on that plate and the words "sixteen years" were imprinted in my mind. For the way in which he said "sixteen years" had neither pride nor pity nor any other noticeable emotional quality to it. It was merely a statement of fact. That moment captured for me the equanimity, patience, and depth of meditative life.

At a lecture one of the brothers said, "Here at the monastery, we take away all freedom of choice about matters such as clothing, food, and what to do with time. This frees us to go within." There's a critical difference between external and internal freedom. The image "Bars do not a prison make" is apt, for monastic life is very much like imprisonment. You are totally controlled in terms of time and space. Yet within these limits you are free from the need to think so much about externals, freeing you to explore yourself.

Take advantage of the excellent retreat facilities available in this country. Many are listed in the directory at the back of this book. Some allow you to be on your own, so it can be like being alone in the wilds. Others offer structured retreats where meditation is taught and strengthened through an intensive training. I have found both kinds of retreats extremely useful. Time to yourself helps you simplify your life. A ten days' sitting with fifty other people and a meditation teacher inspires you and advances your meditation dramatically.

Some religious organizations and growth centers offer such retreats. Many Christian churches and monasteries have retreat facilities open to the lay public. In Burma, retreats are a national pastime. Rather than going on vacation to the seaside or the mountains, the Burmese often use their vacation time for meditative retreats. They renew themselves and return to the world. This is starting to happen in the West.

Retreat centers offer you a totally controlled space with minimal distractions. There are no televisions, radios, newspapers, few chances for idle hanging out, and fewer still for fulfilling most of the desires that interfere with meditation. We normally can't hear the still small voice within because of the blaring trumpets of our desires. In such a setting, where there is nothing to make the trumpet sound, you can more easily hear the still small voice.

As one changes one's goals, much that was once seen as abhorrent becomes very functional—indeed, valued. Once I met a Black Panther. I was impressed with the clarity of his eyes. I said to him, "How did you become so clear?" His answer was, "It was solitary, man." He had been in solitary confinement for a long time and had used that punishment as a chance to deepen his own being.

My life was very simple in my guru's temple in the Himalayas. I slept on a mat, washed from a bucket, ate one meal a day, and sat for long hours looking out the window or studying the Gita. At one point as I was sitting there, I recalled a *Life* magazine article I had once read about some prisoners of war, captured U.S. pilots. Some photographs had leaked out depicting their life. I recalled one major's description of his life as a war prisoner: "I sit in a room all day. I am sleeping on a mat. I am washing from a bucket and eating one meal a day." The article meant to depict the horror of his life, under such dread conditions. I looked at my own life. I had voluntarily chosen to live in exactly the same conditions, and most of the time I was in ecstasy at my situation.

Each day a bus would go by outside the temple. It was my lifeline back to the world. Often when the time came for the bus in the afternoon, I found myself standing at the window watching for it. I would take out my return airplane ticket and hold it as I watched the bus go by. In this way I examined my longing to return to the world. I would fantasize getting on the bus, and maybe thirty or forty hours later arriving back in the United States, where I would jump right back into all the things I had left behind.

At that time the particular image that drew me was dancing to the Grateful Dead in San Francisco's Fillmore Auditorium. I imagined all the things I would do—eating, sex, entertainment, social relationships, visiting with the family, and so on. I could cast myself into any of these roles, run them through in detail and finally get to the point of imagining myself saying, "You know what I would really like? To be living in a temple in India where I could just sit all day." At that point I would put away my ticket and resume my practices.

Sitting quietly, doing nothing,
Spring comes and the grass grows by itself.

—*Zenrin*

The Gospel According to Zen

Is Meditation a Cop-out?

Better to be temporarily selfish than never just.

—Gurdjieff

In Search of the Miraculous,
P. D. Ouspensky

Some people do use meditation as a cop-out. For them meditation is a defense against facing the problems of life. They devote themselves wholeheartedly to meditation as an escape from responsibility. But they defeat their purpose, for you have to be somebody to become nobody. And if you're not somebody enough, you'd better become somebody first. The spiritual path is not a cop-out from life. You need to clean up your life before you attempt to give it up.

The popular image is of the meditator sitting with eyes closed, immersed in himself. Many in the West see meditation as a withdrawal from the world, an avoidance of social responsibility. Such withdrawal may occur temporarily, as when the meditator has periods of retreat. But it is not necessary, nor does it reflect the essence of the meditative state. Rather than make him withdraw from the world, meditation naturally leads the seeker to a deeper appreciation of the interrelatedness of things, of his relation to his family, friends, nation, and the world.

The meditator also comes to honor the individual differences that make up the fabric of society. Within the harmonious flow of the universe each person's part plays its role. For example, because I live in a country that allows me the freedom to meditate, I feel a duty to reciprocate by paying taxes and voting, so as to maintain the whole that allows me that freedom. At the same time, I don't have to go to Washington to protest. That isn't my particular role to play, but I don't object to anyone else doing it. Social action, if done compassionately, also betters society.

Consider compassion and protest. Each of us is predisposed to fill different social roles. One person feels harmony as a mother who keeps a loving home for her family. Another feels that same harmony only when actively protesting social injustice. No role in itself is more conscious than another. A person's consciousness is reflected in the way the role is played. If someone who has a heightened meditative awareness feels drawn to protest against social injustice, such protest would come from a more compassionate sense of the rightness of the action. His meditative awareness allows greater clarity so he can view the social predicament from all sides. This lets the protester act more effectively, since he is not so attached to his own view of how things should be. Gandhi brought together spiritual life and social action in this way. He tried to meditate and always remembered God, even in the thick of a crisis. When he was assassinated, his last words were the name of God.

Meditation changes how you do whatever you do. Look at competitive sports. Two tennis players, for example, may compete fiercely, each preoccupied with winning. Yet if at the same time they appreciate the beauty of the moment—including the fact that they are two human beings collaborating to compete—it changes the nature of the game. Their expanded awareness may also let them appreciate the beauty of the day, and their good fortune in being able to play. This added appreciation enhances the sense of playful competition and frees them of attachment to winning at all costs, an attitude we call poor sportsmanship. They can simply enjoy the moment.

The secret behind successfully performing any act, be it meditation, motherhood, social protest, or tennis, lies in the attitude of the performer, not in the particular act.

St. Abba Dorotheus, a sixth-century monk, said:

Over whatever you have to do, even if it be very urgent and demands great care, I would not have you argue or be agitated. For rest assured, everything you do, be it great or small, is but one-eighth of the problem, whereas to keep one's state undisturbed even if thereby one should fail to accomplish the task, is the other seven-eighths. So if you are busy at some task and wish to do it perfectly, try to accomplish it—which, as I said would be one-eighth of the problem, and at the same time to preserve your state unharmed —which constitutes seven-eighths. If, however, in order to accomplish your task you would

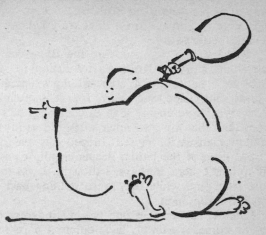

*inevitably be carried away and harm yourself
or another by arguing with him, you should not
lose seven for the sake of preserving one-eighth.*

—Early Fathers from
the Philokalia

In 1967 I spent many months in my guru's
temple in India. I recall receiving a letter from Allen
Ginsberg, describing the Chicago convention and the
revolutionary protest of many people whom I knew.
For a moment, I felt as if I were escaping from the
world by sitting in this temple in India, leading a simple

quiet life. I thought I was copping out. It was as though I were at a rest camp far from the action, and my friends were out on the front lines truly helping mankind find a better world.

At the time I was studying the Bhagavad Gita, which is the story of Krishna's injunction to Arjuna to fight in a battle. As I reflected more deeply, the Bhagavad Gita helped me realize that it is often easier to fight an external enemy than to confront one's inner demons, and that my own inner work did as much for my fellow man as for myself. Indeed this was one of the front lines of the battle, deepening my own inner being to feed others. Perhaps, I thought, I was the one on the front line while they were holding back from ultimate confrontation.

Later I realized that one needn't judge who was better or worse. We simply have different parts to play in the drama.

Calmness of mind does not mean you should stop your activity. Real calmness should be found in activity itself.

—*Shunryu Suzuki*
Zen Mind, Beginner's Mind

Many Stages, Many Paths

There are countless paths, each with its own landmarks, its own route. Meditation unfolds in a sequence, but the specific experiences and their order vary from person to person and from method to method. In devotional meditation or prayer you may be filled with intense love, or with the great pain of separation, or with the presence of the Living Spirit. If on the other hand you meditate using a one-pointedness technique, such as concentration on the breath, you may first experience agitation, then quietness, a deepening silence, more immediate awareness of smaller units of thought, and finally the silent space and emptiness that exists beyond form. In still another approach to meditation, say a movement method like t'ai chi, your first experiences might be of balance, harmony, or flow with the earth, the air, and the surroundings. It is not possible to chart a single path, or to say that every individual will have the same experience. The paths of the heart, the mind, and the body each traverse different terrain to the same goal.

Don't get attached to your way of meditation. Keep in mind that the goal is liberation and that all meditations can be used as you need them to help you in the journey. You can sit and follow your breath to bring your mind to quiet one-pointedness which loosens the hold of all your worldly thoughts. Once the basic tool of one-pointedness is forged, you can use it for any of a number of ends. If you use it to gain insight into the workings of your mind, you ultimately enter the state of Nirvana. Or you might use your one-pointedness to contemplate beings who embody spiritual qualities and develop these qualities in yourself. Or it might work another way: you can begin with prayer, and through the love of Jesus simplify your life to the point that you create no new karma. What may draw you on then is the need for silence, so you seek a simpler meditation, such as following your breath.

I've found that each meditation technique I've ever pursued seriously has helped me by touching another space in my being. Somehow I've danced through them without getting caught in a value system that would say that a single meditative technique is the only way.

You cannot, however, keep collecting methods all the way to enlightenment. Sooner or later you will be drawn to one path or another which is for you the eye of the needle, the doorway to the inner temple. The journey passes from eclectic sampling to a single path. Finally, you recognize the unity of your own way and that of other seekers who followed other paths. At the peak, all the paths come together.

The Indian saints Kabir and Tulsi Dass, as well as St. Theresa, showed an incredibly intense yearning and love for God. Ramana Maharshi, on the other hand, showed the path in which the discriminative mind, through the method of self-inquiry, extricates one from clinging even to the concept of "I." Others, such as the Tibetan sages Padmasambhava and Milarepa, embodied the skillful use of tremendous powers in the service of humanity. Jesus reflected the purest love, compassion, and sacrifice. Buddha showed the path of insight. All these are different routes to a single goal, liberation.

Many, many paths to the mountain top. Each has its own sights, experiences, hazards. Don't get stranded along the way.

In any way that men love me in that same way they find my love: for many are the paths of men, but they all in the end come to me.

—Bhagavad Gita 4:11

Water is for fish
And air for men.
Natures differ, and needs with them.

Hence the wise men of old
Did not lay down
One measure for all.

—*Thomas Merton*

The Way of Chuang Tzu

There is no particular way in true practice.

—*Shunryu Suzuki*

Zen Mind, Beginner's Mind

When you start you most likely won't know which method will be your final one. In the beginning your view of the path is hazy, for you are still caught in your own expectations and models of reality. As your meditation advances you become attuned to your own particular route through. Then as you finish the journey you open to the universality of all lineages.

The best description of that ultimate openness is the life of the Indian saint Ramakrishna. After having followed his own lineage, which honored, worshipped, and loved Mother Kali, he transcended it and went through Moslem, Christian, and a variety of other traditions. Today in the West some people are drawn to fundamental Christianity because of an intense emotional relationship with Jesus, others are drawn to the simple austerity of Zen Buddhism, and some to the intermingling of energy and love in Sufi dancing. When you work with a particular lineage, commit yourself totally to it. Hear it, see it, smell it, taste it, totally surrender into it. Don't worry about your final path. Let the inner guru call you. Through meditation you learn to listen quietly, until the call comes, clear and unmistakable.

> *From of old there were not two paths.*
> *"Those who have arrived" all walked the same road.*

> —*Zenrin*
> The Gospel According to Zen

5

LOSING
YOUR
WAY

Method

It is a rare being who can cross the ocean of existence without a boat. Few of us are ready to see completely through ego's illusion and thereby achieve instant liberation. So we use methods, we use a boat, with the understanding that when we get to the other shore, we'll leave the boat. We're not going to portage; we needn't carry the boat on our heads. We'll be finished with boats.

But the boat can entrap or liberate. Whether you end up as a boatman or as one liberated depends on your original motive for spiritual work. You can become a connoisseur of boats, collecting the very best. Or you can go to the far shore, beyond beyond: "Gate, gate, paragate, parasamgate, bodhi svaha," beyond even the concept of beyond.

Whatever you seek—spiritual realization, liberation, enlightment, merging with God, or however you describe it—don't cling to meditation as a method. At the same time, leave yourself open to any possibilities that come your way. To stand back from any method for fear of entrapment leaves you standing on this side yearning for the far shore. Jump in and trust your inner guide. The purity of your own yearning and of the methods you follow will show you the way.

Methods differ in how big, fancy, or ornate a boat they are. How dependent you become on a method depends on your degree of attachment to stuff, including your method of meditation. You can be attached to meditating on Krishna, chanting to fill your heart with love as the Hare Krishna devotees do. Or you can be attached to the ecstasy that sometimes comes from following your breath with exquisite one-pointedness.

All methods are traps. But for a method to work you must go deeply into it, deep enough to be entrapped. At the same time, trust that your yearning for spiritual self-realization and the nature of the method will ultimately free you from the method itself. For example, a pure guru exists only for your liberation. The guru has no desire to entrap you as a follower or disciple. Yet for your relationship to be productive, it demands your total involvement and surrender. If a teacher is impure, he may want to hold you as a disciple beyond the time you are ready to leave. Then it will be your purity of purpose that turns you away from the teacher.

It's the same with your relationship to meditation. As you reach each new stage, you cling to new highs. Or you may fear not getting enough after investing much of your time and effort. Or you may make the benefits of meditation, such as greater efficiency at work, ends in themselves. These are dead ends on the path.

How you use a method determines whether it

entraps or liberates you. The game isn't to become a method groupie, but to transcend method. To say I'm a meditator—or I'm an anything—is just another trap.

Some, such as Krishnamurti, question whether meditation actually does lead to liberation. They point out that all methods are just more ways of entrapping awareness. Rather than springing us from the traps of ego, they add yet another bar to our freedom. Proponents, such as Patanjali and the Buddha, say these are tools to be used until there is no longer any need for them. My feeling is that it would be best to bypass methods, but there are few of us capable of such a leap of consciousness. The rest of us need methods. These are traps through which we set ourselves free.

A good traveler leaves no track.

—*Lao Tse*

Tao Te Ching

Experience

As your mind quiets more and more in meditation your consciousness may shift radically. With quietness can come waves of bliss and rapture. You may feel the presence of astral beings; you may feel yourself leaving your body and rising into realms above your head; you may feel energy pouring up your spine. You may

have visions, burning sensations, a sharp pain in your heart, deep stillness, stiffening of your body. You may hear voices or inner sounds such as the flute of Krishna, a waterfall, thunder, or a bell. You may smell strange scents or your mouth may be filled with strange tastes. Your body may tingle or shake. As you go deeper you may enter what the southern Buddhists call jhanas, trance states marked by ecstasy, rapture, bliss, and clarity of perception. You may have visions of distant places or find you somehow know things though you can't explain how.

These experiences may seduce you. If you cling to them, fascinated—whether the fascination be out of attraction or repulsion—you invest them with undue importance. When you've had this kind of seductive experience, its memory can be an obstacle to meditation, especially if you try to recreate the experience. To keep going in meditation, you've got to give up your attachment to these states and go beyond. If these experiences come spontaneously, fine. But don't seek them.

I remember taking a fifteen-day insight meditation course. On the twelfth day I experienced a peace that I had never known in my life. It was so deep that I rushed to my teacher and said, "This peace is what I have always wanted all my life. Everything else I was doing was just to find this peace." Yet a month later I was off pursuing other spiritual practices. That experience of peace wasn't enough. It was limited. Any experiential state, anything we can label, isn't it.

My intense experiences with psychedelics led to very powerful attachments to the memories of those trips. I tried to recreate them through yogic practices. It took some years before I stopped comparing meditative spaces with those of my psychedelic days. Only when I stopped clinging to those past experiences did I see that the present ones had a fullness, immediacy, and richness that was enough—I didn't need the memories. Later, during intensive study of pranayama and kundalini, my breath stopped and I felt moments of great rapture. Once again, the intensity of the experience hooked me and I was held back for a time by my attempts to recreate those moments. When I saw that I was closest to God in the moment itself, these past experiences stopped having such a great pull. Again I saw my clinging to memories as an obstacle.

You come to see through your attachment to such experiences and find yourself less interested in striving for them. The despair and frustration that come from desiring a fascinating state and not getting it becomes grist for the mill of insight. It's an irritating process, in a way. You may see things clearly or have a breakthrough into another state for a second or so. But like psychedelics, it leaves you starving. You can grasp it for a moment, but you can't eat the fruit of the garden.

Meditation is not a matter of trying to achieve ecstasy, spiritual bliss or tranquility, nor is it attempting to become a better person. It is simply the creation of a space in which we are able to expose and undo our neurotic games, our self-deceptions, our hidden fears and hopes.

—Chogyam Trungpa

The Myth of Freedom

In Brindavana, the sacred city where Krishna dances with the gopis, there is a dudhwalla, a milk seller. He's a true devotee of Krishna. Once he was selling milk, and because of his purity, Krishna with his shakti Radha came right up to the stand, there on the street in Brindavana, and bought some milk. He actually saw them. His eyes are as though they had been burned out by a brilliant bulb. He can talk about nothing but the moment that Krishna and Radha came to his dudhstand. He's not worried about how much milk he sells any more. He's had the ecstasy of seeing God in the form of light. And that's who he is this lifetime. It's a high place to be.

Shouldn't that be enough? Won't you settle for ecstasy? Bliss? Rapture? Hanging out with the gods? Flying? Bet you always wanted to fly. Reading other people's minds? What power would you settle for? said the devil to Jesus in the desert. You must want something. Whatever you want you get, sooner or later. And there you are. As long as you are not finished with that desire, you are entrapped.

When you are attracted to powers and seduced by pleasures, what had been a vertical path turns horizontal. As long as your goal falls short of full liberation, you will be trapped by these experiences. If you know you want the long-range goal, that knowledge will help you give up the desires for the states along the way. As each desire arises there will be a struggle with your ego. Part of you wants to enjoy the seductive pleasures, part wants to give them up and push on.

One way to handle extraordinary experiences is to be neither horrified nor intrigued by them. The Tibetan Book of the Dead refers to the ten thousand horrible and the ten thousand beautiful visions. In the course of meditation you may meet them all: powers, great beauty, deaths, grotesqueries, angels, demons, all of it. These are just forms, the stuff of the universe. You confront them on the path just as you meet all manner of people when you walk a busy street. Notice them, acknowledge them—don't deny them—and then let them go. To cling to these heavens and hells, no matter how beautiful, slows your progress. Not to acknowledge them, or to push them away, is just a more subtle form of clinging. Follow the middle way. As stuff arises in your mind, let it arise, notice it, let it go. No clinging.

Many sensations come, many thoughts or images arise, but they are just waves of your own mind. Nothing comes from outside your mind.

To realize pure mind in your delusion is practice. If you try to expel the delusion it will only persist the more. Just say, "Oh, this is just delusion." And do not be bothered by it.

—Shunryu Suzuki
Zen Mind, Beginner's Mind

That thou mayest have pleasure in everything,
seek pleasure in nothing.
That thou mayest know everything,
seek to know nothing.
That thou mayest possess all things,
seek to possess nothing.
That thou mayest be everything,
seek to be nothing.

—*St. John of the Cross*

The Ascent of Mount Carmel

Planes

Our senses and thinking mind keep our awareness aligned with the physical plane. But there are planes where beings exist other than the physical. If in meditation you enter other states of consciousness, you may meet such beings who seemingly come to instruct or guide you. At first, they are awesome. They seem to exist either in disembodied states or with luminous or transparent bodies that appear and disappear at will. They do not exist for normal vision.

Because of the uniqueness of these beings you might put more value on their teachings than is merited. Beings on other planes are not necessarily wiser than those on this plane They may be well-meaning, but they may not know any more than you. Because of the way in which you met them, you are filled with awe and reverence, and you might treat their teaching as truth. All they may have to teach you is their existence itself, which shows you the relative nature of reality.

Some whom you meet on planes other than the physical may indeed come from higher, more conscious realms. They may be masters who exist in order to guide you and come forth at critical moments to instruct you. You needn't meet such masters to become liberated. They come to you only if your particular path requires their manifestation.

Just as with teachers on the physical planes, be open. Experience each being you meet and sense in your heart—do we have work to do together or not? If that teacher feels relevant to your spiritual journey, work with him or her until you have fully grasped the teaching. Then thank the teacher and proceed. This is true on every plane of existence.

Power

Even the beginnings of an inner quiet and calm allow you to see much more. You get a new sense of how you create and control your universe. You stop reacting to events simply with blind patterns and habits of thought. Your life becomes more creative. Other powers follow this new creativity as your meditation deepens. They become more and more dramatic, and can include psychic powers, astral travel, and even powers on other planes.

These are traps. They are seductive, especially for people who have felt impotent, inadequate, or weak. Because of their attractiveness these powers tend to make you slow down in your journey in order to enjoy them. This is especially likely when they offer more sensual gratification, for example, if you use the powers to attract new lovers for sexual conquests.

Power entraps even when it is used to do good. Even if you couch the exercise of power in righteous terms, it still involves you more deeply in ego, since you as a separate entity are trying to manipulate your environment. So it is that powers, just like any of the other seductions along the path, are best noted and let go of, rather than acted upon. It's better to go for broke than to take a small profit and run with it.

Meditation may attract those who seek worldly influence because of the psychic powers they can develop. Generals take it up to improve their military efficiency, and so meditation becomes part of the Cold War. Some try to develop telepathic powers or the ability to change things at a distance to win wars or control other people or things with the mind. Meditation might bring you this. So what? With the despair that comes from knowing that the worldly dance, including the greatest powers, is not sufficiently fullfilling, you recognize the deeper potential of meditation: nothing short of, not my, but Thy Will, the Will of God, out of which it all came in the first place. Why settle for less?

> *If you continue this simple practice every day you will obtain a wonderful power. Before you attain it, it is something wonderful, but after you obtain it, it is nothing special.*
>
> —*Shunryu Suzuki*
> Zen Mind, Beginner's Mind

Spiritual Pride

A persistent trap all along the path is pride in one's spiritual purity. It's a form of one-upmanship in which you judge others out of a feeling of superiority. This ultimately limits your spiritual awakening. You can see many people who are caught in this trap of virtue —for example, in the self-righteousness of some churchgoers. In the yoga scene in America there are many groups of people who dress in a certain way, eat in a certain way, are special in some way that gives them an ego-enhancing feeling of purity.

The harmful effect of this trap is not so much to one's social relationships—though they may become strained from this display of subtle arrogance—but rather the effect on oneself. This feeling of specialness or superiority inflates the ego and feeds it with pride. The best antidote to pride is humility, which leads to compassion. The sooner one develops compassion in this journey, the better. Compassion lets us appreciate that each individual is doing what he or she must do, and that there is no reason to judge another person or oneself. Merely to do what you can to further your own awakening.

> *Mad with joy, life and death dance*
> *to the rhythm of this music. The*
> *hills and the sea and the earth*
> *dance. The world of man dances*
> *in laughter and tears.*

> *Why put on the robe of the monk, and*
> *live aloof from the world in lonely*
> *pride?*

> —*Kabir*
>
> One Hundred Poems of
> Kabir

> *The worst man is the one who sees himself as*
> *the best.*

> —*Ali*
>
> Maxims of Ali

> *Whoever has in his heart even so much as a*
> *rice-grain of pride, cannot enter into Paradise.*
>
> —*Muhammad*
>
> Perspectives spirituelles
> et Faits humains

> *We are to practice virtue, not possess it.*
>
> —*Eckhart*
>
> Meister Eckhart: A
> Modern Translation

Highs

For many of us who have come into meditation
through psychedelics, the model we have had for
changing consciousness has been of "getting high." We
pushed away our normal waking state in order to
embrace a state of euphoria, harmony, bliss, peace, or
ecstasy. Many of us spent long periods of time getting
high and coming down. It was like the Biblical story
of the wedding guest who came to the wedding but
was not wearing the proper wedding garments, so he
got thrown out. My guru, in speaking about psychedelics, said, "These medicines will allow you to come
and visit Christ, but you can only stay two hours. Then
you have to leave again. This is not the true samadhi.
It's better to become Christ than to visit him—but even
the visit of a saint for a moment is useful." Then he

added, "But love is the most powerful medicine." For love slowly transforms you into what the psychedelics only let you glimpse.

In view of his words, when I reflected on my trips with LSD and other psychedelics, I saw that after a glimpse of the possibility of transcendence, I continued tripping only to reassure myself that the possibility was still there. Seeing the possibility is indeed different from being the possibility. Sooner or later you must purify and alter your mind, heart, and body so that the things which bring you down from your experiences lose their power over you. Psychedelics could chemically override the thought patterns in your brain so that you are open to the moment, but once the chemical loses its power the old habit patterns take over again. With them comes a subtle despair that without chemicals you are a prisoner of your thoughts.

I recall vividly a very powerful experience in 1962 in the meditation room of our house in Newton. For several hours I sat quiescent in a state of ecstatic transcendence merging into the universe. As the chemical began to wear off, I saw a blood-red wave rolling down the room toward me. In it were thousands of images of me—all of my social and psychological definitions of self. Me on a tricycle, giving a lecture, making love, and so forth. It was as if this wave was about to overrun me and carry me back into myself. I recall putting up my hands, trying to push away the oncoming wave and desperately searching my mind for some mantra or technique that would hold off this incredible force bearing down upon me. But I had no such charm or spell. The wave poured back over me and I came back into my old familiar self. In recent years I have learned how, when the thoughts arise that were contained within that wave, to use a meditative stance to witness them. This gently loosens their hold and brings me back into the moment. Then I see there's nothing special about the high, nothing dreadful about the thoughts in the wave. Just stuff.

The trap of high experiences, however they occur, is that you become attached to their memory and so you try to recreate them. These memories compel you to try to reproduce the high. Ultimately they trap you, because they interfere with your experience of the present moment. In meditation you must be in the moment, letting go of comparisons and memories. If the high was too powerful in comparison to the rest of your life, it overrides the present and keeps you focused on the past. The paradox, of course, is that were you to let go of the past, you would find in the present moment the same quality that you once had. But because you're trying to repeat the past, you lose the moment.

How many times have you felt a moment of perfection—only to have it torn away the next moment by the awareness that it will pass? How many times will you try to get high hoping that this time you won't come down—until you already know as you start to go up that you will come down? The down is part of the high. When in meditation you are tempted by another taste of honey, your memory of the finiteness of those moments tempers your desire. More bliss, more rapture, more ecstasy—just part of the passing show. The moment in its fullness includes both high and low and yet it is beyond both.

Paradise is the prison of the sage as the world is the prison of the believer.

—*Yahja b. Mu'adh al-Razi*

De l'Unité Transcendante
des Religions

Success

Though the numbers are proportionally few, many thousands of us have, through discipline and persistence, arrived at a view of our lives that is open, clear, and detached. In this new space we have a lightness, an ease in carrying out our daily lives, an ability to keep a certain sense of humor about our predicaments. We find that because of the quietness of our minds it's easier to relate to acquaintances, to family, to employers, to friends. It's also easier to bring together our economic scene and the other aspects of our lives.

We begin to feel a little bit like gods on earth, for where we see sadness and suffering around us, we are able to empathize and still feel lightness and joy. It's as if the world is made for our delight, and even our own troubles become a source of amusement. When we look one another in the eye there is clarity and honesty. We have a certain degree of inner peace. Many of us never thought possible this feeling of equanimity, fullness, and delight in life. We have a sense of self-acceptance, spaciousness, and fullness in the moment that makes each day enough. In many ways it seems like liberation.

As I look around at people I know who have been working intensely on themselves for some time, there is a dramatic change. I see beings who were initially preoccupied with their melodramas, whose bodies were their enemies and who were attached to spiritual melodrama, now bright, clear, and strong. Their lives have come together, they have relationships that are fulfilling, moments that are enough, a lightness in their faces. To see them this way fills me with happiness.

Yet I see that this stage is but a preparation for the ultimate climb that leads in the end to total liberation. This stage has a danger: It is too comfortable. It's like a beautiful mountain pasture: there are tents in the pine grove and streams to sit by and plenty of fuel and food. The air is clear, the view is grand. There are birds and wildflowers. These pleasures are a trap.

Many beings tarry here in this role of God on earth for many lifetimes. But ultimately even this heaven is not enough. For there is another path that leads from this pleasant pasture to still higher slopes. There is the final journey.

You should feel no guilt about where you are in your spiritual path. Wherever you are, be it at the beginning of the journey, well on your way, or resting comfortably at some height, you must acknowledge where you are, for that is the key to further growth. You should keep some perspective about the entire journey so that you will not sink into complacency, feeling you have finished the journey when you have not even begun to approach liberation.

The Sage does not talk, the Talented Ones talk, and the stupid ones argue.

—*Kung Tingan*

Judging

Our deep conditioning from school exams, grades, and the like gives us the habit of looking at every achievement competitively, in terms of where we stand. How are we doing: Are we better, equal, or worse than others on the same journey? Such evaluation of our position becomes a real obstacle in spiritual life, for it constantly leads us to look at spiritual evolution in comparative terms. Someone tells you they have visions of lights when they meditate. You never have had such a vision. This fills you with feelings of inadequacy and jealousy. On the other hand, you may sometimes feel yourself leaving your body when you meditate. Your friends don't experience this. This fills you with a subtle spiritual pride that feeds your ego.

In 1970 I traveled around the world on a lecture tour with Swami Muktananda. In his teaching he transmits shakti, or energy, to his students. I recall vividly a living room in Melbourne, Australia, where twenty people were gathered in meditation before him. It was late in the afternoon and he sat crosslegged on a love seat at the end of the room, with eyes closed behind sunglasses, a knit hat on his head, idly strumming a one-stringed instrument. The room was quiet.

Slowly, one by one, the people in the room started to behave bizarrely. One portly gentleman in a dark-blue suit with a watch fob suddenly began to do mudras, traditional Indian hand positions. I recall the look on his face of consternation and perplexity—it was apparent that he knew nothing of these mudras, and was certainly not doing them intentionally. Next to him a gentleman dressed in a tweed jacket and gray flannels with a pipe in his pocket, obviously the perfect professor, suddenly got up and started to do formal Indian dance. Again the look of perplexity, for in no way was he responsible for what he did. Near me was a girl who had come not to see Swami Muktananda, but to be with her boyfriend, who was interested. Suddenly she began to do intense, automatic breathing. Her rapid breathing got to such a height that she literally bounced across the floor of the room with the breaths. Again I saw the look of perplexity.

I watched more and more people experience the touch of Swami Muktananda's shakti, but never felt it myself. None of these things happened to me. I was concerned. After all, if I was "evolved enough" to lecture with Swami Muktananda, why shouldn't I have these dramatic signs of spiritual awakening? The seed of jealousy sprouted in me. Though I didn't admit it, I did my best to induce these symptoms of awakening.

Later I learned that these sometimes bizarre manifestations of shakti were the result of various blockages in people and were in no way necessary on the spiritual path. As time has gone on, I have learned that there is no experience, no symptom, no sign of spiritual growth that is absolutely necessary. Each of us has a unique predicament that stretches back over many lifetimes. Each person is drawn to a different set of practices and responds in his or her own way.

Individual differences are not better or worse, merely different. If we forgo judging, we come to understand that each of us has a unique predicament that requires a unique journey. While we share the overall journey, everyone's particular experiences are his or her own. No set of experiences is a prerequisite for enlightenment. People have become enlightened in all ways. Just be what you are.

The experiences along the way are not enlightenment. So if you don't see lights or meet remarkable beings on other planes, or if your body doesn't shake, or if you don't feel the greatest peace, or even if nothing seems to happen in meditation, don't compare or judge. Just keep going. To compare yourself with others is to forget the uniqueness of your own journey.

Always repenting of wrongs done
Will never bring my heart to rest.

—Chi K'ang

170 Chinese Poems

He who realizes the Lord God, the Atman, the
one existence, the Self of the universe, neither
praises nor dispraises any man. Like the sun
shining impartially upon all things, he looks with
an equal eye upon all beings. He moves about in
the world a free soul, released from all
attachment.

—Srimad Bhagavatam

The Wisdom of God

Love it the way it is.

—*Thaddeus Golas*

The Lazy Man's Guide
to Enlightenment

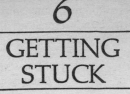

6

GETTING
STUCK

The Body Reacts

The minute that even the most gentle attempt is made
to quiet the mind, to go within, to loosen the hold of
one's overlearned way of thinking and being, new
experiences occur. Many people, after their first hours
of meditation, feel unusual patterns or rushes of energy.
There is no cause to fear. Merely watch and open to
these changing energy patterns. Don't resist them.
Where there is fear, there are blocks in the body, and
energy cannot flow.

Each person has his or her own special weak spot
where tension first manifests. For some it is stomach

upset, for others pain in the neck or in the small of the back, for others headaches. Just sitting quietly for twenty minutes often. creates tensions in a body that is used to being constantly on the move.

Sleep habits may also change. You may need more sleep or less sleep. Even the tiniest quieting of the mind releases energy. If it is able to flow through you freely, you will probably feel energized and sleep less. On the other hand, if your old habits hold on strongly and you struggle against the energy, you get fatigued.

Don't get lost in overreacting to the pains or tiredness. Just make yourself as comfortable as possible and proceed with the meditation. For the most part they are only distractions, not symptoms of a real illness. In each case, gently adapt in whatever way is required. Don't be afraid or exaggerate these things into a melodrama. Don't obsess. These physical symptoms come and go during meditation.

If you treat each such manifestation as real, you'll spend thousands on doctor bills. Once when I was meditating intensely for several months, I began to feel very ill. I went to a doctor who kept making me come back for more tests. He charged me outrageous fees, until I had run up a six-hundred-dollar bill on tests alone, none of which showed anything. I got so frustrated that I just decided to get better. I stopped worrying about my symptoms, and they went away.

This is not to say that you should not treat illness. Remember, your body is your temple—you must take care of it properly. Just give up your melodrama about being sick. If you're ill, get whatever treatment you need. But do so matter-of-factly, and don't use illness as a cop-out to stop meditating.

The body constantly tries to draw attention to itself by its shiverings, its breathlessness, its

*palpitations, its shudders and sweats and cramps;
but it reacts quickly to any scorn and
indifference in its master. Once it senses that
he is not taken in by its jeremiads, once it
understands that it will inspire no pity that way,
then it comes into line and obediently
accomplishes its task.*

—René Daumal

Mount Analogue

*Do not try to drive pain away by pretending that
it is not real;
Pain, if you seek serenity in Oneness, will vanish
of its own accord.*

—Sengstan

Buddhist Texts

*The way that will relieve your woes on the
physical plane will also take you to the highest
spiritual realizations. And the way is simple:
No resistance.*

—Thaddeus Golas

The Lazy Man's Guide
to Enlightenment

The Mind Reacts

Over the years we develop strong habits of perceiving the universe, and we come to be very secure within these habits. We selectively perceive our environment in ways that reinforce them. This collection of habits is what we call ego. But meditation breaks the ego down. As we begin to see through it we can become confused as to what reality is. What once seemed absolute now begins to seem relative. When this happens, some people get confused; others fear they may be going insane.

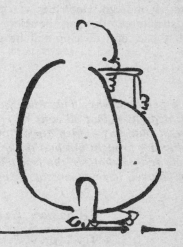

You must expect that growth requires change. A child's structure of reality alters as his or her endocrine system starts to change in puberty, leading sometimes to confusion and emotional upset. So it is with meditation that as you grow into a more conscious being, your old realities crumble and there will be moments of disorientation. The best strategy for dealing with this disorientation is to note it and let it be. Don't try to push it away and retreat into familiar habits. Most people need not fear this disruption. Although you may feel some anxiety, the ego's defense mechanisms usually give way no faster than you can handle it. But if you find these reactions too disturbing you can cut back on the amount of meditation you do, or even stop altogether for a while. When you feel more calm and relaxed, ease back into meditation.

The path to freedom is through detachment from your old habits of ego. Slowly you will arrive at a new and more profound integration of your experiences in a more evolved structure of the universe. That is, you will flow beyond the boundaries of your ego until ultimately you merge into the universe. At that point you have gone beyond ego. Until then you must break through old structures, develop broader structures, break through those, and develop still broader structures.

In fact, a person always finds when he begins to practice meditation that all sorts of problems are brought out. Any hidden aspects of your personality are brought out into the open, for the simple reason that for the first time you are allowing yourself to see your state of mind as it is.

—*Chogyam Trungpa*

The Myth of Freedom

Recently a woman came to see me who considered herself very close to having a nervous breakdown. One of her symptoms was unpredictable amounts of energy, so great at times that though she would ride her bicycle for three or four hours, afterward she would have more energy than when she began. She also cried unpredictably, for no apparent reason. She would sometimes look at some of her clients—she was a therapist—and feel such love for them that she wanted to kiss their feet or worship them. She would wake up at night with visions of beings talking to her, and feel presences in the room. Her vision would keep shifting so that what seemed a reality at one moment would be a dream a moment later. Sometimes she wasn't sure whether something that happened the night before was real or a dream. A constriction in her throat kept rising upward, and she felt energy racing through her spine.

Most of these symptoms, if presented to a traditional psychotherapist, would be treated as pathology. When I heard her description I recognized at once that what was happening to her was the awakening of the kundalini, the energy that resides in the psychic tube in the spine known as the shushumna. I rummaged through my papers and found a list of the symptoms that occur when kundalini awakens. I read her the list, and over 80 percent of her symptoms were on the list. As I read, her anxiety subsided, for suddenly she felt she was no longer crazy. She could now understand that she was in the midst of a spiritual process and there were clear steps for her to take to work with these energies. Just the reduction in anxiety was enough to change the nature of the entire experience for her. She could let the changes happen.

In the initial stages of meditation it is unlikely that you will have any such severe symptoms. But as your meditations get deeper, the ego will cling by whatever means it knows. Very often that clinging will take its form in physical symptoms or intensely negative psychological states. It's as if something that has remained quiescent for a long time is suddenly stirred up and rises to the surface. These long-latent impurities must be skimmed off.

Each of us has psychological weak points. Our weakness may be paranoia, depression, lassitude, confusion, or indecisiveness. I've had clear, decisive people come to me who, after meditating for some time, found themselves becoming less and less certain. Close examination revealed that their previous decisiveness came from being locked into rigid models of reality. As these models crumbled and they began to see the relative nature of the world they once thought they knew, it became more difficult to make decisions. This was only a stage. Later they quieted enough to hear the entire domain of possibilities, not just a narrow slice as before. Their decision-making became even better than before. As each such reaction occurs, merely allow it, sit with it.

> *(Krishnakishore) passed through a God-intoxicated state, when he would repeat only the word "Om" and shut himself up alone in his room. His relatives thought he was actually mad, and called in a physician. Ram Kaviraj of Natagore came to see him. Krishnakishore said to the physician, "Cure me, sir, of my malady, if you please, but not of my Om."*
>
> —*Sri Ramakrishna*
>
> The Gospel of
> Sri Ramakrishna

Distractions

Meditation texts name certain mental states that are hindrances. Try to be aware and work to overcome them in your meditation. The major unhelpful states are: tiredness and torpor; strong desires; distractedness, agitation and worry; and anger, depression, and doubt. Each of these is bound to occur from time to time, and each represents a special danger to meditation practice, because they are so compelling.

Should any of these states of mind arise—e.g., a sexual fantasy, or the thought "I'm too tired to keep meditating, I'll go to sleep instead," or ruminations over some pressing problem—they should be treated like any other distraction. Simply return your full attention to the meditation. These hindering states demand you exert greater effort to get your mind back to meditation than do most of the other random thoughts that cross your mind. Making this effort is the essence of meditation.

I've meditated hours and hours where nothing at all seemed to happen. I became increasingly bored and disgusted. Every tactic I could think of for cutting through these emotional states was useless. I had to examine my inadequacies, my doubts about my practice, my belief that it would lead me to God. I had to confront my reactions to meditation. Take fatigue, for example. It was a chronic problem for me. I remember propping myself up with piles of cushions so that I would not fall over into sleep. I often went to meditation courses because I was afraid that alone I would drift off into sleep. I've since learned to handle drowsy states with breathing techniques. What I experienced as fatigue often was actually a state of deep stillness that I misinterpreted. Instead of taking the feeling of fatigue as an invitation for a nap, I now regard it as a passing state, and keep sitting.

By letting go of whatever thoughts may come, no matter how powerful or fascinating they may be, and constantly returning to the meditation, our mental habits lose their hold over us. We create space for new possibilities, new realities, new being.

In Bodhgaya, where Buddha was enlightened, perhaps a hundred of us gathered at a monastery for meditation training. For ten days at a time we meditated intensively from five-thirty in the morning until ten at night. During these ten-day periods on about the eighth day the teacher would instruct us to spend a sixty-minute period in the hall without moving at all. I recall vividly one such period. The room was crowded, it was darkened—a gentle night. Outside I could hear the sound of the village, the creaking of the wooden wheels of the oxcarts, drivers yelling at their water buffalo, the laughter of children at play. I sensed a gentle, timeless civilization close to the earth.

Inside the teacher was reminding us, "Be aware of your breath. Do not move." From the distance I became aware of the buzz of a mosquito, the sound becoming louder. The horrible thought arose in my mind, "I hope the mosquito lands on someone else if he must land at all." Then there was guilt, and then with the next following of the breath, the thought of guilt faded. The mosquito approached. My consciousness once again was entrapped by the sound of the mosquito. It landed on my cheek. "Do not move," the teacher intoned.

I could feel the mosquito walking over my skin looking for an appropriate place to feed. My automatic impulse to brush away or kill mosquitoes came to mind. I wrestled with my mind to bring it back to my breath. Then I felt the mosquito inserting its proboscis into my skin. Slowly I felt it getting heavier as it filled with my blood. I wrestled to bring my mind back to my breath, but it kept being caught by the drama that was unfolding on the surface of my skin. Slowly the mosquito withdrew, was still for a moment, and then staggered across my skin preparing for takeoff with its new burden—my blood. I felt the fullness of the engorged mosquito. It flew away.

Just beneath the surface of my skin there came a sensation. Itching, itching. I wrestled to bring the mind back to my breath. Itching, itching. I watched the itch arise, become overwhelmingly insistent, and then slowly subside, as the alien fluids were absorbed into my system.

How much I learned in that tiny bit of suffering! By holding back my reaction I saw the entire sequence clearly. What grace that mosquito provided in allowing me to examine the passing nature of phenomena.

*If at prayer we do nothing but drive away
temptations and distractions, our prayer is well
made.*

—St. Francis de Sales

Conformity to the
Will of God

*We must do our business faithfully, without
trouble or disquiet, recalling our mind to God
mildly, and with tranquillity, as often as we find
it wandering from Him.*

—Brother Lawrence

The Practice of the
Presence of God

*When you are practicing zazen, do not try to stop
your thinking. Let it stop by itself. If something
comes into your mind, let it come in, and let it
go out. It will not stay long. When you try to stop
your thinking, it means you are bothered by it.
Do not be bothered by anything.*

—Shunryu Suzuki

Zen Mind, Beginner's Mind

*The man of wandering mind lies between the
fangs of the Passions.*

—Santi-deva

The Path of Light

*Constantly struggle with your thought and
whenever it is carried hither and thither, collect
it together. God does not require from novices
prayer completely free from distractions. Do
not despond when your thought is distracted, but
remain calm, and unceasingly restore your
mind to itself.*

—St. John of the Ladder

On the Prayer of Jesus

*A wandering thought is itself the essence
of Wisdom—
Immanent and intrinsic.*

—Milarepa

The Hundred Thousand
Songs of Milarepa

Doubt

You can't expect that your ego is going to lie down
and stop resisting immediately. It finds new and more
subtle ways to use your every weakness. At many
points in your spiritual journey your faith may be
tenuous and your commitment minimal, and your zeal
may evaporate.

One of the ego's favorite paths of resistance is to
fill you with doubt. When you want to sleep late, you'll
find reasons not to get up to do your sadhana. You

won't see the usefulness of meditation any more. You'll doubt your teacher, yourself, and the Spirit. You'll doubt God. And on and on and on.

These doubts have to be dealt with, for some may be valid. For example, you may be right to doubt your teacher. Your teacher may not be worthy of his or her following. On the other hand, this very doubt may be a mind game to keep you from a deeper commitment. In truth, only you know which it is. There is a place in you that knows whether you are conning yourself in order to cop-out, or whether you're indeed dealing with a legitimate awareness of limitations.

Doubt demands you examine what you are doing with a critical eye. In this examination, include the doubt itself. If the doubt seems just another dodge of your ego, suspend it and proceed. The antidote to doubt is faith, but it should be an informed faith, not blind.

Let go the things in which you are in doubt for the things in which there is no doubt.

—Mohammed

The Forty-Two Traditions
of An-Nawawi

It is when your practice is rather greedy that you become discouraged with it. So you should be grateful that you have a sign or warning signal to show you the weak point in your practice.

—*Shunryu Suzuki*

Zen Mind, Beginner's Mind

Once a man was about to cross the sea. Bibhishana wrote Rama's name on a leaf, tied it in a corner of the man's wearing-cloth, and said to him: "Don't be afraid. Have faith and walk on the water. But look here—the moment you lose faith you will be drowned." The man was walking easily on the water. Suddenly he had an intense desire to see what was tied in his cloth. He opened it and found only a leaf with the name of Rama written on it. "What is this?" he thought, "Just the name of Rama!" As soon as doubt entered his mind he sank under the water.

—*Sri Ramakrishna*

The Gospel of
Sri Ramakrishna

Fear

Some people from time to time feel fear during meditation. Fear takes all kinds of objects. Fear of hypnosis, faddism, insanity, losing control, irresponsibility, losing friends, loss of identity or of will, apathy, or

passivity. Fear of being lost in the void or the emptiness. Nameless fear, of nothing particular. Fear that
nothing will happen. Fear that something really will
happen that will change you.

Such fears will grab at you and influence you to
stop meditation. Examine these fears; be open to
them. But don't worry; they will pass. The changes
that meditation brings will not be such that there is
anything to fear. Roosevelt was right: "We have nothing to fear but fear itself." For the defenses of your
ego are sturdy enough that you have ample opportunity to offset any negative effects of meditation.

My suggestion is to relax and enjoy the journey.
As fears arise, allow them their space. Understand
that, like all the other feelings meditation brings you
—confusion, pleasure, pain, excitement, boredom—
your fears, too, will pass.

*It was a dark night, early summer, finally turning
warm. As Grandpa Joe slipped out of the car,
I called to him to ask for his advice. I had
been warned that the bears of the mountains
were now active especially at night. It was
dangerous to walk in the woods in the dark.
And furthermore, last summer a bear had actually
come and circled the very tipi where I was now
living, for it is pitched a good twenty minutes'
walk further up the mountain from the other
Lama dwellings.*

*"Grandpa," I asked, "tonight I must walk
alone in the dark a long way to get to my tipi.
Perhaps I will meet a bear. What should I do?
Should I talk to the bear? Should I send it love?"*

*Grandpa leaned back and we shared a
gentle space of silence together. Then he gave
me this advice. "No talk to bear. Talk to God!"*

—Saraswati

*It is not that you must be free from fear. The
moment you try to free yourself from fear, you
create a resistance against fear. Resistance, in any
form, does not end fear. What is needed,
rather than running away or controlling or
suppressing or any other resistance, is
understanding fear; that means, watch it, learn
about it, come directly into contact with it. We
are to learn about fear, not how to escape from
it, not how to resist it through courage and
so on.*

—Krishnamurti

Loss of Meaning

Very often people report to me that meditation has brought an emptiness into their life. Everything seems meaningless. It takes great faith to ride through such heavy periods of spiritual transformation.

I recall the near anger I had towards spirituality as I saw my favorite rushes fall away. Things I had previously gotten great thrills from became empty. For example, many years back one of my aesthetic highs was to visit Tanglewood, the music festival where the Boston Symphony played. I recall in particular a beautiful evening when I lay under the elm trees on a blanket with wine and cheese and listened to the symphony in the outdoor shell play Berlioz' *Requiem*. I was in ecstasy.

A few years ago, some twenty years later, I was passing by Tanglewood and remembered that moment. I decided to drop by to attend an evening concert. Much to my delight, I found they were to play the Berlioz *Requiem* that evening. I immediately got some wine and cheese, took a blanket, and arrived very early so I would have a choice elm to lie under. The evening was beautiful, soft and warm. The music began to play.

Much as I tried, I could not recapture the ecstasy. The experience was incredibly beautiful, delightful and enjoyable. But it wasn't as I remembered it. I had to realize that my memory of that moment was so high because by comparison the rest of my life was much lower. But now things had changed and each moment of every day had started to have a quality of newness and radiance and intensity. The driving to the concert, the buying of the wine, the lying under the elm were equally as high as the concert. Instead of peaks and valleys, I had a plateau.

Meditation brings this change. Each moment starts to have a richness or thickness of its own. Fewer moments are special as more of them become richer. This lessens the rushes, the highs and lows. As they disappear we sometimes feel a sadness and depression, a sense of having lost the richness and the romance of life. Indeed, an awakened being is not romantic, for nothing is special any more. Every moment is all of it. No romance. Just the coming and the going. Coming and going.

In a way it is sad to see one's story line turn into empty form. The dark night of the soul is when you have lost the flavor of life but have not yet gained the fullness of divinity. So it is that we must weather that dark time, the period of transformation when what is familiar has been taken away and the new richness is not yet ours.

"Perhaps your Reverence has met a certain lady?"
Mahatissa the Elder replied:
"I know not whether a man or woman passed.
A certain lump of bones went by this way."

—*Buddhaghosa*

The Path of Purity

He who contemplates the Lotus Feet of God
looks on even the most beautiful woman as
mere ash from the cremation ground.

—*Sri Ramakrishna*

The Gospel of
Sri Ramakrishna

Before a man can find God, . . . all his likings
and desires have to be utterly changed . . . All
things must become as bitter to thee as their
enjoyment was sweet unto thee.

—*John Tauler*

Life and Sermons of
Dr. John Tauler

The attainment of enlightenment from ego's
point of view is extreme death, the death of self,
the death of me and mine, the death of the
watcher. It is the ultimate and final
disappointment.

—*Chogyam Trungpa*

The Myth of Freedom

On Not Finding Your Guru

Seeking one's guru is like going on pilgrimage. It is a useful journey, but you don't have to take it to finish the path. There is a good possibility you will never meet your guru. But because you do not meet your guru does not mean you do not have one. Any person that reaches toward God, toward liberation, toward the spirit, is noticed, and a contact is made with the vehicle or form that will ultimately draw you home.

You needn't know your guru. It is only necessary that your guru know you. Only your need to maintain control compels you to try to know your guru. Your journey is one of purification, and you can proceed whether you know your guru or not. Don't worry about it. Your guru will become known to you, if and when necessary. If the guru were to manifest too soon, you might get lost in an interpersonal devotion that would just be another trap for you. You must trust that the process is benevolent. When needed, the guru appears. It's a benign conspiracy.

I once asked my guru, "How do you know if a person is your guru?" He answered that it is simply whether this person can take you all the way. Taking you all the way does not mean that the guru does it for you. Rather the guru *is* the way. The guru's very being creates a space that is the doorway to your freedom.

Along the way you may meet your guru and feel overwhelming love for him or her. This makes you cling to the guru. In the end you must go beyond the separateness of the forms you have loved. To go all the way is to go beyond the concept of guru. Ramana Maharshi said it: God, Guru, Self—all the same thing.

> *For thirty years I went in search of God, and when I opened my eyes at the end of this time, I discovered that it was really He who sought for me.*
>
> —*Bayazid al-Bistami*
>
> Translations of Eastern Poetry and Prose

> *I had heard about a superior type of man, possessing the keys to everything which is a mystery to us. This idea of a higher and unknown strain within the human race was not something I could take simply as an allegory. Experience has proved, I told myself, that a man cannot reach truth directly, nor all by himself. An intermediary has to be present, a force still human in certain respects, yet transcending humanity in others. Somewhere on our Earth this superior form of humanity must exist, and not utterly out of our reach. In that case shouldn't all my efforts be directed toward discovering it? Even if, in spite of my certainty, I were the victim of a monstrous illusion, I should lose nothing in the attempt. For, apart from this hope, all life lacked meaning for me.*
>
> —*René Daumal*
>
> Mount Analogue

*In time, and always just at the right moment, a
teacher or maggid arrives. He may manifest in
many ways, as old Kabbalistic documents
indicate. One may not see him more than once,
or realize one has known him all his life. It
can be one's grandfather or a fellow student,
the man crossing the sea with you on a boat, or
someone you thought a fool. He may arrive at
your front door or already be in the house.*

—Z'evben Shimon Halevi

The Way of Kaballah

7

GETTING FREE

Keep Your Ground

If you feel free only when you meditate, you're not really free. Freedom does not come from turning your back on your responsibilities. The game is to be in the world but not of it. Even when you find yourself feeling spaced out, disoriented, or untogether, you can make an extra effort to meet the needs of the moment, whether it's the baby's diapers that need changing or your income tax that is due. Don't make meditation a cop-out from life.

You can allow yourself adjustment periods when

you don't have to function quite as well as at other times, especially just after periods of intense retreat. Eventually you learn to function in the world even right after the deepest meditation. That's the goal: balancing inner and outer. You're part of society, you're part of a family, you're part of all sorts of groups. Do what you must to meet your responsibilities, but do it as an exercise that furthers your own liberation as well. The true freedom of awareness that you seek is possible only when you acknowledge and fulfill honorably all aspects of the dance of life. It is in the perfection of form that we are free.

The time of business does not with me differ from the time of prayer, and in the noise and clatter of my kitchen, while several persons are at the same time calling for different things, I possess God in as great tranquillity as if I were upon my knees at the blessed sacrament.

—Brother Lawrence

The Practice of the
Presence of God

Do not permit the events of your daily lives to bind you, but never withdraw yourselves from them. Only by acting thus can you earn the title of "A Liberated One."

—Huang Po

The Zen Teaching
of Huang Po

The true saint goes in and out amongst the people and eats and sleeps with them and buys

*and sells in the market and marries and takes
part in social intercourse, and never forgets God
for a single moment.*

—*Abu Sa'id ibn Abi
l-Tkayr*

Studies

*I did not go to the "Maggid" of Meseritz to
learn Torah from him but to watch him tie his
boot-laces.*

—*A Hassidic saint*

Major Trends in
Jewish Mysticism

Facing Weaknesses

We have all been enchanted with getting high, having
a free awareness, and so we have tried to repress or
deny lows when our awareness once again gets caught
in this or that. We love the illusion of being high but
are afraid of coming down. As your journey proceeds,
you realize that you can't hold on to your highs and deny
your lows. Your lows are created by the remaining
attachments that blind your awareness. Facing your
lows—your anger, loneliness, greed, fears, depressions,
and conflicts—is the most productive fire of purification you can find.

As your connection with the spirit deepens, you might even choose to seek out those things that bring your attachments to the surface, so that you might confront them and free your awareness from them. It's a tricky business—playing with fire. You must feel your own way, unless you have a guide to say when to go and when to stop. If you don't have a guide, trust your own judgment. For example, if anger still traps your awareness, you might put yourself in situations which usually elicit anger and then attempt to maintain clear awareness.

If you confront your attachments out of guilt, out of "oughts" or "shoulds," or through some externally imposed discipline, it won't work. For these confrontations are difficult and your motives to confront them must come from deep within. It takes the innermost resolve to resist your powerful temptations, or separate your awareness from your strong desires, be they lust, anger, or whatever. Your gains through meditation give you the enthusiasm that can bring a breakthrough into another plane, or the heartfelt desire to go in deeper, or the hunger to change your life. But it still takes much courage and fortitude to face the deepest attachments head on.

When you feel that your life is committed to the spirit you can no longer avoid confronting these weaknesses. Your strategy changes, you seek to move faster, wishing to confront head-on the things that bring down your awareness. You can no longer let them have their way. So you ask for a hotter fire, a fiercer confrontation. Even though this is often painful rather than pleasurable, it's all right, for you are reaching toward that freedom which lies beyond pleasure and pain. When you want to burn away the grip of your ego on your awareness you'll endure whatever is needed to clean up your life.

Truth alone is the austerity of the Kali Yuga.

—*Sri Ramakrishna*

Women Saints of
East and West

Handling Energy

Meditation is like diving deep in the ocean. To allow you to go to the depths and come back up smoothly your body must acclimate at each stage. As you adjust to each new level, you are filled with a greater energy.

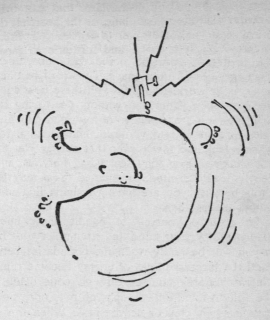

The predicament is that as you receive greater energy during meditation, it carries over to the times you are not meditating, when your old habits of mind to which you are still attached hold sway. The temptation is to use these new energies to strengthen your old habits, to use the meditative energy in the service of your ego. For example, you may find that these new energies enhance your sexual excitement, enthusiasm, and proficiency or your social power or charisma. This undoubtedly is one of the attractions of meditation.

But if your yearning is to go to the depths of your own soul—if your journey is to seek what Buddha had, what Christ had, what Ramakrishna had, what Abraham had, what Mohammed had—then you must beware of dissipating these energies through your old habits. You must channel them to go deeper. The energies that come from going near God can take you even nearer to God.

The ego is designed to survive in the midst of this energy. It's like a spacecraft with walls of thick steel to protect it from the incredible bombardment of the high energies of outer space. The art of meditation, however, is to work gradually with these new energies to free awareness from ego without destroying it.

If your mind and heart are not open enough, the energies that surge into you can take negative forms. They may feel like raw power that causes you fits of violent shaking. You may feel edgy, nervous, unable to sleep, speedy, excited, or agitated. You may feel a paranoia because you are having insights that no one you know understands.

To prepare yourself to handle these energies positively, purify your mind and strengthen your body. Then you will be ready when the boundaries between you and the larger sources of energy become thin. As this intense energy courses through your being, you will be able to handle it, though you may notice symptoms such as shaking or nervousness. When this happens to me, I focus on my heart, breathe in and out of it, filling with love on each breath. Great force can come to you, but when it is balanced with love you won't feel overwhelmed. With love, you are more open to the energy. Then you will grow in power—the power of love. You are on the way home.

Live as quiet a life as you can during intense periods of meditative practice. Get enough rest. You may encounter new spaces that will consume or create huge amounts of energy. Your body one moment may be totally exhausted and the next moment full of energy and refreshed. Your behavior may become erratic. Sometimes when I'm in intense spaces, my body is just barely strong enough to stand what it undergoes. Then I'll suddenly fall into a sound sleep that lasts maybe fifteen minutes. When I come out of it my whole body is vibrant with energy, fully revitalized.

Some people feel the need for a guide who senses when they are getting more energy than they can balance. Such a guide sees what they need to do to acclimate to new levels of energy. For most of us, our intuitive common sense will handle the moderate changes that we face.

The practice of meditation will open us gradually to more and more of the energy of the universe. If we remember the highest wisdom—that energy and love are one—this journey will be without fear.

Faith and Persistence

Many times in the course of meditation you will think of things you'd rather be doing. There may be moments of boredom, of sexual desire, doubt, or fatigue. At these moments you must call upon your faith. Faith in what? Faith in the power of meditation to change your awareness and your perspective about reality.

It is to strengthen this faith that you study books such as this rather than simply do your practices. Study brings you a deeper understanding of why you meditate and what to expect. When you read other people's stories of a meditative life you get a sense of the possibilities for your own. These inspirations can generate sufficient faith to override the difficult moments in meditation. Understanding feeds your faith.

Along with faith comes the requirement for dogged persistence. At first meditation may bring you mild highs or some relief from suffering. But there may come a time—just as there does in the development of any skill—when there will be a plateau. You may be bored, discouraged, or even negative and cynical. This is when you will need not only faith, but persistence. Often you will find yourself in training that forces you to sit when you wish you didn't have to. You subject yourself to this because something deeper within tells you to go on. It forces you to persist despite your abhorrence of the process. This persistent effort brings greater faith.

Even to the end of the journey faith is vulnerable. For example, though your faith may be strong enough to sit in meditation, if you mix with people who sneer at it, their skepticism may weaken your resolve. But if you stay with meditation, faith in your path will strengthen until you can withstand any criticism, even your own doubt and dark night of the soul.

When meditation works as it should, it will be a natural part of your being. There will no longer be anything apart from you to have faith in. Hope starts the journey, faith sustains it, but it ends beyond both hope and faith.

A young lad was sent to school. He began his lessons with the other children, and the first lesson the teacher set him was the straight line, the figure "one." But whereas the others went on progressing, this child continued writing the same figure. After two or three days the teacher came up to him and said, "Have you finished your lesson?" He said, "No, I'm still writing 'one.' " He went on doing the same thing, and when at the end of the week the teacher asked him again he said, "I have not yet finished it." The teacher thought he was an idiot and should be sent away, as he could not or did not want to learn. At home the child continued with the same exercise and the parents also became tired and disgusted. He simply said, "I have not yet learned it, I am learning it. When I have finished I shall take the other lessons." The parents said, "The other children are going on further, school has given you up, and you do not show any progress; we are tired of you." And the lad thought with sad heart that as he had displeased his parents too he had better leave home. So he went into the wilderness and lived on fruits and nuts. After a long time he returned to his old school. And when he saw the teacher he said to him, "I think I have learned it. See if I have. Shall I write on this wall?" And when he made his sign the wall split in two.

—Hazrat Inayat Khan

The Sufi Message of
Hazrat Inayat Khan

A group of us were in a sauna bath—just hanging out, going out into the sun, coming back into the bath—and a telegram arrived for me saying, "Rohatsu Dai Seshin is being held at Mt. Baldy in Los Angeles. We are holding a space for you." This is the most difficult of the zen sittings each year. It was to start the next day. So I got on a plane and went to Los Angeles.

I arrive at the zen monastery having sacrificed a sauna bath in the warm desert for this cold mountain outside of Los Angeles. I expect a greeting like, "Oh, Ram Dass, we're so happy you could come!"—a little bit of ego feeding. Instead I'm met by a guy in a black outfit with a clipboard and a shaved head who says, "Dass, Ram; you will be in bunk six. Here is your robe. Brother John will show you how to put it on and you are to be in the zendo in six minutes."

So I think, OK, baby, I'll play. I go in and I set up my bunk. You're not supposed to look at anybody or talk to anybody for nine days. Nine days. Every morning it's pitch black and all these people in black outfits are rushing to toilets, toothpaste, zendo at two in the morning and it's freezing. If you don't sit straight they beat you with a stick. There's snow all around and I had a cold. I'm getting sicker and sicker and plotting how to get out of this. Should I have a telegram sent saying I have been called away on an emergency, or remember I had a lecture or something?

Four times a day you go in to visit Joshu Sasaki Roshi, a tough, squat Japanese of about sixty-five. It's called dokusan. He had given us the koan "How do you know your Buddha nature through the sound of a cricket?" When it comes my turn, I go in, bow the proper number of times, and sit down. He's got a bell and a stick, and he says, "Ah, Doc-tor. How you know your Buddha nature through sound of cricket?" I had been sitting out there waiting my turn, thinking, now how would you know . . . You're not supposed to do that but I figured, what the hell, here is a Jewish Hindu in a Zen Buddhist scene—I'll give him a

Tibetan Buddhist answer. So I concluded that the best thing to do when he asked me was to hold my hand up to my ear, like the Tibetan Milarepa listening to the sounds of the universe outside his cave. The Roshi says only, "sixty percent," and rings the bell that means I should leave.

It goes on like this for days. I'm getting sicker and sicker and madder and madder and just bored and disgusted. Even though my sitting is stronger, I can't solve the damned koan. Finally about the fourth or fifth day, I walk up to see the Roshi. I still haven't solved the koan. I stand up there and think, "I don't give a damn what the answer to that koan is. Screw this whole scene. I've had enough."

I walk in and he says, "Ah, Doc-tor, how you know your Buddha nature through sound of cricket?"

And I say, "Good morning, Roshi." Like, let's cut the crap. Good morning, enough already.

"Ah, Doc-tor. Finally you are becoming a beginning student of zen."

Grace is proportionate to exertion.

—Sathya Sai Baba

Do not do things off and on. Have your sadhana every day with greater and greater intensity.

—Swami Ramdas

Guide to Aspirants

> *The result is not the point; it is the effort to improve ourselves that is valuable. There is no end to this practice.*
>
> —*Shunryu Suzuki*
>
> Zen Mind, Beginner's Mind

> *To endure is the disposition of the sage.*
>
> —The I Ching

Trust Your Heart

In the first part of your journey you may be quite eclectic, trying out many methods. Don't consider these changes from one method to another a weakness. Nor is it a weakness to stay with one method if it feels right to you. But it is a weakness to stay with a method that doesn't feel right, or to shift methods to avoid going too far with any one of them. How do you know when to shift, when to stay? Listen to your inner voice, your heart, and be truthful with yourself. This self-reliance and honesty will guide you not only in these early stages, but all the way to enlightenment. Each person has to be very honest and honor his or her stage of evolution. Nobody can live another's life. You've got to live your own.

When I went to Bodhgaya in India I took course after course in meditation. After a while I started to eat more and more, get up later and later, and waste more time each day, until the message was clear. This was no longer the time for intense meditation. It was time for me to take it easy. To try to meditate too intensely before you are ready will bring you similar tensions and difficulties. On the other hand, not meditating when the pull to do so is strong may raise the same difficulties.

Be prepared for the possibility that what seemed to be the right practice or strategy at one moment may not feel so a moment later. The process is dynamic and changing. Sometimes, for example, you may feel a very deep pull toward meditation. You may join a spiritual group only to find that the group's goals are far more limited than your own. As your practice takes on a dimension beyond that of the group's you will have to seek more profound methods and teachers.

Be prepared to give up your models of the path as you travel it. There is no shame in admitting your mistakes. Mahatma Gandhi once led a protest march in which many thousands of people left their jobs and homes to endure great hardship. As the march was well underway, Gandhi called a halt and disbanded it. His lieutenants came to him and said, "Mahatma-ji, you can't do this; the march has been planned for a long time and there are so many people involved." Gandhi's answer was, "My commitment is to truth as I see it each day, not to consistency."

All that you seek is already within you. In Hinduism it is called the Atman; in Buddhism, the pure Buddha-mind. Christ said, "The Kingdom of Heaven is within you." Quakers call it the "still, small voice within." This is the space of full awareness that is in harmony with all the universe, and thus is wisdom itself. Every new level of meditation, every new understanding of who you really are, attunes you more delicately to this space so that you can hear and be guided by your inner voice more clearly. Time and time again your attachments may veil this truth from you. Your attachments lead you to seek outside of yourself for answers that can only come from your own heart. Each time you lose contact with that inner awareness, you need only meditate. For through meditation you will hear that inner "click," that sense of rightness about what you are doing. Your answers are unique. Listen with your heart.

> *We have what we seek. It is there all the time, and if we give it time it will make itself known to us.*
>
> —*Thomas Merton*

> *If you do not get it from yourself*
> *Where will you go for it?*
>
> —*Zenrin*
>
> The Gospel According to Zen

Humor

Did you ever have a bad day? Everything seems to go wrong and you are completely lost in anger, frustration, and self-pity. It gets worse and worse, until the final moment when, say, you have just missed the last bus. There is some critical point where it gets so bad the absurdity of it all overwhelms you and you can do nothing but laugh. At that moment you uplevel your predicament, you see the cosmic joke in your own suffering.

Meditation, because of the space it allows around events, gives you the chance to see the humor of your predicament. Awareness of the passing show of one's own life allows a lightness to enter in where only a moment before there was heaviness.

Humor puts things in perspective. There are many levels of humor—there is a humor of survival, a humor of sex and gratification, a humor connected with power. Beyond all these there is a humor that is filled with compassion. It is reflected in the tiny upturn in the mouth of the Buddha, for he sees the humor in the universal predicament: all beings are lost in illusion, yet he knows that they will awaken from that illusion for they are, at heart, already enlightened. He knows that what seems so hard to them is from another perspective their own path to liberation.

Often the perspectives about yourself and the universe that you arrive at through meditation make you want to giggle or laugh. This giggle is without malice. It's a cosmic giggle, one that I identify with my guru, Maharaji. For his giggle was not of this world. It was not a social or personality giggle, but rather a cosmic chuckle, the delight in the fun of it all. His giggle was from the place that gives us the term "lila," the divine dance of life.

If it were not laughed at, it would not be sufficient to be Tao.

—*Lao Tse*

Tao Te Ching

Maharaj-ji was sitting with a group of devotees when suddenly he asked, "Who's coming, who's coming?" No one could be seen. Just then the servant of one of his devotees came. The minute Maharaj-ji saw him he yelled, "I won't go. I know he's dying. I won't go." The servant was surprised because no one knew that his employer had just had a heart attack and had called for Maharaj-ji. Everyone pleaded with Maharaj-ji to go, but he continued to refuse. Finally he picked up a banana and said, "Here, give him this, he'll be all right." The servant rushed home with the banana. It was mashed up and fed to the dying man, and as he took the last bite he died.

—*a devotee*

*The monks of a large Gelugpa monastery were
appalled one morning to find a man on top of
the prayerflag pole in their main courtyard. Since
this was considered a very bad omen they
determined at once to hold a ceremony to
exorcise this apparition. Five thousand monks
gathered that afternoon in the courtyard and
en masse chanted the Heart Sutra. At the end of
the recitation, in accordance with tradition they
proclaimed two verses to accomplish the
exorcism.*

> *By the power of our words may this evil
>   being come down.*
> *By the power of our contemplation of these
>   words may this evil being come down.*

*As they chanted the first verse, the man on
the flagpole (who was the Mad Yogi of Bhutan)
slid halfway down. As they chanted the second,
he went back to the top.*

—Chogyam Trungpa

Visual Dharma: The
Buddhist Art of Tibet

*A certain Bektashi dervish was respected for his
piety and appearance of virtue. Whenever
anyone asked him how he had become so holy,
he always answered: "I know what is in the
Koran."*

One day he had just given this reply to an enquirer in a coffee-house, when an imbecile asked: "Well, what is in the Koran?"

"In the Koran," said the Bektashi, "there are two pressed flowers and a letter from my friend Abdullah."

—Idries Shah

A rabbi visited a village reputed to have a miracle-working tzaddik, and asked: "What miracles has your tzaddik actually performed?"

"Our tzaddik has fasted every day for three whole years now!"

"Three years?! But that's impossible. He'd be dead by now!"

"Certainly he would! But our tzaddik knows that if he fasted every day that demonstration of saintliness would put everyone else to shame; so he eats only to spare everyone's feelings—and conceals the fact that privately he's fasting."

—Leo Rosten

The Joys of Yiddish

Anyone walking about Chinatown in America will observe statues of a stout fellow carrying a linen sack. Chinese merchants call him Happy Chinaman or Laughing Buddha.

This Hotei lived in the T'ang dynasty. He had no desire to call himself a Zen master or to gather many disciples about him. Instead he walked the streets with a big sack into which he would put gifts of candy, fruit, or doughnuts. These he would give to children who gathered around him in play. He established a kindergarten of the streets.

Whenever he met a Zen devotee he would extend his hand and say: "Give me one penny."

Once as he was about his play-work another Zen master happened along and inquired: "What is the significance of Zen?"

Hotei immediately plopped his sack down on the ground in silent answer.

"Then," asked the other, "what is the actualization of Zen?"

At once the Happy Chinaman swung the sack over his shoulder and continued on his way.

—Paul Reps

Zen Flesh, Zen Bones

8

THE JOURNEY OF CONSCIOUSNESS

We are departing for the skies. Who has a mind for sightseeing?

—*Rumi*

Picture a beautiful warm summer day. A group of people has decided to climb a nearby mountain. The going is easy, the day gentle. After several hours they reach a plateau with a rest station. Here they find a

restaurant, comfortable chairs, rest rooms, telescopes —all the conveniences. The view is inspiring. The air is cooler and clearer than down below. A sense of well-being, of health and energy, animates the climbers body and soul. For many in the group this is enough. They return home refreshed and satisfied. They are Sunday climbers.

A few remain, having discovered another path. Or perhaps it is the same path that began far down in the valley. Impelled by the need to explore, they thrust forward onto it. After a while the air grows cooler still. The trees thin out. Clouds obscure the sun from time to time. The path keeps rising, getting steeper and steeper. It is not yet beyond the skill of those who are determined to go on.

They reach a second rest area, with no conveniences other than an outhouse and an outdoor fireplace. The comraderie is now deeper. Their eyes feast on a grander view. The villages in which they grew up nestle tiny and remote from this new distance. It is their past they see in a new perspective. They see the limits of their lives in the valley far below. Few people

leave this station to travel higher. Most stay for awhile, then go back down.

Some remain—a handful. They seek and find a hidden path disappearing above. Are they ready to ascend the flat faces of rocks, to creep along narrow ledges, to explore caves high above, to crawl up to the snow line and beyond?

They feel some fear and loneliness now, some confusion. They ask themselves why they left the conviviality of the rest stop to tackle this painful, dangerous journey—or is it a pilgrimage? Their physical hardships reflect their spiritual struggle. The obstacles of rock and cliff mirror the possibility of great injury, worse than before because the openness and risk is greater.

Added now is an inner battle. The climbers feel they have taken on an adversary. The mountain has become something to be mastered and controlled. Of the handful of people that climbs to this height, only one or two can reach the top. Those few who go for broke, who want to reach the top, will use their every tool to its utmost. They want all of it, the top of the mountain, the mystic experience every great climber has known.

We have in America little appreciation, less experience, and no models for this ultimate journey. This final path is reflected in Christ's forty days in the desert, by the many years of intense spiritual work which Gautama Buddha underwent before enlightenment, by the years in which the great saint Swami Nityananda sat in a tree like a monkey, living close to the edge of insanity, or by Ananda Mayee Ma, who roamed about lost to self and family in trance. Asia has innumerable stories of these few beings who made such a fierce journey—a journey that can only be made if you are propelled by an inner fire, a yearning and pull for liberation that is so powerful there is no way to deny it.

After one arrives at the summit, after going through the total transformation of being, after becoming free of fear, doubt, confusion, and self-consciousness, there is yet one more step to the completion of that journey: the return to the valley below, to the everyday world. Who it is that returns is not who began the climb in the first place. The being that comes back is quietness itself, is compassion and wisdom, is the truth of the ages. Whatever humble or elevated position that being holds within the community, he or she becomes a light for others on the way, a statement of the freedom that comes from having touched the top of the mountain.

The return completes the cycle. It is this cycle which brings the spirit to earth and allows the divine to feed once again the hopes and aspirations, the barely sensed possibility, that exists in each human being. This is the way of the bodhisattva, the maggid, the shayk, the enlightened soul, the saint.

You cannot stay on the summit for ever; you have to come down again . . . So why bother in the first place? Just this: what is above knows what is below, but what is below does not know what is above.

One climbs, one sees. One descends, one sees no longer but one has seen. There is an art to conducting oneself in the lower regions by the memory of what one saw higher up. When one can no longer see, one can at least still know.

—René Daumal

Mount Analogue

There is no real coming and going.
For what is going but coming?

—*Shabistari*

The Secret Rose Garden of
Sa'd Ud Din
Mahmud Shabistari

Keeping Still is the mountain.

—The I Ching

But can one say that such a being has returned from beyond? In truth, he or she is beyond return. The one who arrives at the top is not the being who set out at the bottom. One who arrives at the top goes through the fear of death, and sees what only a few ever see, knows what only a few ever know. Such a being returns to the world to live in humility and simplicity. For to have faced the forces of the universe and found a way to harmonize with them is to find one's true place, to be in the flow. This is the achievement which is no achievement. This very special journey allows such a being to be nothing special.

Up to the very end of the climb up the mountain of liberation the most subtle suffering still remains, for there is still an individual who identifies with his or her own separateness. There is still clinging. There is still a final bond to break. At the moment of scaling the highest peak or walking the narrowest ledge the climber must let go of everything, even self-consciousness, in order to become the perfect instrument of the climb. In the ultimate moments of the climb, he or she transcends even the identity of climber. As Christ said, one must truly die and be born again.

The absence of identity with personal ego means that the being is free, is pure compassion, pure love, pure awareness. For such a being, everything is in the moment. There is a richness in which past, present, and future all co-exist. You cannot say of a moment of full awareness that something is not present, nor can you say that something stands out. You can focus on one thing or another, or on the emptiness of the form, or on the many planes within the form. The focus of a totally free being is guided by the need of the moment, by the karma of the individual he or she is with. For such a being, life is a constant unfolding. No need to think about what to do. It's all intuitive. It's as simple as the innocence and freshness that a young child experiences. Only in this silence—the silence that lies behind thought—can one hear the symphony of the universe, can one hear the whisper of the Word, can one approach the inner temple wherein dwells the soul.

The moment is timeless. But within timelessness there is time. The moment is spaceless. But within the undifferentiated boundaries of infinite space lies form, with its demarcations. There is clarity, so that everything is discrete and can be seen clearly if one focuses. There is liberation; there is perfect faith; no fear of change, no clinging to the moment. The moment is enough. The next moment is enough also. And the judgment of "enough" is gone—choiceless awareness.

*Grown men may learn from very little children,
for the hearts of little children are pure, and,
therefore, the Great Spirit may show to them
many things which older people miss.*

—Black Elk

The Sacred Pipe

It is all an open secret.

—*Ramana Maharshi*

Talks with Sri
Ramana Maharshi

Such unbounded spacious awareness contains an intense love of God, equanimity, compassion, and wisdom. In it there is openness and harmony with the whole universe. Beings whose awareness is free enter into the ocean of love that has no beginning or end— love that is clear like a diamond, flowing like the ocean, passionate as the height of the sexual act, and soft like the caress of the wind.

This is the all and everything. It is the love that includes hate, for it is beyond polarity. It is the love that loves all beings.

There is a universal tradition of people who complete the path of meditation, who transcend their intellects, open their hearts, and come into tune with that from which the universe flows. Such beings are sages, enlightened, realized, free, children of God. They are God people.

One day I was sitting in the courtyard across from my guru, Maharaji. Many people were sitting around him, joking and talking with him, rubbing his feet, giving him apples and flowers. He was giving things right back and I could see the love flow back and forth. But I sat across the courtyard, in a very impersonal state.

I thought, "That's all well and good, but it is just attachment to form. I've done that. I must go beyond that. He is nothing special, although he is everything. I can be at his feet anywhere in the universe. The way in which he and I are connected has nothing to do with form. We are one in awareness."

At that moment I saw Maharaji whispering to an old devotee who came running across the courtyard and touched my feet. I asked, "Why did you do that?" He replied, "Maharaji said, 'Touch Ram Dass' feet. He and I understand each other perfectly.' "

From having met Maharaji I have a sense of what a free being is like, what a pure awareness is like that does not cling to time, to space, to identity. I sense what it is to live so totally in the moment, that you do not cling at all.

Anjani says of him:

There can be no biography of Maharaji. Facts are few, stories many. He seems to have been known by different names in many parts of India, appearing and disappearing through the years. His Western devotees of recent years knew him as Neem Karoli Baba, but mostly as "Muharaj-ji"—a nickname (meaning "great king") so commonplace in India that one often can hear a tea vendor addressed thus. Just as he said, he was "nobody."

He gave no discourses; the briefest, simplest stories were his teaching. Usually he sat or lay on a bench wrapped in a plaid blanket while a few devotees sat around him. Visitors came and went, food was given them and a few words, a nod, a slap on the head or back, and they were sent away. There was gossip, laughter—he loved to joke. Orders for running the ashram were given, usually in a piercing yell across the compound. Sometimes he sat in silence, absorbed in another world to which we could not follow, but bliss and peace poured down on us.

Who he was was no more than the experience of him, the nectar of his presence, the totality of his absence—enveloping us now like his plaid blanket.

—Anjani

The true men of old
Knew no lust for life,
No dread of death.
Their entrance was without gladness,
Their exit, yonder,
Without resistance.
Easy come, easy go.
They did not forget where from,
Nor ask where to,
Nor drive grimly forward
Fighting their way through life.
They took life as it came, gladly;
Took death as it came, without care;
And went away, yonder,
Yonder!

They had no mind to fight Tao.
They did not try, by their own contriving,
To help Tao along.
These are the ones we call true men.

Minds free, thoughts gone
Brows clear, faces serene.
Were they cool? Only cool as autumn.
Were they hot? No hotter than spring.
All that came out of them
Came quiet, like the four seasons.

—*Thomas Merton*

The Way of Chuang Tzu

THE DIRECTORY

1

INTRODUCTION

Though the sages speak in divers ways, they express one and the same Truth.

—Srimad Bhagavatam

This directory is an endeavor to provide at least some access to the spiritual resources within our community. It consists of two parts, a guide to groups that teach meditation, and a list of retreat facilities.

Many groups of meditators meet, many teachers instruct, and many organizations offer opportunities for retreats, not all are listed here. This is an incomplete list, compiled from other lists, advertisements, public relations, and the old faithful *Spiritual Community Guide.*

There has been no effort to judge the many resources in the United States and Canada in selecting these listings, nor in the presentation of them. Some groups which might seem to be emphasized are not well esteemed by the compilers. Others, which are, may be found described just once and very briefly. This is done on faith that each of us can best judge for himself or herself. So, dive in, and trust yourself to know how to swim.

Beyond the use of this directory, you may find that friends, local churches, newspapers and magazines, bulletin boards, schools (especially free schools), health-food stores, etc. will offer something to meet your interest. The Yellow Pages contain useful information too—under such headings as Camps; Churches; Judo, Karate, and Jiu-Jitsu; Meditation Instruction; Religious Organizations; Retreat Houses; Synagogues; Yoga Instruction; etc.

If you are unable to find a suitable group nearby, the following list provides the names of several groups offering correspondence courses in some aspect of meditation. Some other group which particularly interests you might also have correspondence courses, literature, or book lists, not to mention summer retreats and the like—which are not indicated in this directory.

Ananda Co-op Village, Nevada City, CA; see Local Listings.

Arcana Workshops, Beverly Hills, CA; Local Listings.

Arcane School, New York, NY; Local Listings.

Astara, Upland, CA; Local Listings.

Center for Spiritual Awareness, Lakemont, GA; Local Listings.

Holy Order of Mans; National Listings.

Meditation Group for the New Age, Ojai, CA; Local Listings.

Pansophic Institute, Reno, NV; Local Listings.

Self-Realization Fellowship; National Listings.

SYDA Foundation; National Listings.

Society of Pragmatic Mysticism, New York, NY; Local Listings.

The Theosophical Society; National Listings.

University of the Trees, Boulder Creek, CA; Local Listings.

A limited list of reasonably priced tape cassettes on basic meditation techniques by teachers from varying traditions is available from Hanuman Tape Library, Dept. M, Box 61498, Santa Cruz, CA 95061.

2

GROUPS THAT TEACH MEDITATION

This list has two parts—the National Listings and the Local Listings. The National Listings includes those groups which are both nationwide and quite large. They are arranged alphabetically by name. The Local Listings is made up of smaller groups, those having no more than two dozen or so centers if that many. They are arranged alphabetically by state, city, and name. For the most part churches are not included here as they are too numerous to list.

National Listings

ANANDA MARGA
854 Pearl St.
Denver, CO 80203
Tel. (303) 623–6602

Ananda Marga is an international organization whose aim is to elevate and purify individuals through detailed meditation instruction and, at the same time, to serve and reform society in order to help create a new social order based on love. All instruction is free of charge. Yogic postures designed to fit the individual, health and dietary procedures, and advanced meditation techniques are taught by highly qualified teachers.

Ananda Marga's social service projects, which include schools, orphanages, group homes, prison and drug rehabilitation programs, and disaster-relief teams are based upon the concept that the served and the server are one. The organization was founded in 1955 by Shri Anandamurti. There are over 100 Ananda Marga Centers in North America. Check the phone book or write for the address of the nearest office.

ARICA
24 West 57th Street
New York, NY 10019
Tel. (212) 489–7430

Arica, founded in 1971 by Oscar Ichazo, teaches a new theory and method for achieving clarification of consciousness. Intensive Arica trainings last from a few hours to 40 days or more. Programs include such practices as karma processing, energy generation and transmutation, physical exercise, relaxation, meditation, and *zhikr*. Open House is held in New York every Tuesday and Thursday night, beginning at 7:00 P.M. Write for the address of the nearest Arica teaching center.

DIVINE LIGHT MISSION
INTERNATIONAL HEADQUARTERS
PO Box 532
Denver, CO 80201
Tel. (303) 623–8280

Founded by the young Guru Maharaji Ji. Divine Light Mission offers initiation—a threefold method of understanding: meditation to connect with the inner essence of life, service to learn and practice selfless action, satsang to listen to and give discourse on the experience. There are hundreds of Divine Light Mission Centers throughout the country. Check the phone book or write for the address of the nearest center.

HOLY ORDER OF MANS
20 Steiner St., PO Box 14606
San Francisco, CA 94114
Att.: Director of Education
Tel. (415) 431–1917

Under the mantle and guidance of the Master Jesus Christ, the order accepts all true spiritual paths and teachers. Likewise the approach to meditation is universal. Stated simply, to meditate is to ask a question and receive an answer from the Self which is always perfect and which is part of God. Meditation and the other spiritual tools of man are taught in the local Brotherhouses on Tuesday and Thursday evenings at 7:00 P.M. in cities across the country. For the address of the nearest Brotherhouse write to the above address. There is also the Discipleship Movement, which is the lay order for correspondence study (see Holy Order of Mans, Cheyenne, WY in the Local Listings). Spiritual instruction and meditation is also given by the priest or brother in the local Christian Community in various cities. For the address of the nearest Christian Community, write to the Christian Community Bureau (see Local Listing in Ft. Worth, TX). *God bless you in your striving.*

INTEGRAL YOGA INSTITUTE
227 W. 13th Street
New York, NY 10011
Tel. (212) 929–0585

The Integral Yoga Institutes are founded and guided by Rev. Sri Swami Satchidananda. Integral Yoga is a synthesis of the various branches of yoga, designed to bring about the harmonious development of every aspect of the individual: physical, emotional, social, intellectual and spiritual. The practices suggested and taught by the I.Y.I. include hatha (physical postures, breathing techniques, and deep relaxation), raja (concentration and meditation), japa (mantra repetition), karma (selfless action), bhakti (chanting and other devotional practices), and jnana (study of self-inquiry) yogas. Daily classes are held at the 15 Institute branches and 20 Integral Yoga Groups and Teaching Centers in the yogas mentioned above as well as Yoga diet, scripture study, and satsang (spiritual sharing). Guests are also invited to visit the Integral Yoga Homes connected with many of the Institute branches. Check the phone book or write for the address of the nearest institute. There also are Satchidananda Ashrams in Eureka Springs (Arkansas), Santa Barbara (California), and Pomfret Center (Connecticut). See local listings for their addresses. Sri Swamiji explains the goal of Integral Yoga as:

> *A body of perfect health and strength, mind with all clarity and control, intellect sharp as a razor, will of steel, heart full of love and compassion, a life dedicated to the common welfare and realization of the true Self.*

ISKCON
INTERNATIONAL SOCIETY FOR KRISHNA CONSCIOUSNESS, INC.
3764 Watseka Ave.
Los Angeles, CA 90034
Tel. (213) 871–0717

ISKCON (popularly known as the Hare Krishna Movement) was founded in 1965 by His Divine Grace A.C. Bhaktivedanta Swami Prabhupada, who came from India on the order of his spiritual master to preach love of God to the people of the West. Sri Krishna, as the Supreme Personality of Godhead, is the central focus of the organization and its activities. A blissful spiritual relationship with Him is enjoyed through bhakti yoga—humble, devotional, personal service to the Lord, especially through congregational chanting of the mantra "Hare Krishna, Hare Krishna, Krishna

Krishna, Hare Hare, Hare Rama, Hare Rama, Rama Rama, Hare Hare." Visitors are welcome during the day, sunrise meditation 7:00 A.M. daily, bhakti yoga class 7:00 P.M. Monday–Saturday. All are invited to attend the "joyful festival and sumptuous feast" held each Sunday at 4:00 P.M. Check in the phone book or write for the address of the nearest branch.

> *Abandon all varieties of religiosity and simply*
> *surrender unto Me. I will protect you from all*
> *sinful reaction. Do not fear.*
>
> —*The Bhagavad Gita,*
> 18.66

MATAGIRI
Mt. Tremper, NY 12457

Matagiri is a small community dedicated to the experiment of living the Integral Yoga of Sri Aurobindo within the framework of a collective. Since its inception in 1968, Matagiri, located on 42 wooded acres near Woodstock, has served as a link to provide information on the Sri Aurobindo Ashram and information on Auroville—the "City of Human Unity" now evolving in South India as an expression of the teaching of Sri Aurobindo and the Mother. Visitors are welcome. Accommodations are limited and simple, so reservations must be made in advance. As Matagiri is not a retreat, much of a typical day is devoted to work done in a spirit of consecration and detachment. Collective meditations are held Wednesday and Saturday at 7:30 P.M. and daily at 3:30 P.M. Matagiri is not a national headquarters, but it is listed here since it will be able to supply addresses of other Sri Aurobindo centers upon request.

> *The sadhana of this Yoga does not proceed*
> *through any set mental teaching or prescribed*
> *form of meditation, mantras or others, but by*

*aspiration, by a self-concentration inwards or
upwards, by self-opening to an Influence, to the
Divine Power in the heart, and by rejection of all
that is foreign to these things. It is only by faith,
aspiration and surrender that this self-opening
can come.*

—Sri Aurobindo

NICHIREN SHOSHU OF AMERICA
525 Wilshire Blvd.
Santa Monica, CA 90401
Tel. (213) 451–8811

NSA is a school of Buddhism in which the emphasis
is on life in and of the world, life devoted to happiness.
Happiness is "the attainment of enlightenment through
perfection and the realization of all desires." The way
to this ideal is the chanting of mantra. Check the phone
book or write for the location of the NSA branch
nearest you.

SATHYA SAI BABA CENTRAL COMMITTEE OF AMERICA
PO Box 668
Soquel, CA 95073

Sathya Sai Baba is a world teacher with millions of
followers in India and around the globe. The path of
Sai Baba is the path of devotion using bhajan and
service as a vehicle. Sathya Sai Baba organizations do
not seek publicity or advertisement. For information
about Sai Baba and his centers, write the above address.

*There is only one caste the caste of Humanity,
There is only one religion the religion of Love,
There is only one language the language of the
Heart.*

—Sathya Sai Baba

SELF-REALIZATION FELLOWSHIP
3880 San Rafael Ave.
Los Angeles, CA 90065
Tel. (213) 225–2471

Paramahansa Yogananda founded SRF in the U.S. in 1920. His special mission was to teach the science and techniques of kriya yoga. He was chosen by Babaji to introduce kriya yoga to the world in this age and to show that the experience of God is the same, regardless of differing dogmas. The goal of the Self-Realization kriya yoga teaching, which embraces in a balanced way the essence of all other forms of yoga, is direct personal experience of God. For those who wish to know more about the life and teachings of Yogananda, his inspirational classic *Autobiography of a Yogi* is recommended. SRF offers printed lessons based on Yogananda's teachings. Write for free literature.

SILVA MIND CONTROL
1110 Cedar Ave.
Laredo, TX 78040
Tel. (512) 722–6391

During intensive training classes, students are taught to produce and maintain tranquil, positive mental states and to develop ESP. This is done by learning to function at alpha and theta frequencies of the brain. The training is accomplished without the use of biofeedback equipment. Classes available throughout the world. Check the phone book or write for the address of the nearest office.

SIVANANDA YOGA VEDANTA CENTER
8th Avenue
Val Morin, Quebec J0T 2R0
Canada
Tel. (819) 322–3226

A nonsectarian organization practicing a synthesis of yoga which combines all the different paths of yoga into one homogenous workable pattern as prescribed by Swami Sivananda. Swami Vishnu-Devananda is the founder-president of the center. Yoga classes, retreats, and teacher training programs are available. A prison yoga project is run by members of the center. There are branch centers and retreats located around the world. Write for locations.

SRI CHINMOY CENTRE
PO Box 32433
Jamaica, NY 11431
Tel. (212) 523–3471

Sri Chinmoy, Bengali author and spiritual teacher, teaches the path of grace. Through Divine Love, one-pointed devotion, and unconditional surrender to the highest, the disciple comes to the realization of his eternal oneness with the Supreme. This is the path of the heart. Sri Chinmoy holds a meditation every Friday night at 7:30 P.M. in the All Angels Church, 81st St. and West End Ave. in Manhattan. Admission is free. There are sixty Sri Chinmoy Centres around the country. Check in the phone book, call, or write for the address of the nearest one.

SUFI ORDER
PO Box 396
New Lebanon, NY 12125

The Sufi Order, directed by Pir Vilayat Inayat Khan, is dedicated to the awakening of the consciousness of humanity. The successor of Hazrat Inayat Khan, who founded the Sufi Order in the West in 1910, Pir Vilayat leads frequent meditation seminars, camps, and retreats in North America and Europe, giving training in meditation, counseling, and darshan. Sufi Order centers throughout the United States, Canada, and Western Europe offer a program of spiritual training, hold weekly classes in Sufi teachings and meditation, and celebrate Universal Worship paying homage to all the world's great religions and teachers. The national headquarters of the Sufi Order are located at the Abode of the Message, a new age community in upstate New York. Please write the headquarters for the location of the nearest center.

> *Toward the One, the Perfection of Love, Harmony and Beauty, the Only Being, united with all the Illuminated Souls who form the Embodiment of the Master, the Spirit of Guidance.*
>
> —*Sufi invocation*

SYDA FOUNDATION
SIDDHA YOGA DHAM CALIFORNIA
1107 Stanford
Oakland, CA 94608

Mailing address:
S.Y.D.A. Foundation
PO Box 11071
Oakland, CA 94611
Tel. (415) 655–8677

Baba Muktananda teaches that the entire universe can be experienced as the Self through meditation. This path, called siddha yoga, is initiated when the inner spiritual energy, kundalini, is awakened. Once the process has begun, the experiences needed for personal growth, both in meditation and in daily life, unfold automatically. Free regular programs of chanting, meditation and instruction are offered at Baba Muktananda's many meditation centers and residential ashrams. They also offer Siddha Yoga intensives where the spontaneous kundalini awakening (Shaktipat) is transmitted. Write for the location of the nearest center.

THE THEOSOPHICAL SOCIETY IN AMERICA
PO Box 270
Wheaton, IL 60187
Tel. (312) 668–1571

The Theosophical Society is a nonsectarian body of seekers after truth, promoting brotherhood and striving to serve humanity. Its declared objectives are to form a nucleus of the Universal Brotherhood of Humanity to encourage the study of comparative religion, philosophy, and science, and to investigate unexplained laws of nature and the powers latent in man. The society sees every religion as an expression of the Divine Wisdom. H.P. Blavatsky and Annie Besant have been among the leaders of the movement. Several correspondence courses in Theosophy are offered, such as "The Study and Practice of Meditation" ($8.00). There are also courses offered at the National Headquarters, frequently including one in meditation. There are over 130 branches, study centers, and camps of the Theosophical Society in America. Check the phone book or write for the address of the nearest branch.

3HO FOUNDATION
INTERNATIONAL HEADQUARTERS
1620 Preuss Rd.
Los Angeles, CA 90035
Tel. (213) 273–9422

3HO (Healthy, Happy, Holy Organization) was founded in 1969. Yogi Bhajan is the director of spiritual education. His teachings incorporate meditation, the chanting of mantra, Sikh Dharma, tantra, and the awakening of kundalini energy through the use of various yogic postures in combination with specific breathing exercises. Great emphasis is placed on respect for woman and her dignity as the Grace of God. There are over 108 3HO Centers and ashrams in the United States, Canada,

Europe and Mexico. Check the phone book or write for the address of the nearest center.

> *Keep up! There is no liberation without labor . . . and there is no freedom which is free.*
>
> —*The Siri Singh Sahib*
> (Yogi Bhajan)

TM®
(TRANSCENDENTAL MEDITATION)
17310 Sunset Blvd.
Pacific Palisades, CA 90272
Tel. (213) 459–4387

There are over 460 centers teaching the TM technique in the United States and Canada. Check the phone book under Transcendental Meditation or write for the location of the nearest center.

VAJRADHATU
KARMA DZONG
1345 Spruce St.
Boulder, CO 80302
Tel. (303) 444–0210

Karma Dzong is the largest of the Vajradhatu centers under the direction and spiritual guidance of Chogyam Trungpa, Rinpoche, who is a scholar and meditation master trained in the philosophical traditions of the Kagyu and Nyingma sects of Tibetan Buddhism. Vajradhatu also includes 14 large urban centers called Dharmadhatus, and 18 smaller centers called Dharma Study Groups in cities across the United States and Canada. For more information and location of the centers of Chogyam Trungpa, Rinpoche, see Karme-Choling, Barnet, VT; Naropa Institute, Boulder, CO; or Maitri Center, Wingdale, NY, in the Local Listings or write to Vajradhatu.

VEDANTA SOCIETY OF SOUTHERN
CALIFORNIA
1946 Vedanta Pl.
Hollywood, CA 90068
Tel. (213) 465–7114

Vedanta is the philosophy which has evolved from the
Vedas, a collection of ancient Indian scriptures, perhaps the oldest religious writings in existence. The
fundamental truths of Vedanta are that the Godhead,
the underlying reality, is omnipresent within each of
us, within every creature and object, so man in his
true nature is God; it is the purpose of man's life on
earth to unfold and manifest this Godhead, which is
eternally existent within him, but hidden; and truth is
universal in that men seek the Godhead in various ways,
but what they all seek is the same. The Vedanta centers
in the United States, of which the Vedanta Society of
Southern California is one, are united under the spiritual guidance of the Ramakrishna Order of India. In
charge of each Vedanta Center is an ordained monk
of the Ramakrishna Order of India. At several of the
centers, resident students live under the supervision of
swamis who train them in the practice of meditation,
worship, and service. Each center has a schedule of
services, classes, and meditations open to the public.
For the location of the nearest center write to the
Vedanta Society in Hollywood.

Local Listings

ARIZONA

SRI RAM ASHRAMA
Box AR
Benson, AZ 85602
Tel. (602) 586–2575

Under the guidance of Swami Dayanand.

UNIVERSAL SERIES CENTER
UNIVERSAL TRUTH FOUNDATION
4340 North 7th Ave.
Phoenix, AZ 85013
Tel. (602) 264–6542

Many classes, including meditation.

UNIVERSITY OF LIFE CHURCH
1124 N. 3rd Ave.
Phoenix, AZ 85003
Tel. (602) 254–9667

Meditation classes.

AMMAL'S GARDEN
PO Box 18344
Tucson, AZ 85731

Nightly meditations and instruction available at this small community that welcomes all visitors. Please write if you are passing through town.

MIND AND BODY SCIENCE
7334 E. 6th Ave., Suite 2
Scottsdale, AZ 85251
Tel. (602) 946–7730

Mind and Body Science offers many classes in psychic and yogic topics. Meditation instruction available. Dr. Robert H. Frey is the founder.

ARKANSAS

SATCHIDANANDA ASHRAM
PO Box 190
Eureka Springs, AK 72632
Tel. (501) 789–5272

A spiritual community founded and guided by Swami Satchidananda. For further information see the National Listing for Integral Yoga Institute.

DIMENSIONS OF EVOLVEMENT
Box 342
Jasper, AK 72641
Tel. (501) 466–5201

Meditation and spiritual-growth courses and retreats. Workshops provided in various cities.

CALIFORNIA

STARCROSS MONASTIC COMMUNITY
HUMANIST INSTITUTE
Annapolis, CA 94512
Tel. (707) 886–5330

Founded by Brother Tolbert McCarroll. Meditation and other aspects of spiritual growth are taught in ongoing weekly groups, weekend workshops, short-term residential programs and a full-time spiritual apprentice program. Workshops are also regularly held in Richmond, VA, and occasionally in other locations. These programs are organized through the Humanist Institute, which is a venture of the Starcross Monastic Community. There is also the opportunity for those who have taken part in these programs to go on individual retreats and to temporarily share in the life of the community. The emphasis is on relating the mystical quest to everyday life. Both Eastern and Western traditions are explored with special focus on Taoism and fourteenth-century Western teachers like Meister Eckhart. See listing in Richmond, VA.

INTERNAL SCHOOL
1251 9th St.
Arcadia, CA 95521
Tel. (707) 822–2908

Buddhist meditation center.

TATAGATAS
PO Box 216
Ben Lomond, CA 95005
Tel. (408) 336–2336

Ed Dalton leads three-day communication sesshins
(formerly called enlightenment intensives). Participants work on the question "Who Am I?" or one of
a related nature.

AQUARIAN MINYAN OF BERKELEY

Call Judith, (415) 525–6434, for information.
Friday-evening meditation in the Jewish tradition.

BERKELEY ZENDO
1670 Dwight Way
Berkeley, CA 94703
Tel. (415) 845–2403

A resident zendo affiliated with the Zen Center of
San Francisco. Regular schedule of zazen (Soto tradition), services, lectures, and instruction.

MEHER BABA INFORMATION
Box 1101
Berkeley, CA 94701

Meher Baba, an Indian master who stated that he
was "The Ancient One" or God-Man who periodically incarnates on this earth to be a living example
of the One Truth, did not give any specific meditation. To follow him is to live a life of love and
service. In his words, "meditation may be described
as the path an individual cuts for himself while trying to go beyond the limitations of the mind." A list
of books and information on Meher-Baba-oriented
meetings and activities including centers in Myrtle
Beach, SC; Ojai, CA; and New York, NY, is available upon written request. See also listing in Cambridge, MA.

THE SUFI ISLAMIA RUHANIAT SOCIETY
Berkeley contact:
Tel. (415) 527–2569

For further information see the listing for The Sufi
Islamia Ruhaniat Society in San Francisco, CA.

VIPASSANA FELLOWSHIP OF AMERICA
66 Menlo Pl.
Berkeley, CA 94707
Att.: Yvonne Ginsberg
Tel. (415) 526–6235

The fellowship sponsors vipassana (insight) meditation evenings and weekends, plus intensive retreats,
in the Bay Area. In the Northeast, spring retreats
are taught by Dhiravamsa (formerly head of the
Thai Buddhist Mission to England) and Mitchell
Ginsberg (who has taught vipassana in England,
France, and the United States). The retreats are
small and personal. The formal practice consists in
developing open awareness in both sitting and walking. In addition to this traditional practice, applica-
tions of vipassana awareness to personal conflicts
and growth are also employed.

ARCANA WORKSHOPS
407 N. Maple Dr.
Suite 214
Beverly Hills, CA 90210
Tel. (213) 273–5949 or 540–8689

Arcana Workshops is a meditation training center
offering group experience in the following pursuits:
scientific meditation training in weekly workshops
and correspondence courses; study and practice of
advanced psychology, observation of mental and
emotional attitudes that tend toward health or dis-
ease, systematic study of the inner constitution of
the human being, development of insight and intuition; recording and publishing of group thinking

distilled from group study and meditation; experiments in intergroup cooperation toward development of intergroup ethics. The overall aim of Arcana is to relate spiritual goals to community needs through group work, thereby enabling the individual to make his/her maximum contribution to the building of a more compassionate society.

SHERBORNE STUDIES GROUP
PO Box 3513
Beverly Hills, CA 90212

Inspired by Gurdjieff and Bennett and associated with the Claymont Society, Charles Town, WV.

UNIVERSITY OF THE TREES
PO Box 644
Boulder Creek, CA 95006
Tel. (408) 338–3855

A three-year course in meditation and self-unfoldment written by the founder and director, Christopher Hills. Courses available by correspondence. Meditation classes for children. The meditations practiced come from many traditions including Christian, Hindu, and Tibetan. There is an open session of chanting and meditation each Friday evening, which includes a talk by Mr. Hills.

SAMBOSA TEMPLE
28110 Robinson Canyon Rd.
Rt. 2
Carmel, CA 93921

A Korean Zen Buddhist temple. For more information see International Zen Center of New York in New York City.

TASSAJARA ZEN MOUNTAIN CENTER
Carmel Valley, CA 93924

For information see Zen Center, San Francisco, CA.

ISLAMIC SOCIETY OF CALIFORNIA
781 Bolinas Rd.
Fairfax, CA 94930
Att.: Mah' Jabin
Tel. (415) 454–6666

Jamu Salam, the Redwood Mosque run by the Islamic Society, offers Arabic and Quoranic studies, Friday Juma prayer and feast, Sunday meetings, and Wednesday-morning Grace (Baraka) class for women. Facilities also available for seminars and retreats.

SEICHO-NO-IE
14527 S. Vermont
Gardena, CA 90247
Tel. (213) 323–8486

A worldwide organization with millions of members, Seicho-no-ie was founded by Dr. Masaharu Taniguchi. The practice of shinsokan, a form of meditation, is the method by which members strive to realize the Truth, the Truth that one is a child of God, pure and sinless.

VEDANTA SOCIETY OF SOUTHERN
CALIFORNIA
1946 Vedanta Place
Hollywood, CA 90068
Tel. (213) 465–7114

For further information see the National Listings.

EWAM CHODEN TIBETAN BUDDHIST
CENTRE
254 Cambridge St.
Kensington, CA 94708
Tel. (415) 527–7363

Classes in meditation, the Tibetan Book of the Dead, Buddhist Dharma, and the Tibetan language conducted by Lama Kunga Thartse, Rinpoche, the designated reincarnation of Sevan Repa, Heart Disciple of Milarepa. On Sunday there is a meditation open to everyone.

ANANDA ASHRAMA
5301 Penna Ave.
PO Box 8555
La Crescenta, CA
Tel. (213) 248–1913

Srimata (Rev. Mother) Gayatri Devi, Spiritual Leader. Two public services each week: Sunday at 11:00 A.M. and Thursday at 8:00 P.M. The Thursday service includes group meditation and a talk on some aspect of the spiritual life. Ananda Ashrama houses a community of resident monastics and householder families which follows the teaching of Sri Ramakrishna. Their spiritual guide, Srimata Gayatri Devi, is in residence about half of each year. There is another center in Cohasset, MA.

SOCIETY OF THE SMILING BUDDHA
464 Marine St.
La Jolla, CA 92037
Tel. (714) 459–6414

A zen center founded by Joshu Sasaki Roshi of the Cimarron Zen Center (see listing in Los Angeles, CA).

ZEN CENTER OF LONG BEACH
1942 Magnolia Ave.
Long Beach, CA 90806
Tel. (213) 599–3275

Dr. Soyu Matsuoka, Roshi, Director. Daily zazen schedule. Also periodic lectures and sesshins.

Silence is thunder.

BODHI
Box 638
Los Altos, CA 94022
Tel. (415) 325–5339

Kobun Chino Otogawa is the teacher for Bodhi, which is comprised of zen centers in Los Altos, Potter Valley (Spring Mountain Sangha), Santa Cruz, California, and Fremont, Michigan (So Getsu-in). (See listings.) The Los Altos group (Haiku Zendo) was founded in 1965 by Shunryu Suzuki-roshi. There is a daily zazen schedule. Zazen instruction is given Wednesday evenings at 6:30, followed by zazen and a lecture by Chino-sensei or another member of the group. Sesshins are held several times a year. Members' homes are open for sitting in Menlo Park and Santa Clara. Bodhi is in the process of purchasing land for a new meditation center.

CALIFORNIA BOSATSUKAI
5632 Greek Oak Dr.
Los Angeles, CA 90028

Founded by Nyogen Senzaki in the 1930s, California Bosatsukai offers sesshins in the Rinzai tradition, directed by Nakagawa Soen, Roshi, when he is in this country.

CENTER FOR YOGA
230½ N. Larchmont Blvd.
Los Angeles, CA 90004
Tel. (213) 464–1276

The Center for Yoga has a complete curriculum for hatha yoga classes including classical and Iyengar techniques; meditation training, holistic health workshops, weekend retreats, summer programs at Earth Camp One, teacher training courses, Krishnamurti video tapes, music concerts, prominent speakers, and various other programs and events. See separate listing in Santa Barbara, CA.

CIMARRON ZEN CENTER
2505 S. Cimarron St.
Los Angeles, CA 90018
Tel. (213) 732–2263

This Rinzai zen center is under the guidance of
Joshu Sasaki Roshi. There is a daily meditation
schedule, with morning and evening zazen, and a
Sunday morning beginners' class. During the summer
and winter months Roshi is available to give sanzen
every Sunday morning and frequently during the
week. Most people here are engaged in koan practice as directed by Roshi. This is the urban sister-
center of Mt. Baldy Zen Center (see listing under
Mt. Baldy, CA). Roshi also guides the Society of
the Smiling Buddha (see listings in La Jolla, CA;
and San Diego, CA) and the Zen centers in Jemez
Springs, NM, and Vancouver, BC (see listings).

> *As a butterfly lost in flowers*
> *As a child fondling mother's breast*
> *As a bird settled on the tree*
> *Sixty-seven years of this world I*
>   *have played with God.*
>
>   *—Joshu*

GOLD WHEEL TEMPLE
5743 Huntington Dr.
Los Angeles, CA 90032

Chinese Buddhist temple. For more information see
the listing for Sino-American Buddhist Association
in San Francisco, CA.

INTERNATIONAL BUDDHIST
MEDITATION CENTER
928 S. New Hampshire Ave.
Los Angeles, CA 90006
Tel. (213) 384–0850

Founded and directed by the Ven. Thich Thien-An, a Vietnamese Buddhist priest and philosophy professor. Regular morning meditations as well as weekend and seven-day sesshins. This is a nonsectarian center. One may choose from a variety of meditation practices from each of the three main Buddhist traditions (Theravada, Mahayana, and Vajrayana). Dr. Thich Thien-An helps each person select the practice best suited to his or her character.

INTERNATIONAL SOCIETY FOR KRISHNA CONSCIOUSNESS
3764 Watseka Ave.
Los Angeles, CA 90034
Tel. (213) 871–0717

For further information see the National Listings.

KARGYUDPA ORDER
Los Angeles, CA

For more information on centers under the guidance of Lama Kalu Rinpoche, see Kagyu Kunkhyab Chuling in Vancouver, BC.

KOYASAN BUDDHIST TEMPLE
342 E. First St.
Los Angeles, CA 90012

Directed by Bishop Seysu Takahashi of the Shingon school.

SATHYA SAI BABA CENTER & BOOKSTORE
7911 Willoughby Ave.
Los Angeles, CA 90046
Tel. (213) 656–9373

For further information see the National Listings.

SELF-REALIZATION FELLOWSHIP
3880 San Rafael Ave.
Los Angeles, CA 90065
Tel. (213) 225–2471

For further information see the National Listings.

SRI MAHISHI RUBY FOCUS CIRCLE
1265 N. Sweetzer Ave. #14
Los Angeles, CA 90069
Tel. (213) 656–8786

Meditation instruction and practice in use of the
Paramantra system.

TAHL MAH SAH TEMPLE
354 S. Kingsley Rd.
Los Angeles, CA 90005

A Korean Zen Buddhist temple. For more information see International Zen Center of New York in
New York City.

3HO FOUNDATION
INTERNATIONAL HEADQUARTERS
1620 Preuss Rd.
Los Angeles, CA 90035
Tel. (213) 273–9422

For further information on 3HO see the National
Listings.

ZEN CENTER OF LOS ANGELES, INC.
905 S. Normandie Ave.
Los Angeles, CA 90006
Tel. (213) 387–2351

Taizan Maezumi Roshi, director of ZCLA, is a Soto
Zen priest and a recognized master in both the Soto
and Rinzai lineages of Zen Buddhism. The influence
of both these traditions is reflected in the practice at

the Zen Center. There is an ongoing resident training program for intensive practice and an extended resident training program for those with outside employment. Families are welcome and child care is provided. There is a daily schedule of meditation which includes sitting periods in the morning, afternoon and evening, open to members and non-members alike; and, for members and trainees, daily interviews with Roshi are available. In addition, a week-long sesshin (meditation retreat) is held monthly. There is also a varied format of seminars, and for newcomers there are monthly introductory workshops.

LOS GATOS ZEN GROUP
16200 Matilija Drive
Los Gatos, CA 95030
Att.: Arvis Justi
Tel. (408) 354–7506

Meetings every Sunday 8:00 A.M.–10:00 A.M. Instruction for beginners. Three-day sesshins in spring and fall with Maezumi Roshi—other times to be arranged. Meetings consist of meditation and chanting—tea and discussion optional.

SHREE GURUDEV ASHRAM CALIFORNIA
19330 Overlook Road
Los Gatos, CA 95030
Tel. (408) 354–1109

Center of Swami Muktananda which offers a correspondence course in Siddha Yoga.

MT. BALDY ZEN CENTER
PO Box 429
Mt. Baldy, CA 91759
Tel. (714) 985–6410

The center was established in 1970 to provide a more monastic setting for the training of students than was available at Cimarron Zen Center in Los Angeles, which is also under the guidance of Rinzai Zen Master Joshu Sasaki Roshi. The program is highly structured, the atmosphere austere, and the discipline rigorous. Persons wishing to visit Mt. Baldy are invited to attend a special zazen period and instruction for beginners any Sunday beginning at 9:00 A.M. The center is also open to those who wish to come and practice on weekends. Weekend students must participate in the center's schedule but are not required to share in the work. The fee for a weekend stay is $35. Reservations are required. Each summer the communities under the direction of Joshu Sasaki Roshi sponsor Summer Seminars on the Sutras at Mt. Baldy Zen Center, Mt. Baldy, Calif. The goal of the seminar is to provide a tranquil meditative setting for students who wish to study Buddhism under Joshu Roshi and emminent scholars who are invited to lead the sutra study. Zazen is held each morning and evening, and a Dai-Sesshin follows the academic program. Each year a university co-sponsors the Seminars making college credit available to interested qualified students. Correspondence should be addressed to:

Summer Seminars on the Sutras
2245 West 25th Street
Los Angeles, CA 90018
(213) 734–6704

CHO-KE MOUNTAIN ZENDO
108 South B St.
Mt. Shasta, CA 96067

Under the guidance of the Rev. Don Gilbert, who follows the teaching of his Korean zen master, the Ven. Dr. Seo.

SHASTA ABBEY
HEADQUARTERS, REFORMED SOTO ZEN
CHURCH AND THE ZEN MISSION SOCIETY
PO Box 478
Mt. Shasta, CA 96067
Tel. (916) 926–4208

Under the guidance of the founder, Roshi Jiyu-
Kennett, Abbess, Shasta Abbey is a seminary and
training monastery for the Zen Buddhist priest-
hood following the Reformed Soto Zen tradition. It
has programs for both priest trainees and lay students open to men and women, and weekend introductory retreats specifically designed to teach zen
meditation and its application in daily life. There are
also advanced retreats and seven-day intensive sesshins and a lay student residence program. Reservations are required for all programs. See listings of
affiliated priories in Oakland, CA; and Cottage
Grove, OR.

ANANDA COOPERATIVE VILLAGE
900 Alleghany Star Rt.
Nevada City, CA 95959
Tel. (916) 265–5877

The 125 or so people who live in this spiritual community in the foothills of the Sierra Nevada are
disciples of Paramahansa Yogananda (author of
Autobiography of a Yogi) and practice his techniques of kriya yoga. Swami Kriyananda, who
founded the community in 1968 and lives in full-
time residence, is a direct disciple of Yogananda.
Members are monastics or householders some of
whom have children in Ananda's three schools.
Ananda's Institute of Cooperative Spiritual Living
offers programs and workshops throughout the summer. In addition to a year-round, fully-staffed retreat
(see Retreat Facilities), the community offers the
public an Apprentice Program—two or more months
of life at Ananda working, learning, meditating, and

sharing, a strict but rewarding schedule for those on the meditative path. A yoga home-study course called "14 Steps to Self Mastery" is also offered. Ananda is dedicated to the fulfillment of Paramahansa Yogananda's dream:

> *To spread a spirit of brotherhood among all people and to aid in establishing in many countries, self-sustaining world-brotherhood colonies for plain living and high thinking.*

INNER LIGHT FOUNDATION
PO Box 761
Novato, CA 94947
Tel. (415) 897–5581

The Inner Light Foundation is a nondenominational, nonprofit corporation. It was formed in 1967 by the friends and associates of Betty Bethards, the psychic channel and meditation teacher. The principle objective of the Inner Light Foundation is to engage in spiritual, educational, charitable, and scientific activities which foster, develop, and achieve in mankind an awareness of his unity with God, the Universal Consciousness. This is accomplished through lectures, conferences, educational programs, counseling, scientific research, meditation, and meditation groups.

BERKELEY BUDDHIST PRIORY
3538 Telegraph Avenue
Oakland, CA 94609
Tel. (415) 655–1286

Affiliated with Shasta Abbey, the Soto zen training monastery of Roshi Jiyu-Kennett. Daily meditation and services, weekend retreats, and classes in various aspects of zen training. Resident lay program. Private instruction in meditation available by appointment. Monthly newsletter.

SIDDHA YOGA DHAM CALIFORNIA
1107 Stanford Ave.
Oakland, CA 94608
Mailing address:
S.Y.D.A. Foundation
PO Box 11071
Oakland, CA 94611
Tel. (415) 655–8677

This is Swami Muktananda's main ashram in America. For further information see S.Y.D.A. Foundation in the National Listings.

YESHE NYINGPO
ORGYEN CHÖ DHING
6448 Hillegass Ave.
Oakland, CA 94618
Tel. (415) 654–1755

Tibetan Buddhist Center founded by His Holiness Dudjom, Rinpoche. See listing in New York City for more information.

KROTONA INSTITUTE OF THEOSOPHY
PO Box 433
Ojai, CA 93023
Tel. (805) 646–1139 or 646–2653

Krotona is a theosophical educational center in a retreat setting which offers a variety of courses dealing with ancient wisdom. For more information see the National Listing for the Theosophical Society in Wheaton, IL.

MEDITATION GROUP FOR THE NEW AGE
PO Box 566, Dept. H
Ojai, CA 93023

A meditation course by correspondence in techniques and aspects of meditation. Attention is focused on service to humanity. First year free.

CHURCH OF HANUMAN
c/o Whole Life Center and School
3437 Alma St.
Palo Alto, CA 94306
Tel. (415) 493–0561

Classes in meditation, spiritual healing, and Sufi dancing.

THE SUMMIT LIGHTHOUSE
PO Box 7000
Pasadena, CA 91109
Tel. (213) 798–0971

The Summit Lighthouse publishes the teachings of the ascended masters of the Great White Brotherhood as taught by Elizabeth Clare Prophet. Study, meditation, and the science of the spoken Word in decrees and mantras are an essential part of their program to help the individual realize his God-potential and soul freedom and to assist people of every race and religion to live in harmony with cosmic law.

SPRING MOUNTAIN SANGHA
11525 Mid-Mountain Rd.
Potter Valley, CA 95469
Tel. (707) 743–1438

Spring Mountain is one of the zen centers comprising Bodhi, which is guided by Kobun Chino Otogawa. Chino-sensei visits and conducts sesshin several times a year. This is a residential community which is open to people in the area. There is a daily zazen schedule. See the listing for Bodhi in Los Altos, CA.

JOSHU ZEN TEMPLE
2303 Harriman Lane
Redondo Beach, CA 90278

Under the guidance of Joshu Sasaki Roshi. For more information see Cimmarron Zen Center, Los Angeles, CA.

THE SUFI ISLAMIA RUHANIAT SOCIETY
HURKALYA
St. John's Church (Sat. 8:00 P.M.)
14 Lagunitas Road
Ross, CA 94957
Tel. (415) 453–2097

For further information see the listing for The Sufi
Islamia Ruhaniat Society in San Francisco, CA.

SACRAMENTO YWCA
1122–17th St.
Sacramento, CA 95814
Tel. 442–4741

Hatha and raja yoga. The instructor, Shirani, is a
disciple of Paramahansa Yogananda and student of
Swami Kriyananda.

SANATANA DHARMA FOUNDATION and
KAYAVAROHAN, a spiritual community
3100 White Sulphur Springs Road
St. Helena, CA 94574
Tel. (707) 963–9487

Residents welcome, as are visitors, to take part in
daily programs with Yogeshwar Muni or weekend
events in yogic health, clearing, meditation techniques, Enlightenment Intensives, etc. Call or write
for information.

BUDDHIST CHURCHES OF AMERICA
1710 Octavia St.
San Francisco, CA 94109
Tel. (415) 776–5600

Headquarters of the Shin (Pure Land) school in
America.

CALIFORNIA INSTITUTE OF ASIAN
STUDIES
3494 21st St.
San Francisco, CA 94110
Tel. (415) 648–1489

President, Dr. Frederic Spiegelberg. M.A. and Ph.D.
programs in philosophy and religion, East/West
psychology, Buddhist and Vedic studies.

HELIOTROPE
21 Columbus
San Francisco, CA 94111
Tel. (415) 398–7042

An open university offering a great variety of courses,
including yoga, meditation, and Jewish Merkedah
meditation.

HOLY ORDER OF MANS
PO Box 14606
San Francisco, CA 94114
Att.: Director of Education
Tel. (415) 431–1917

For further information see the National Listings.

KAGYU DRODEN KUNCHAB
San Francisco, CA

For more information on centers under the guidance
of Lama Kalu Rinpoche, see Kagyu Kunkhyab
Chuling in Vancouver, BC.

PARAS RAJNEESH MEDITATION CENTER
PO Box 22174
San Francisco, CA 94122
Tel. (415) 664–6600

Bhagawan Shree Rajneesh, an Indian spiritual teacher of tantric and Sufi heritage, has devised his own occult tools specifically for the Western psyche. Chaotic Meditation, his technique, involves deep and fast breathing and spontaneous body movement in a group to create a situation in which catharsis can happen. After the group dancing and emotional play have reached a peak, there is silence and one can fall spontaneously into meditation. A dozen Paras Rajneesh Meditation Centers are located across the country. Write for the address of the nearest center.

Love is not a relationship but a state of being.

—*Rajneesh*

PSYCHOSYNTHESIS INSTITUTE
3352 Sacramento St.
San Francisco, CA 94118
Tel. (415) 922–9182

A synthesis of many traditions, Psychosynthesis was developed by Roberto Assagioli. See Canadian Institute of Psychosynthesis, Inc., Montreal, Quebec, Canada, for a further description of the Psychosynthesis practices.

SHUGEN CHURCH OF AMERICA
KAILAS SHUGENDO
2362 Pine St.
San Francisco, CA 94115
Tel. (415) 922–5008

San Francisco Kailas Shugendo is guided by Vajrabodhi Ajari (Dr. Pemchekov Warwick). The spiritual disciplines practiced include climbing mountains while chanting mantras, fire ceremony, walking on the sacred fire, going under ice-cold waterfalls, and the making of a lot of joyful music.

SINO-AMERICAN BUDDHIST ASSOCIATION
GOLD MOUNTAIN MONASTERY
1731 15th St.
San Francisco, CA 94103
Tel. (415) 621–5202 or 861–9672

The Sino-American Buddhist Association is head-quartered at Gold Mountain Monastery in San Francisco and at the City of Ten Thousand Buddhas on Wonderful Enlightenment Mountain in Talmage, CA. The Ven. Ch'an Master Hsüan Hua is the abbot of Gold Mountain Monastery and Tathagata Monastery (Talmage, CA), the chairman of the Sino-American Buddhist Association, the founder and dean of the International Institute for the Translation of Buddhist Texts, San Francisco), and Chancellor of Dharma Realm Buddhist University (Talmage, CA). As training centers, the International Institute, the monasteries, and Gold Wheel Temple in Los Angeles have daily programs which include three hours of meditation, three hours of chanting, and lectures. The monasteries periodically convene meditation sessions lasting from one to twelve weeks. Besides observing the traditional Mahayana Buddhist precepts, many residents of the monasteries, the Institute, and Gold Wheel also observe other vigorous practices such as eating one meal a day before noon and never lying down to sleep. A major task carried on by the Sino-American Buddhist Association, the parent organization, is the translation of Buddhist texts into English and other Western languages. The City of Ten Thousand Buddhas is S.A.B.A.'s country community located in the beautiful Ukiah Valley of Mendocino County, CA. The City is planned to serve as a foundation for world Buddhism when it is fully operating. See City of Ten Thousand Buddhas, Talmage, CA.

THE SUFI ISLAMIA RUHANIAT SOCIETY
MENTORGARTEN
410 Precita Ave.
San Francisco, CA 94110
Tel. (415) 285–5208 or 648–3933

The Bay Area Sufi community was long guided by Murshid Samuel L. Lewis, whom many people met in the movie *Sunseed*. It is presently directed by Murshid Moineddin Jablonski and Masheikh Wali Ali Meyer. Public meetings, which include meditation and/or meditative dances and music, are held on a weekly basis in San Francisco, Ross, and Berkeley. There is a charge of $1.50 for these classes. For information on these meetings, the new school for Sufi studies, other classes, camps, and seminars, contact The Sufis (see also listings in Berkeley, and Ross, CA).

VISION MOUND CEREMONY
The Dawn Horse Bookstore
1443 Polk St.
San Francisco, CA 94109

Vision Mound Ceremony is a spiritual community devoted to the study and practice of the teaching of Bubba Free John (Franklin Jones). The radical path of understanding which Bubba teaches consists of spiritual practice, satsang, and the transforming relationship between the disciple and the guru. Meditation is done within the context of this life and according to the dharma of understanding.

> *Real meditation is an intense fire. It is a marvelous intelligence, a brilliance, a genius, a living force. It is not a pious attempt to quiet your little thoughts. It blasts the hell out of those thoughts! Truth is an intelligence that needs only to look at some obstruction for it to dissolve and this is the process that comes awake in satsang.*
>
> —*Bubba Free John*

ZEN CENTER
300 Page St.
San Francisco, CA 94102
Tel. (415) 863–3136

Founded by Shunryu Suzuki Roshi. Teacher and director: Zentatsu Baker Roshi. Large, resident zen center. Daily zazen and services open to everyone. Lecture and zazen instruction on Saturday morning. See *Zen Mind, Beginner's Mind* by Suzuki Roshi for a description of the practice followed at the center as well as at Green Gulch Farm, Tassajara Zen Mountain Center, and Berkeley Zendo.

> *The way we eat in zen, the way we handle things, the eating bowl should just rest in your hand. When you use the whole of your hand, the bowl is holding your hand and your hand is holding the bowl. There is some intimacy, some equality and participation of hand and bowl.*
>
> *— Baker Roshi*

CHRISTANANDA YOGA ASHRAM
977 Asbury Street
San Jose, CA 95126
Tel. (408) 292–6359

Sri Yogi Raj Evangelos Alexandrou combines the teachings of yoga and the Hesychast contemplative tradition (or the "Prayer of the Heart" of Eastern Christianity. A yoga teachers course is available at the Christananda community where people can live in and participate with Christian Tantra illuminaries. There is deep meditation techniques from Tantra Yoga, Tao, Zen, Sufi, dancing and singing in joyous celebration and Christian mysticism. Meditation Workshops and intensives are given every first Friday of each month and every third Friday of each month for three days.

STILLPOINT MEDITATION INSTITUTE
604 S. 15th St.
San Jose, CA 95112
Tel. (408) 287–5307

Buddhist vipassana (insight) meditation center. One-day to one-month retreats under the guidance of Sujata. Program limited to six persons a month.

YOGA HOUSE
418 Mission St.
San Rafael, CA 94902
Mailing address:
PO Box 3391
San Rafael, CA 94902

Hatha yoga and meditation classes given free by Yoga Master Dadaji Vimalananda and students in Marin County and in San Francisco. Free meditation and chanting class every Sunday with Dadaji, 6:00–8:00 P.M. Nondenominational.

CENTER FOR YOGA
PO Box 30588
Santa Barbara, CA 93105
Tel. (805) 967–5420

For further information see listing in Los Angeles, CA.

SANTA BARBARA ZENDO
333 E. Anapamu
Santa Barbara, CA 93101
Tel. (805) 966–7221

Daily meditations.

SATCHIDANANDA ASHRAM
1705 San Marcos Pass
Santa Barbara, CA 93105
Tel. (805) 967–3344

A spiritual community founded and guided by Swami Satchidananda. For further information see the National Listing for Integral Yoga Institute.

THE HANUMAN FELLOWSHIP
PO Box 1569
Santa Cruz, CA 95061

A nonprofit organization devoted to the arts, education, and service. The Fellowship, based on the study and practice of Ashtanga Yoga as taught by Baba Hari Dass, offers quarterly retreats, yoga classes, and performances of the Ramayana. It also publishes and distributes its own books and runs a volunteer service for the elderly and handicapped. Satsang (questions and answers, music, dance, and food) is available to the public every Sunday at noon.

SANTA CRUZ VIPASSANA MEDITATION GROUP
Santa Cruz, CA
Tel. (408) 426–1630

Weekly sittings with Stephen Levine.

SANTA CRUZ ZEN CENTER
113 and 115 School St.
Santa Cruz, CA 95060
Tel. (408) 426–0169

Santa Cruz is one of the zen centers comprising Bodhi, which is guided by Kobun Chino Otogawa. There is a daily zazen schedule. Zazen instruction is given on Tuesday evening at 7:00, followed by zazen and a lecture by Chino-sensei or another member of the group. Sesshins are held here or in Los Altos. For further information see the listing for Bodhi in Los Altos, CA.

NICHIREN SHOSHU OF AMERICA
525 Wilshire Blvd.
Santa Monica, CA 90401
Tel. (213) 451–8811

For further information see the National Listings.

VAJRAPANI INSTITUTE FOR WISDOM
CULTURE
PO Box 295
Santa Monica, CA 90406
Tel. (213) 393–2418

The institute, under the guidance of Lama Thubten Yeshe and Lama Thubten Zopa Rinpoche, organizes courses, seminars, and retreats of Tibetan Buddhist meditation. It also publishes a quarterly newsletter and distributes translations of texts and other books on Tibetan Buddhism.

GENJO-JI
SONOMA MOUNTAIN SANGHA
6367 Sonoma Mtn. Rd.
Santa Rosa, CA 95404
Tel. (707) 545–8105

A Buddhist lay sangha practicing with Jakusho Kwong, sensei. Rurally located within the Valley of the Moon.

ZEN CENTER
GREEN GULCH FARM
Star Rt. (Muir Beach)
Sausalito, CA 94965
Tel. (415) 383–3134

The purpose of Green Gulch Farm is to provide another type of practice situation for San Francisco Zen Center students as well as to provide a zendo for the neighboring communities. There is a daily schedule of meditation, farm work, and kitchen work at this resident zendo. Lecture and zazen instruction are given on Sunday mornings.

*Abandon all hope, abandon any kind of loca-
tion. It is just a wonderful experience to realize
that you are actually lost, just swimming. We
do not know, here with this beautiful stone
Buddha, with each other in this room, where
this is. Do you know where this is, where we
are? If you think you know, that is not right.*

—*Baker Roshi*

MIDDLEBAR BUDDHIST MONASTERY
2503 Del Rio Dr.
Stockton, CA 95204
Tel. (209) 462–8208

Middlebar is of the Soto sect of Zen Buddhism. The
training under Roshi MacDonough is on a personal
basis, which limits the number of monks the master
can accept. Persons interested in this type of training
should contact the monastery. There are also programs of daily zazen and study groups open to non-
resident students of both sexes. There are also
periodic week-long meditation retreats for men.

CITY OF TEN THOUSAND BUDDHAS
DHARMA REALM BUDDHIST UNIVERSITY
TATHAGATA MONASTERY
PO Box 217
Talmage, CA 95481
Tel. (707) 462–0939

The City of Ten Thousand Buddhas is a center for
world Buddhism containing 67 large buildings spread
over 267 acres in the Ukiah Valley, Mendocino
County. Dharma Realm Buddhist University and
Tathagata Monastery are located at the City as well
as Instilling Virtue Elementary School. A high school
and hospital are also planned. Dharma Realm Buddhist University offers graduate and undergraduate
degrees in many areas of study with special emphases

in Buddhist studies, Chinese studies, and Oriental and Western art. For more information see the listing for Sino-American Buddhist Association, San Francisco, CA.

ASTARA
800 W. Arrow Hwy.
Upland, CA 91786
Tel. (714) 981–4941

Astara is "a center of all religions and philosophies, a school of the ancient mysteries and an institute of psychic research" founded and guided by Robert and Earlyne Chaney. Meditation instruction available. Meetings Sunday at 11:00 A.M. Correspondence courses, seminar, workshop, and retreat facilities available.

SUFISM REORIENTED
1300 Boulevard Way
Walnut Creek, CA 94595
Tel. (415) 938–4820

A disciplined, traditional Sufi order, reoriented by Avatar Meher Baba, under the leadership of Murshida Ivy, O. Duce.

INSTITUTE OF MENTALPHYSICS
59700 29 Palms Hwy.
PO Box 640
Yucca Valley, CA 92284
Tel. (714) 366–8471

A teaching center and spiritual retreat in the high desert where yoga breaths, meditation, and other spiritual practices lead to the highest development of the total person, body, mind, and spirit, one is evolutionarily able to achieve.

COLORADO

NAROPA INSTITUTE
1111 Pearl Street
Boulder, CO 80302
Tel. (303) 444–0202

Naropa Institute, a division of Nalanda Foundation, began its first session of classes with over 2000 students and 60 faculty members in June, 1974, in Boulder. The environment of learning and personal growth is founded on the interaction of contemplative, artistic and academic traditions. This direct experience can form a sound basis for integrating the complementary intellectual and sensory-intuitive approaches to living in the world. In turn, scholarship provides clarification of individual experience. Courses at the Institute include—philosophy and psychology, meditation, Buddhist studies, dance, martial arts, music, theatre, visual arts and poetics. In 1976 year-round courses of study began, and in the summer of 1977, Naropa Institute graduated its first class. B.A. and M.A. degrees were granted in the fields of psychology, Buddhist studies, as well as certificates in poetics, dance, theatre and visual arts. For more information concerning Trungpa Rinpoche's centers, see the Vajradhatu Karma Dzong in the National Listings.

THE TEMPLE OF KRIYA YOGA
209 Canyon Blvd.
Boulder, CO 80302

Mailing address is Salina Star Route, Boulder, CO 80302. Regular services are held on Sundays at 11:00 A.M. for Aratee Puja and satsang, and on Wednesdays at 7:00 P.M. for chanting and meditation. Classes, counseling, and individual instruction in yoga, meditation, mystical philosophy, the spiritual sciences, and sane, joyous living. Also see listing in Chicago, IL.

VAJRADHATU
KARMA DZONG
1345 Spruce St.
Boulder, CO 80302
Tel. (303) 444–0210

For further information see the National Listings.

ANANDA MARGA
854 Pearl St.
Denver, CO 80203
Tel. (303) 623–6602

For further information see the National Listings.

DENVER ZEN GROUP
1233 Columbine
Denver, CO 80206
Tel. (303) 333–4844

For further information see The Zen Center, Rochester, NY.

DIVINE LIGHT MISSION
INTERNATIONAL HEADQUARTERS
PO Box 532
Denver, CO 80201
Tel. (303) 623–8280

For further information see the National Listings.

ORDER of FRANSISTERS and
FRANBROTHERS
Mailing address:
2168 S. Lafayette St.
Denver, CO 80210

The order was founded in 1963 upon the prayer of St. Francis but is interreligious, embracing all faiths,

East and West. The intention of Fransisters and Franbrothers is identity with their Ideal, feeling that daily living is an offering of Love. It is important to do one's best and for Life to know that one of Its extensions is coming closer to Its Source. Teaching, healing, and retreats are main activities. Book lists and literature available. Please send a stamped, self-addressed envelope with request.

CONNECTICUT

NEW HAVEN ZEN CENTER
193 Mansfield St.
New Haven, CT 06511
Tel. (203) 787–0912

A Korean Zen Buddhist center. For more information see International Zen Center of New York in New York City.

SATCHIDANANDA ASHRAM—YOGAVILLE
PO Box 108
Pomfret Center, CT 06259
Tel. (203) 974–1005

A spiritual community founded and guided by Swami Satchidananda. For further information see the National Listing for Integral Yoga Institute.

PERSONAL DEVELOPMENT CENTER, INC.
Box 251
Windham Center, CT 06280
Tel. (203) 423–4785

Free courses to qualified students in tao, raja, tantric yoga. Tuition courses offered in hatha and prenatal yoga, call (203) 887–4971.

DISTRICT OF COLUMBIA

BUDDHIST VIHARA SOCIETY
5017 16th St., N.W.
Washington, DC 20011
Tel. (202) 723–0773

Open daily, service on Sunday, regular meditation classes in the practice of mindfulness of breath as taught in Theravadin Buddhism. The teacher is the Ven. Henepola Gunaratana from Sri Lanka.

Y.S.M., INC.
YOGA SCHOOL OF WASHINGTON
100 Vermont Ave. NW
2nd Floor
Washington, DC 20005

Classes in hatha yoga, meditation, pranayama, teacher training, and yoga philosophy.

FLORIDA

INVITATION CENTER
PO Box 552
Anna Maria, FL 33501
Tel. (813) 778–2422

Invitation Center stresses no method but finds refuge in the acceptance of life as it is. It exists as a point around which a natural community could form. No effort is being expended for this to happen at present. Visits by written request only.

YOGASHAKTI ASHRAM
827 S. Federal Hwy.
Deerfield Beach, FL 33441
Tel. (305) 421–9878 or 421–2567

Yoga-oriented teaching inspired by Ma Yogashakti Saraswati. Daily classes in hatha yoga, meditation, and philosophy. Satsang every Sunday.

CHELA CENTER
614 E. Atlantic Blvd.
Pompano Beach, FL 33060
Tel. (305) 782–3041

Chela Center, a service-oriented humanistic business
and esoteric school, is open Monday to Friday,
11:00–7:00; Saturday 11:00–4:00; closed Sunday.
The school program includes subjects in the fields
of meditation, yoga, health, etc.

UNITY CHURCH OF POMPANO
261 S.E. 13th Ave.
Pompano Beach, FL
Tel. (305) 943–3715

Dedicated to the Christian fellowship of man. Weekly
open house with a group meditation.

GEORGIA

ZEN CENTER OF ATLANTA
141 Inman Dr.
Decatur, GA 30030
Tel. (404) 378–1332

Rev. Michal Elliston, Director. Affiliated with the
Zen Center of Long Beach, California.

CENTER FOR SPIRITUAL AWARENESS
Box 7
Lakemont, GA 30552
Tel. (404) 782–4723

Meditation taught each summer by director Roy
Eugene Davis, a disciple of Paramahansa Yogananda. The teaching by Dr. Davis is in the Siddha
tradition with emphasis on jnana yoga and raja yoga.
Among the center's publications is the "Home Study
Course in Spiritual Awareness" which consists of
twelve monthly lessons in yoga and meditation.

THE BRIDGE MEDITATION CENTER
PO Box 808
Riverdale, GA 30274

Korean Zen tradition as presented by Zen Master, Rev. Mi Ju Cozad, Dharma heir of Zen Master Ven. Ta Hui: Daishi, who is in turn Dharma heir of Zen Master Ven. Dr. Seo. The Bridge Meditation Center has a residency training program for students interested in special training in the field of meditation, new thought principles, aquarian age living, Christ truth teachings, Zen and Tibetan Buddhist philosophy, and universal scriptures. The residency training program also extends to those whose life calling is in teaching and ministering, and has a special orientation in training lay ministers and teachers in meditation. The Bridge offers quarterly "retreat-sesshins" and workshops in this area, also private individual retreats and counseling. For more information write or call (404) 996–7839. Address all inquiries to the Spiritual Program Director.

HAWAII

MAUI ZENDO of the DIAMOND SANGHA
RR 1, Box 702
Haiku, HI 96708
Tel. (808) 572–8163

For further information see Koko An Zendo, Honolulu, HI.

KOKO AN ZENDO of the DIAMOND SANGHA
2119 Kaloa Way
Honolulu, HI 96822
Tel. (808) 946–0666

Located near the University of Hawaii. Up to six residents maintain an early-morning and evening schedule of zazen and house-maintenance with some twenty other members participating from the community. The Koko An Zendo and the Maui Zendo form the Diamond Sangha. They are affiliated with the Harada-Yasutani tradition of Zen Buddhism. Robert Aitken completed his formal zen training with Yamada Koun, Roshi, in 1974 and now conducts sesshins and guides students as Roshi of both centers. Visitors should write or phone first.

**SOTO MISSION of HAWAII, SHOBOJI
ZEN BUDDHIST TEMPLE**
1708 Nuuanu Ave.
Honolulu, HI 96817

Soto Zen Center.

SHING LUNG GOMPA
Wood Valley Temple
PO Box 701
Pahala, HI 96777
Tel. (808) 928–8536

The Ven. Nechung Rinpoche Supreme Abbot, Spiritual Director. A Tibetan Buddhist meditation center.

WOOD VALLEY TEMPLE
General Delivery
Pahala, HI 96777

Founded by the Ven. Nechung Rinpoche, this Tibetan Buddhist Center maintains a regular schedule of meditation, teachings and Tibetan language lessons, as well as occasional special ceremonies and weekend retreats. Located in a cool, very quiet bamboo and eucalyptus forest, the temple serves as a country retreat center for those who want an environment for intensive study and meditation. Reasonable single and group rates.

ILLINOIS

BUDDHIST TEMPLE of CHICAGO
1151 W. Leland Ave.
Chicago, IL 60640
Tel. (312) 314–4661

This is a nonsectarian temple, but there is a regular zazen schedule with instruction for beginners.

BUL TA SAH TEMPLE
3437 N. Daneman Ave.
Chicago, IL 60618

A Korean Zen Buddhist temple. Mr. di-Hak Son, Dharma teacher. For more information see International Zen Center of New York in New York City.

INTERNATIONAL BABAJI KRIYA YOGA SANGAM
1118 W. Armitage
Chicago, IL 60614
Tel. (312) 549–0031

Guided by Yogi S.A.A. Ramaiah, disciple of Master Babaji Nagaraj of the Himalayas. Kriya yoga involves hatha, kundalini, mantra, dhyana, pranayama, and bhakti yogas. There are several branches in California and New York, etc. Write for address of the nearest branch.

TEMPLE of KRIYA YOGA
505 N. Michigan Ave.
Chicago, IL 60611

Classes, counseling, and individual instruction in yoga meditation, and the spiritual sciences. Sri Goswami Kriyanand, head priest and spiritual preceptor.

ZEN CENTER OF CHICAGO
2230 N. Halsted St.
Chicago, IL 60614
Tel. (312) 348–1218

Directed by Rev. Kongo Langlois, Roshi, and affiliated with the Zen Center of Long Beach, CA; the
Zen Center offers zazen on Sunday at 10:00 A.M.
and 4:00 P.M. and on Tuesday and Thursday evenings at 7:30 P.M. Weekend sesshins are conducted
every other month from September through May.

CHICAGO ZEN GROUP
2029 Ridge
Evanston, IL 60201
Tel. (312) 475–3015

For further information see The Zen Center, Rochester, NY.

HIMALAYAN INTERNATIONAL INSTITUTE
OF YOGA SCIENCE AND PHILOSOPHY
1505 Greenwood Rd.
Glenview, IL 60025
Tel. (312) 724–0300

Swami Rama, spiritual head and founder of the
Himalayan Institute, teaches the system of super-
conscious meditation. Retreats and weekend seminars in yoga philosophy and meditation, eight-week
meditation courses and hatha yoga courses, biofeedback training and special programs. Write for address
of center near you.

THE THEOSOPHICAL SOCIETY IN AMERICA
PO Box 270
Wheaton, IL 60187
Tel. (312) 668–1571

For further information see National Listings.

INDIANA

THE TIBET SOCIETY
Goodbody Hall 101
Indiana University
Bloomington, IN 47401
Tel. (812) 337–2233

Directed by Thubten Jigme Norbu (Tagster, Rinpoche), who is the older brother of the Dalai Lama. Former Abbot of Kumbuh Monastery in eastern Tibet, he is now an author and professor.

KENTUCKY

CORNUCOPIA INSTITUTE
St. Mary, KY 40063
Tel. (502) 692–6006

The Cornucopia Institute (formerly Living Love Center in Berkeley, California) was founded and is guided by Ken Keyes, Jr., author of *The Handbook to Higher Consciousness*. The basic approach of the Living Love Way is that our separateness and unhappiness is primarily caused by the demands we make on ourselves, other people, and the world in general. Because our expectations are based on our inner models of how things "should" be, we are constantly disappointed by ourselves and others. During the weekend consciousness workshops given both at the Institute and throughout the country, Ken and his associates show participants how to free themselves from security, sensation and power demands and expectations that prevent life from working smoothly and peacefully—a synthesis of Eastern philosophy and Western psychology with clear, effective techniques.

MARYLAND

JANUS GROWTH CENTER
21 W. 25 Street
Baltimore, MD 21218
Tel. (301) 366–2123

Savitria Meditation Program offers an alternative approach to drug-abuse treatment. Treatment is aimed not at the symptomatic behavior patterns of the drug abuser, but at the roots of those patterns. The problematic nature of drug usage is de-emphasized in favor of the experience of self-discovery. The program seeks to provide an environment to nurture the beginning of such a process. The purpose is to help to awaken and redirect the individual's creative tendencies. The approach is holistic, focusing on the physical, mental, and spiritual human experience. The twelve-week sessions offer a diversified process that includes meditation, art therapy, Guided Imagery with Music, movement and body awareness, psychodrama, dance, Gestalt, dream work, and individual counseling.

KOINONIA
PO Box 5744
Baltimore, MD 21202
Tel. (301) 486–6262

A 26-year-old spiritual and educational community on 45 wooded acres just north of Baltimore. Work centers on developing the strengths and skills for conscious, joyous, creative living. Here, many "new age" and traditional paths and forms of worship meet and share energy as the community strives to reverence and to experience the Universal Spirit in its many dancing manifestations. Year-round terms of studies and of disciplines along with numerous retreats, festivals, seminars, lectures, and other special programs. Koinonia is recognized as a place of college-level learning. Transfer credit to other schools is possible.

MASSACHUSETTS

CAMBRIDGE ZEN CENTER
7 Ashford Terr.
Allston, MA 02134
Tel. (617) 254–0363

A Korean Zen Buddhist center. For more information see International Zen Center of New York in New York City.

CHRISTIAN COMMUNITY OF BOSTON
1377B Commonwealth Ave.
Allston, MA 02134
Tel. (617) 783–5810

Classes held every Tuesday and Thursday at 7:30 P.M. on the inner Christian mysteries and their application to one's daily living situations. Christianity as a vehicle for the expression of Light, Life, and Love. Meditation, daily Communion 6:15 and 11:00 A.M.; Sunday services at 11:00 A.M.

BOSTON ZEN GROUP
17 Oak Knoll
Arlington, MA 02174
Tel. (617) 646–2908

For further information see The Zen Center, Rochester, NY.

INSIGHT MEDITATION SOCIETY
Pleasant St.
Barre, MA 01005

A meditation center available for scheduled meditation instruction and for individual retreats in the Theravadin Buddhist tradition.

OM THEATER WORKSHOP BOSTON SUFI ORDER CENTER FOR THE ESOTERIC ARTS
551 Tremont Street (4th floor)
Boston, MA 02116
Tel. (617) 482–4778

Sufi dancing and group meditation Tuesday night, $1. Enquirer's class for Sufi path, Tuesday night. Universal worship service, Sunday at 11:00 A.M. Actor and teacher-training courses uniting modern theater training with meditative practices.

SERVERS OF THE GREAT ONES, INC.
47 Roslin Street
Boston, MA 02124
Tel. (617) 436–5204

Servers of the Great Ones, Inc., is a group whose meditations and activities focus on service to humanity. Eastern and Western techniques are used to develop receptivity to soul contact and the ability to channel spiritual energies toward those areas of the planet most in need; for example, to the United Nations, to any nations in conflict, to bring about racial harmony, and to humanity in general. Meditation meetings are held every Wednesday evening at 7:30 free of charge. These meditations, based on impersonal service to humanity, are followed by discussions on such esoteric subjects as Qabbalah, tarot, I Ching, and the Path of Discipleship. At the time of the full moon, we link up with meditation groups around the world by using the Great Invocation. A full moon newsletter is available free of charge. In the spring of 1978, we are offering a correspondence course on the practical application of spirituality, entitled Foundations of the Wisdom. Those interested in receiving these materials should write or call us. In cooperation with a number of local groups, a healing meditation for the City of Boston is held every Friday between 7:00 and 9:00 P.M. People are encouraged to send light and love to Boston, each in their own way. Another intergroup activity is the sponsoring of public gatherings annually on World Goodwill Day, the full moon of Gemini. Those in other cities might consider similar intergroup projects.

CAMBRIDGE VIPASSANA GROUP
Cambridge Vipassana Fellowship of America
c/o Paul Gron
32 Tufts St.
Cambridge, MA 02139
Tel. (617) 354–4014

Evening meditations.

MEHER BABA INFORMATION CENTER
7 Inman Square
Cambridge, MA 02139
Tel. (617) 354–8661

The center provides a reading room and gathering place for those interested in learning more about Meher Baba. Informal meetings are held weekly for those interested in Meher Baba's life, work, and messages. The meetings often include films and music. See also listings in Berkeley, CA.

VEDANTA CENTRE–ANANDA ASHRAMA
130 Beechwood St.
Cohasset, MA 02025
Tel. (617) 383–0940

For more information see La Crescenta, CA.

MAHA SIDDHA NYINGMAPA MEDITATION CENTER
PO Box 256
Conway, MA 01341
Att.: Jean Cowles

Director the Ven. Dodrup Chen Rinpoche. Informal teaching in Nyingmapa tradition, occasional seminars and ceremonies when Rinpoche is in residence. In process of building temple in nearby Berkshire Hills.

SATSANG SATSEVA, INC.
200 Bay Rd.
Hadley, MA 01035
Tel. (413) 586–5214

A service collective offering meditation and counseling.

MAHA YOGA ASHRAM
PO Box F
Newton, MA 02158

The Maha Yoga Ashram is a spiritual and educational center founded on the principles and practices of the eightfold path of raja yoga by Yogiraj Shri T. R. Khanna. Its activities include hatha yoga classes, meditation sessions, satsang, chanting, weekend retreats, intensives, guest lecturers, and special programs. The ashram is a self-supporting community which functions as a resident family unit as well as a student center.

MICHIGAN

SIDDHA YOGA DHAM ANN ARBOR
902 Baldwin
Ann Arbor, MI 48104
Tel. (313) 994–5625 or 994–3072

Ashram of Swami Muktananda. See National Listings for further information.

SO GETSU-IN
Box 39
Fremont, Michigan 49412

So Getsu-in is one of the zen centers comprising Bodhi. There is a daily zazen schedule. Chino-sensei comes to visit and conduct sesshin during the year. For further information, see the listing for Bodhi in Los Altos, CA.

NEW DIRECTIONS THRU MEDITATION, INC.
c/o Costello
3658 Samuel
Rochester, MI 48063
Tel. (313) 852–2412

Relational Meditation (relating to self, to others, to the universe). Workshops, seminars, lectures, courses. Director: the Rev. Michael J. Gramlich.

MINNESOTA

MINNESOTA ZEN MEDITATION CENTER
3343 E. Lake Calhoun Pky.
Minneapolis, MN 55408
Tel. (612) 822–5313

Regular activities include zazen (two sittings in both the morning and the evening), chanting and service, instruction in zazen (Soto tradition), and two lectures each week by resident teacher Dainin Katagiri, Roshi. Two-day sesshins are held the third weekend of the month, seven months of the year, and there are four seven-day sesshins each year. Roshi holds formal interviews with students during sesshins and at other times will hold formal or informal interviews with zen students or other interested persons upon request.

MISSOURI

UNIVERSAL GREAT BROTHERHOOD ADMINISTRATIVE COUNCIL OF USA
Box 9154
St. Louis, MO 63117

The Universal Great Brotherhood, A.U.M. Solar Line is an international, cultural, and educational organization opened to the public in 1948 by Dr. Serge Raynaud de la Ferriere. Its goal is the re-education of humanity toward world peace through a synthesis of science and religion, emphasizing the techniques of yoga, meditation, cosmobiology, t'ai chi, I-Ching, karate, Qabbalah, psychology, and art. Pre-Initiatic and Initiatic Schools are open to those who are ready to pursue the path of service to humanity. Affiliated branches are located in Los Angeles, CA; Tucson, AR; Oklahoma City, OK; Chicago, IL; Cleveland, OHIO; Ann Arbor, MI; and Brooklyn, NY. The international headquarters is located in Mexico City, MEXICO. Please write for addresses and further details.

NEBRASKA

OMAHA ZEN GROUP
1915 N. 84th St.
Omaha, NE 68114
Tel. (402) 393–4842

There is zazen each morning of the week. Once a month Katagiri Roshi comes from the Minnesota Zen Meditation Center in Minneapolis to lead zazen, give lectures, and sometimes hold sesshin.

NEVADA

PANSOPHIC INSTITUTE
PO Box 2971
Reno, NV 89505

An international educational organization which has undertaken a program to disseminate the concepts of Tibetan Buddhism into Western culture. The director of the institute, the Ven. Simon Grimes, teaches classes in meditation and Tibetan yoga. Some correspondence courses are also available.

NEW HAMPSHIRE

SANT BANI ASHRAM
Franklin, NH 03235
Tel. (603) 934–2948

Sant Bani Ashram, founded by and dedicated to Param Sant Kirpal Singh, who left his earthly body in 1974, is the international headquarters of the ashrams currently under the spiritual guidance of Sant Ajaib Singh, a disciple of Kirpal Singh. It offers initiation into the path of Surat Shabd Yoga, a path of love and discipline that embraces the essence of the teachings of all True Masters. Sant Bani Ashram has sixteen centers in the United States and Canada. For their locations, see the Local Listings or write. Call to arrange for visits.

SANT BANI ASHRAM
Hanover, NH

See listing in Franklin, NH.

NEW JERSEY

LABSUM SHEDRUB LING
LAMAIST BUDDHIST MONASTERY OF
AMERICA
140 E. 3rd St.
Howell, NJ 07731
Tel. (201) 363–6075

Founded by the Tibetan Buddhist lama the Ven. Geshe Wangyal. Practice includes prayer, study, and translation of Buddhist scriptures, as well as meditation. Seminars and summer programs, taught by an ecumenical faculty of Buddhist priests, college professors, etc., are offered on a regular basis. See also Lamaist Buddhist Monastery in Washington, NJ.

SHANTI YOGA INSTITUTE AND RETREAT
943 Central Ave.
Ocean City, NJ 08226
Tel. (609) 399–1974

Institute Director Shanti Yogi teaches individuals and classes in hatha yoga, raja yoga, and meditation following the path of surrender. Meditations open to the public are held every Sunday evening. See listing in Philadelphia, PA.

LAMAIST BUDDHIST MONASTERY OF
AMERICA RETREAT HOUSE
Rt. 1, Box 306A
Washington, NJ 07882
Tel. (201) 689–6080

Retreat house and residence of lama, the Ven. Geshe Wangyal. For further information see Labsum Shedrub Ling, Howell, NJ.

NEW MEXICO

JEMEZ BODHI MANDALA
Box 44
Jemez Springs, NM 87025

A zen center under the guidance of Joshu Sasaki Roshi. For more information see Cimarron Zen Center, Los Angeles, CA.

LAMA FOUNDATION
Box 444
San Cristobal, NM 87564

Lama Foundation hosts summer meditation seminars and retreats by teachers from various traditions. It is open to visitors every Sunday.

NEW YORK

BUDDHIST ASSOCIATION OF THE UNITED STATES
3070 Albany Crescent
W. 231st St.
Bronx, NY 10463
Tel. (212) 884–9111

The temple has an open meditation and lecture Sunday afternoon. The teachings are from the Ch'an school of Chinese Buddhism, a school which emphasized the practice of meditation. Instruction in the meditation of counting the breaths is available.

BUFFALO MEDITATION SOCIETY
464 Statler Hilton
Buffalo, NY 14202
Tel. (716) 854–8195

Monday evening classes in the fall and spring are offered in the basic practice of Buddhist Vipassana meditation.

THE HUMAN DIMENSIONS INSTITUTE,
ASSOCIATED WITH DAEMEN COLLEGE
(FORMERLY ROSARY HILL COLLEGE)
4620 W. Lake Rd.
Canandiagua, NY 14424
Tel. (716) 394–8173

HDI is a nonprofit, independent educational organization known for its efforts to understand the "whole"
person, his inner condition and cosmic connections
—physical, emotional, mental, and spiritual. It op-
erates through scientific research, publications, public
lectures, in-depth seminars, experience groups, and
continuing courses for all age groups, conducted at
Daemen College and surrounding institutions. There
is often an introductory to meditation course available.

YOGI GUPTA ASHRAM, INC.
94–29 50th Avenue
Elmhurst, NY 11373
Tel. (212) 592–3217

Classes in hatha yoga and meditation.

THE ESSENE SCHOOL
65–11 175 St.
Flushing, NY 11365
Tel. (212) 762–0320

Courses in meditation, healing, cosmic consciousness, astrology, and other metaphysical subjects. All
courses are taught by Martin Schulman.

KARMA TRIYANA DHARMACHAKRA
RD 7, Knapp Rd.
Hopewell Junction, NY 12533
Att.: Lama Tenzin Choney, President

Karma Triyana Dharmachakra is the parent organization undertaking to build a monastery which will
be the seat of His Holiness the Gyalwa Karmapa—

the head of the Kagyupa order of Tibetan Buddhism —in North America. This monastery will be traditionally Tibetan, and will be a major center of Tibetan Buddhist Dharma practice and culture in the West. Lama Tenzin Choney is His Holiness' representative for the monastery project, and with him are Lama Kathar and Lama Gangha. Inquiries about the monastery or about His Holiness' itinerary may be directed to him at the above address.

SRI CHINMOY CENTRE
PO Box 32433
Jamaica, NY 11431
Tel. (212) 523–3471

For further information see the National Listings.

THE ZEN STUDIES SOCIETY
DAI BOSATSU ZENDO KONGOJI
Beecher Lake, Star Rt.
Livingston Manor, NY 12758
Tel. (914) 439–4566

For further information see The Zen Studies Society, New York, NY.

MATAGIRI
Mt. Tremper, NY 12457

For further information see the National Listings.

SUFI ORDER
PO Box 396
New Lebanon, NY 12125

For further information see the National Listings.

ARCANE SCHOOL
866 United Nations Plaza
Suite 566/7
New York, NY 10017

The Arcane School was established by Alice A. Bailey in 1923. The function of the school is to assist those at the end of the probationary path to move forward on the path of discipleship, and to assist those already on that path to move on more quickly and to achieve greater effectiveness in service. The training, which is conducted by correspondence, is based on three fundamental requirements—occult meditation, study, and service to humanity.

ARICA
30 W. 57th St.
New York, NY 10019
Tel. (212) 489–7430

For further information see the National Listings.

ARUNACHALA ASHRAMA
BHAGAVAN SRI RAMANA MAHARSHI
CENTER, INC.
342 E. 6th St.
New York, NY 10003
Tel. (212) 477–4060 or 854–0322

Established for the sake of the wholehearted practice of Self-Enquiry and submission and surrender to the supreme Self as taught by Bhagavan Sri Ramana Maharshi, Sri Arunachala Ashrama presently maintains an ashrama center in New York City and an ashrama farm in the Annapolis Valley, Nova Scotia, Canada (see separate listing). A rigorous schedule is followed in each of the ashramas similar to that of Bhagavan Sri Ramana Maharshi's ashrama in Tiruvannamalai, India. Sri Bhagavan's central teaching of Self-Enquiry or "Who am I?" is the focal point of the devotees' lives.

> *Divine Grace is essential for Realization. It leads one to God-realization, but such Grace is vouchsafed only to him who is a true devotee or a yogin, who has striven hard on the path towards freedom.*
>
> —*Bhagavan Sri Ramana Maharshi*

FIRST ZEN INSTITUTE OF AMERICA
113 E. 30th St.
New York, NY 10016
Tel. (212) 684–9487

Rinzai zen center with regular schedule of zazen and sesshins for members. Meditation instruction is available. Persons who wish information should come on Wednesdays, 7:45 P.M. Mailed inquiries should include stamped, self-addressed envelope. Contact Mary Farkas.

GOODWILL MEDITATION GROUP
866 United Nations Plaza
Suite 566/7
New York, NY 10017

A worldwide group of people who link together in thought each week at noon on Wednesday to meditate upon the energy of goodwill. The group's purpose is to stimulate and increase the use of goodwill in a troubled world.

INDO-AMERICAN YOGA-VEDANTA SOCIETY
330 W. 58th St.
New York, NY 10019
Tel. (212) 265–7719

Classes in yoga asanas, pranayama, chanting, mantra meditation, and lectures by Swami Bua.

INTEGRAL YOGA INSTITUTE
227 W. 13th St.
New York, NY 10011
Tel. (212) 929–0585

For more information see the National Listing.

INTERNATIONAL ZEN CENTER OF
NEW YORK
40 E. 20th St.
New York, NY 10003
Tel. (212) 677–0650

The International Zen Center of New York is under
the direction of Zen Master Soong San. There is
daily morning and evening formal practice, and a
lecture every Sunday night. Two monks of the Korean
Buddhist Chogye order reside at the temple, which
serves both Korean and American students. Six three-
day intensive training periods are held each year.
See addresses of affiliate centers in Carmel, CA; New
Haven, CT; Chicago, IL; Cambridge, MA; and
Providence, RI.

JAIN MEDITATION INTERNATIONAL
CENTER
120 E. 86th St., 2nd floor
New York, NY 10028
Tel. (212) 722-7474

The center is under the direct guidance of Gurudev
Chitrabhanu, the first Jain spiritual teacher to come
to the West. Classes in yoga, meditation, philosophy
and vegetarian cooking. Gurudev Chitrabhanu
teaches at the center a number of times each week,
regularly leads retreats there, and gives an open
lecture every Friday evening. Write or call for a list
of affiliated centers on the East coast and in Colorado.

KARGYU DSAMLING KUNCHAB
35 W. 19th St.
New York, NY 10011

For more information on centers under the guidance
of Lama Kalu Rinpoche, see Kagyu Kunkhyab
Chuling in Vancouver, BC.

LINDISFARNE IN MANHATTAN
49 W. 20th St.
New York, NY 10011
Tel. (212) 929–2722

Lindisfarne, founded by William Irwin Thompson, is a contemplative and educational community devoted to the study and realization of a new planetary culture. The Center holds meetings and conferences, publishes books and tapes, offers public lectures, concerts, and readings; and for participating members: daily meditation, seminars, and the use of its library.

NAQSHBANDI (SUFI CENTER)
c/o Klarreich
99 Macdougal St., Apt. 5
New York, NY

NEW YORK BUDDHIST CHURCH
332 Riverside Dr.
New York, NY 10025
Tel. (212) 749–8719

Directed by the Rev. H. Seki of the Shin (Pure Land) school.

NEW YORK ZEN CENTER
440 West End Ave.
(entrance 267 W. 81st St.)
New York, NY 10024
Tel. (212) 724–4172

Soto zen temple under the guidance of the Rev. Kando Nakajima. Beginners are asked to attend a weekly introductory lecture given every Monday, after which they are welcome to participate in any of the activities of the center. There is zazen Monday through Friday evenings at 7:45 P.M. with lectures Wednesday evening and Sunday morning. Friday evening includes a personal interview (optional). The third Sunday of each month is an all-day sesshin.

SIDDHA YOGA DHAM OF NEW YORK
324 W. 86th St.
New York, NY 10024
Tel. (212) 873–9188

Ashram of Swami Muktananda. See National Listings for further information.

SOCIETY OF PRAGMATIC MYSTICISM
200 W. 58th St., Apt. 9B
New York, NY 10019
Tel. (212) 246–5464

Pragmatic Mysticism is a truth teaching based on the Bible and the eternal laws of God. It is the practice of the presence of God in everyday life with conscious effort and direction. The society was founded by Mildred Mann and offers her teachings through lectures and through correspondence classes. Prayers and meditation are part of the teachings.

THE TIBET CENTER, INC.
114 E. 28th St.
New York, NY 10016
Tel. (212) 684–8245

Khyongla Rato, Rinpoche, a Tibetan Buddhist lama, teaches here. He is a noted author and scholar of the Gelugpa sect.

YESHE NYINGPO
ORGYEN CHO DZONG
19 W. 16th St.
New York, NY 10011

Orgyen Cho Dzong, the New York center of the Yeshe Nyingpo organization, is the American seat of His Holiness Dudjom, Rinpoche, head of the Nyingmapa order of Tibetan Buddhism. The center is guided by Thinley Norbu, Rinpoche, when His Holiness is elsewhere. Each Tuesday night at 7:30 meditation is held, open to the public. Yeshe Nyingpo also has a center in Berkeley, CA, called Argyen Cho Dhing, under the guidance of Gyatrul, Rinpoche.

THE ZEN STUDIES SOCIETY
NEW YORK ZENDO SHOBO JI
223 E. 67th St.
New York, NY 10021
Tel. (212) 861-3333

The Zen Studies Society has two zendo (zen training centers), one in New York City and another in the Catskill Mountains. At each zendo, study and practice is under the guidance of Eido Roshi and his master, Soen Roshi, who visits periodically. The zen training is basically in the Rinzai tradition. It takes a flexible attitude to adapt some necessary elements to suit American lay people's needs, but the authenticity of Rinzai Zen Buddhism is maintained. New York Zendo Shobo Ji (City Zendo) offers part-time zen practice for those who live and work in the city, while Dai Bosatsu Zendo Kongo Ji (Catskill Monastery) is the first Zen Buddhist monastery in this country designed to offer traditional zen full-time monastic life in a Japanese-style temple to American lay students. There are two training periods in the City Zendo when public zazen meetings are held every Thursday night during which everyone is welcome ($2.00 contribution). Other meetings are only for Sangha Members' practice. Dai Bosatsu Zendo Kongo Ji has two uninterrupted training periods of three months each, separated by two three-month Zen Community Life periods that are less formal. During the training periods, sesshins are held at which outside experienced zen students are welcomed. See listing for the Catskill Monastery under Zen Studies Society, Livingston, Manor, NY.

ICSA (INTEGRAL CENTER OF
SELF-ABIDANCE)
102 David Dr.
North Syracuse, NY 13212
Tel. (315) 458-4098

Since 1958 the ashram-home of Srimati Margaret Coble. Margaret's programs emphasize the One Presence–Power–Reality. Training is offered in meditation and other disciplines.

THE ZEN CENTER
7 Arnold Pk.
Rochester, NY 14607
Tel. (716) 473–9180

The Ven. Philip Kapleau, Roshi, teaches an integral zen grounded in the doctrines and disciplines of both the Soto and Rinzai sects, which includes koan practice for experienced students. The Rochester center offers a daily schedule of meditation and chanting with periodic four- and seven-day sesshins open to members. Introductory workshops are also available. Write for location of nearest affiliate center.

THE MAITRI CENTER FOR PSYCHOLOGY
Old Forge Rd.
Wingdale, NY 12594
Tel. (914) 832–6588

The Maitri program consists of the practice of the Maitri postures and sitting meditation within a small community setting. The Maitri postures are an approach to meditation originally adapted for highly disturbed individuals by Chogyam Trungpa, Rinpoche, from traditional Tibetan techniques. Particular postures and rooms evoke different psychological spaces which, according to Buddhist tantric teaching, are the foundation of thought and emotion. Through the Maitri program, students explore the major types of psychological space; the nature of sanity, neurosis, and psychosis; and the Buddhist approach to helping people. The programs take place on a 90-acre converted farm in Connecticut. For more information on Trungpa Rinpoche's centers, see Vajradhatu Karma Dzong in the National Listings and Karme-Choling, Barnet, VT, and Naropa Institute, Boulder, CO, in the Local Listings.

OHIO

NEW WORLD CENTER
3408 Telford St.
Cincinnati, OH 45220
Tel. (513) 961–6400

Weekend retreats for spiritual consciousness, theory and practice of meditation along with yoga, progressive relaxation, breathing exercises, acupressure, inner awareness, natural diet and healing, and other practices for spiritual development.

LIGHT OF YOGA SOCIETY
12429 Cedar Rd.
Cleveland Heights, OH 44106

Founded by Alice Christensen, a disciple of Swami Rama, the society offers instruction in yoga, breathing, meditation, mantra, and the fundamentals of philosophy as well as a special "Easy Does It" yoga system for people over sixty.

PATHWAYS
1392 Warren Road
Lakewood, OH 44107
Tel. (216) 226–1224

A basic course is offered in which techniques are taught which allow one to become aware of and communicate with one's inner world. The program is designed for our active, dynamic western lifestyle.

OREGON

SAGINAW ZEN PRIORY
32646 Saginaw West Rd.
Cottage Grove, OR 97424
Tel. (503) 942–7515

Affiliated with Shasta Abbey, the Soto zen training monastery and seminary of Roshi Jiyu-Kennett. Located south of Eugene. Daily meditation and services, weekend retreats, weekly sesshins, and classes in various aspects of zen training. Resident lay program. Private instruction in meditation available by appointment. The priory also runs a weekly meditation group in Portland and a prison meditation group in Salem. The priory may be moving to Eugene in the near future.

PENNSYLVANIA

THE GURDJIEFF WORK
Northeon Forest
RD 4, Box 517
Easton, PA 18042
Tel. (215) 258–9559

Meeting for aspirants every Wednesday, 8:00–9:00 P.M.

GURU BAWA FELLOWSHIP
5820 Overbrook Ave.
Philadelphia, PA 19131
Tel. (215) 879–9960

The Fellowship is the ashram-residence of Guru Bawa who has spent the greater part of his life as a spiritual teacher in Sri Lanka. Guru Bawa emphasizes the living of Universal Divine Qualities and Characteristics.

SHANTI YOGA INSTITUTE
58 W. Penn St.
Philadelphia, PA 19144
Tel. (215) 848–3931

Founded by Shanti Yogi. Classes in hatha yoga and meditation. See listing in Ocean City, NJ.

PYRAMID ZEN SOCIETY
PO BOX 8220
Pittsburgh, PA 15217
Tel. (412) 421–2039

The Pyramid Zen Society, also known as TAT (Truth and Transmission), was founded by Richard Rose. The group uses a meditational technique and a confrontation technique that are designed to find the Real Self. The society has several branches in Ohio and across the country. Write for address of nearest branch.

THE HINDU AMERICAN RELIGIOUS INSTITUTE
222 State Street
West Fairview, PA 17025
Tel. (717) 732–3926

The Hindu American Religious Institute, near Harrisburg, is the residence of His Holiness Shankaracharya Swami Swanandashram. Swamiji, as he prefers to be called by his students, lived for twenty years in the Himalayan Mountains of India and Tibet. He has practiced yoga and meditation for over thirty years. One of India's High Holy Men, Swamiji is a world traveler, author, and lecturer who is Prasthanatrayee in Sankara philosophy (equivalent to M.S. in Sanskrit and Ph.D. in Sankara philosophy). He has taught Indian philosophy at Berkeley, California, and he currently offers classes and private instruction in the practical application of yoga, with the aim of helping others realize the true nature of the self. Swamiji says "That Unchangeable Eternal Consciousness you are, know thyself. We live to know what is the truth behind life. We hear the truth; we meditate upon the truth; and we realize the truth. That is the aim of life."

KRIPALU YOGA ASHRAM/RETREAT
PO Box 120
Summit Station, PA 17979
Tel. (717) 754–3051

Established in 1970 by Yogi Amrit Desai, Kripalu Yoga Ashram Retreat is a spiritual retreat which offers Shaktipat Kundalini Yoga and Kripalu Yoga in a program of integrated yoga seminars, retreats, intensives, communications skills training, and wholistic health programs as well as providing a residency program. The institute for yoga teachers' training offers courses for beginning and advanced teachers as well as teacher certification programs. Two rural and secluded settings provide 150 men, women, and children with a serene environment supportive of true inner unfoldment. The 240-acre Kripalu Yoga Retreat, located in the Blue Mountains of Pennsylvania, is open to visitors year-round. Kripalu Centers are located from Nebraska across the Northeast. Write for center addresses.

PUERTO RICO

KAGYU PEN DAY CHULING
N. San Juan, PR

For more information on centers under the guidance of Lama Kalu Rinpoche, see Kagyu Kunkhyab Chuling in Vancouver, BC.

RHODE ISLAND

PROVIDENCE ZEN CENTER
40 Hope St.
Providence, RI 02903
Tel. (401) 351–5646

A Korean Zen Buddhist center. For more information see International Zen Center of New York in New York City.

SOUTH CAROLINA

MEHER-CENTER-ON-THE-LAKES
PO Box 487
Myrtle Beach, SC 29577
Att.: Elizabeth C. Patterson

This beautiful center provides individual retreats, for the lovers of Meher Baba, around his home in America.

TENNESSEE

SWAMI SHANTIANANDA CENTER
Rt. 1
Woodbury, TN 37190
Tel. (615) 563–5154

Daily meditation, yoga, chanting, self-awareness, and talks by Swami Shantiananda. Visitors please write before coming.

TEXAS

CHRISTIAN COMMUNITY BUREAU
817 Penn St.
Fort Worth, TX 76102

For further information see Holy Order of Mans in the National Listings.

THE YOGA INSTITUTE
2168 Portsmouth
Houston, TX 77098
Tel. (713) 526–6674

Classes and weekend intensives. Techniques taught include meditation, hatha yoga, relaxation, and breath and body awareness.

SILVA MIND CONTROL
1110 Cedar Ave.
Laredo, TX 78040
Tel. (512) 722–6391

For further information see the National Listings.

DESERT DANCE
PO Box 77
Terlingua, TX 79852

Desert Dance, a nonprofit organization, offers nomadic learning expeditions through the Chihauhuan Desert, using the desert wilderness experience as a means of stimulating one's personal evolution.

VERMONT

KARME-CHOLING
(formerly Tail of the Tiger)
Star Rt.
Barnet, VT 05821
Tel. (802) 633–2384

A rural, residential community of students of Chogyam Trungpa Rinpoche. It furnishes a rich environment for making friends with oneself through group and individual relationships, work projects, retreats, seminars, and a regular schedule of group meditation (Buddhist tradition). The daily schedule now includes 4½ hours of meditation and 1½ hours of study; there are also three one-month-long dathuns (all-day sittings). Trungpa Rinpoche comes occasionally to lead seminars. Individual meditation instruction is available from staff members authorized by Trungpa Rinpoche to teach meditation. Visitors are welcome at Karme-Choling at any time. The guest rate is $10 a day or $60 a week. Because of limited space, advanced reservations are required. For more information concerning Trungpa Rinpoche's centers, see Vajradhatu Karma Dzong in the National Listings, and Maitri Center, Wingdale, NY, and Naropa Institute, Boulder, CO, in the Local Listings.

VERMONT INSTITUTE OF COMMUNITY INVOLVEMENT
PO Box 2287
South Burlington, VT 05401

The Noogenesis program uses transpersonal and humanistic psychology, biofeedback, psychic systems, ritual and meditation, dance and movement. It offers a B.A.-level program during the academic year and has intensive summer and weekend workshops.

VIRGINIA

PREMA DHARMASALA AND FELLOWSHIP ASSOCIATION and the PREMA WORLD COMMUNITY
Rt. 4, Box 265r
Bedford, VA 24523
Tel. (703) 297–5982

Residential ashram for monastics and spiritual center for lay-members, founded by Sri Vasudevadas, who shares his relationship with all five major Sufi Orders, and the love of his Guru, Paramahansa Yogananda, with the sincere aspirant of this day and age. Year-round retreat center; satsangs, classes, tapes and publications; consultation and research. Reservation required for all visits.

STARCROSS MONASTIC COMMUNITY
HUMANIST INSTITUTE
Richmond, VA

For information regarding activities in Richmond, VA, contact Starcross Monastic Community, Annapolis, CA (see separate listing).

SHANKARACHARYA PITHAM
SADHANALAYA ASHRAM
Rt. 1, Box 158
Rockbridge Baths, VA 24473
Tel. (703) 348–5522

For further information see The Holy Shankaracharya Order, Stroudsburg, PA.

ASSOCIATION FOR RESEARCH AND
ENLIGHTENMENT, INC.
PO Box 595
Virginia Beach, VA 23451
Tel. (804) 428–3588

The association is a nonprofit open-membership organization made up of individuals interested in spiritual growth, parapsychological research, and the work of Edgar Cayce. The aim is to make available to anyone the information given by the late psychic Edgar Cayce. His gift of the spirit was his ability to enter into profoundly deep meditation and from this higher state of consciousness to give discourses. Central to the philosophy of these readings is the premise that man is a spiritual being whose purpose on earth is to reawaken and apply this knowledge. Meditation as well as other principles of physical, mental, and spiritual attunement are studied and practiced. The association offers an open meditation with the staff, daily healing prayer groups, retreats, workshops, study groups, and lectures throughout the country. Its Meditation Room is open daily for individual meditation.

WASHINGTON

RAJ-YOGA MATH AND RETREAT
PO Box 547
Deming, WA 98244

A semi-monastic community and retreat area secluded from worldly karma. Sadhana consists of a balance of bhakti, jnana, and karma yoga; uses hatha and raja yoga; and emphasizes japa and guru yoga. Only sincere, open, responsible and mature aspirants are acceptable. Six month resident training sessions offered quarterly. Yogi Father Satchakrananda (Spiritual Director) "teaches not by example but by the fire of negation."

ZEN CENTER OF EVERGREEN
326 Viewridge Drive
Everett, WA 98203
Tel. (206) 252–6741

Directed by Eric Thompson. Affiliated with the Zen Center of Long Beach, California.

SAKYA TAGCHEN CHOLING CENTER
4416 Burke Ave. N.
Seattle, WA 98103
Tel. (206) 634–3063

This Tibetan Buddhist center for the study of Vajrayana Buddhism and Tibetan culture is under the guidance of Jigdal Dagchen Sakya, Rinpoche. N. Trinlay, Rinpoche, and Dezhung Tulku, Rinpoche, also teach at the center. And we are awaiting the arrival of T. G. Dhongthog, Rinpoche, at any time.

WEST VIRGINIA

THE CLAYMONT SOCIETY FOR CONTINUOUS EDUCATION, INC.
PO Box 112
Charles Town, WV 25414

The society, a nonprofit, tax-exempt educational institution, is organized according to the principles of the Fourth Way. Schools of the Fourth Way are concerned with evolution—a movement back against the stream of involution—as the many seeking the one. The Claymont School offers a nine-month course in the principles and techniques of Spiritual Psychology, according to the ideas of George I. Gurdjieff, and John G. Bennett, and is directed by seekers who studied under them. Inquiries are welcome; they should be addressed to the Registrar.

WISCONSIN

GANDEN MAHAYANA CENTER
5136 Lake Mendota
Madison, WI 53705

Under the auspices of the Tibetan lama Geshe Chundup Sopa, the Ganden Mahayana Center is being developed in order to preserve the traditional teachings of Buddhism, as it existed in India and Tibet, and to offer these doctrines and practices to the people of the West.

MADISON ZEN GROUP
1820 Jefferson St.
Madison, WI 53711
Tel. (608) 255–4488

For further information see The Zen Center, Rochester, NY.

WYOMING

HOLY ORDER OF MANS
DISCIPLESHIP MOVEMENT
PO Box 308
Cheyenne, WY 87007

For further information see Holy Order of Mans in
the National Listings.

CANADA

BRITISH COLUMBIA

VISHVA HINDU PRAISHAD OF
BRITISH COLUMBIA
3885 Albert St.
North Burnaby, BC
Canada

Regular services in Hindu tradition each Sunday
morning and Wednesday evening, group chanting,
classical astanga yoga classes, etc.

KOSMUNITY
PO Box 40
Proctor, BC
V0G 1V0 Canada
Tel. (604) 229–4361

Kosmunity follows the Essene tradition of purity in
diet, lifestyle, and spiritual learning. Functions uni-
versally through rural centers working on the land,
conducting retreats, arts and crafts, and parayoga
studies.

KAGYU KUNKHYAB CHULING
2865 W. 4th Ave.
Vancouver, BC
Canada
Tel. (604) 732–0414

Kagyu Kunkhyab Chuling is a Tibetan Vajrayana Buddhist meditation center under the spiritual guidance of Lama Kalu Rinpoche, who is the senior meditation master and spiritual teacher of the Kargyudpa order. Although Kalu Rinpoche is not always in the West, other Tibetan lamas lead regular meditations at some of the twenty or more centers established by Kalu Rinpoche. A country retreat center, under construction on nearby Salt Spring Island, will offer advanced instruction, group seminar retreats, and training for lamas within this tradition. This educational and monastic center will be a major seat of the Kagyu order in North America. Write for the address of this center and others.

ZEN CENTRE OF VANCOUVER
104 West 10th Ave.
Vancouver 3, BC
Canada

See Cimmarron Zen Center, Los Angeles, CA.

NOVA SCOTIA

ARUNACHALA ASHRAMA
BHAGAVAN SRI RAMANA MAHARSHI
CENTER, INC.
RR 1
Bridgetown, NS
B0S 1C0 Canada
Tel. (902) 665–2090

For further information see the listing for the Arunachala Ashrama in New York, NY.

ONTARIO

THE SON LOTUS SOCIETY
378 Markham St., Apt. B–1
Toronto, Ont.
M6G 2K9 Canada
Tel. (416) 923–7571

Samu Sunim, a Korean Zen Buddhist monk, conducts zen meditation on a regular weekly basis here and at one other location in Toronto. Twice a month there are all-day sittings and every two months there is a seven-to-ten-day Yongmaeng chongjin. A beginner's class is held Tuesday and Thursday evenings. Samu Sunim combines Son practice with agriculture and handicrafts, not distinguishing between practice and work. All forms of practice are employed according to individual karma and capacities.

TORONTO ZEN CENTER
569 Christie St.
Toronto, Ont.
M6G 3E4 Canada
Tel. (416) 653–0866

For further information see The Zen Center, Rochester, NY.

QUEBEC

THOMAS MERTON CENTER
RR 3
Magog, Que.
Canada
Tel. (819) 843–2435

Taught by Linda Sabbath, four-week, semi-monastic intensive retreats in contemplative prayer are planned on an individual basis according to the needs and capacities of each student. They follow the basic system of Patanjali's yoga, adapted for contemporary Western consciousness, and utilize the spiritual traditions of St. John of the Cross and St. Theresa of Avila. The program is structured for clergy, seminarians, and professed religious and exceptional lay persons.

CANADIAN INSTITUTE OF
PSYCHOSYNTHESIS INC.
3496 Avenue Marlowe
Montreal, Que.
H4A 3L7 Canada
Tel. (514) 488–4494

Psychosynthesis is a comprehensive psychological and spiritual approach to the development of the whole person. It is a synthesis of many traditions. The individual is helped to contact the integrating center within the psyche, which can harmonize and direct the various aspects of the personality. The institute's purpose is to manifest the spiritual essence, or Self, as fully as possible in the world of everyday living. Some of the techniques used are: guided imagery, dream work, movement, role playing, symbolic art work, Self-identification, training of the will, journal keeping, development of intuition, and meditation. See also Psychosynthesis Institute, San Francisco, CA.

MONTREAL ZEN GROUP
3432 Marlowe St.
Montreal, Que.
H4A 3L7 Canada
Tel. (514) 488–7311

For further information see The Zen Center, Rochester, NY.

SIVANANDA YOGA VEDANTA CENTER
8th Ave.
Val Morin, Que.
J0Y ZR0 Canada
Tel. (819) 322–3226

For further information see the National Listings.

3

RETREAT
FACILITIES

The following facilities provide individual and/or group
retreats (or facilities for them). Individual retreats may
range from isolation to directed programs of yoga and
meditation—as are offered by many of the organizations listed in the preceding section. If you cannot tell
from the description what a facility that you are interested in offers, write and ask. Some retreats are geared
only to people who are part of their own tradition or
interested in partaking in it. Many of them have very
limited space and are heavily booked. Some are closed
in the winter.

Never just arrive at a retreat facility—be sure to
write or call first. Try not to require special arrange-
ments at a facility that is not prepared to provide them.
If nothing else suits you, a closed door, tent, or cabin
is all that is needed.

> *There is nowhere perfect rest save in a heart
> detached.*
>
> *—Eckhart*

This list is largely composed of Catholic retreat
facilities suitable for individual retreats or a "day of
renewal," as well as (in most cases) for groups. In
addition, there are facilities run by other churches,
synagogues, spiritual groups, and social organizations
such as the YMCA.

ALABAMA

BLESSED TRINITY SHRINE RETREAT
Holy Trinity, AL 36895

Sister Cira Anthony, MSBT, Dir. 45 rooms.

SACRED HEART RETREAT HOUSE
2300 Spring Hill Ave.
Mobile, AL 36607

Sister M. Pauline Thompson, VHM, Dir. Capacity 55.

ARIZONA

PICTURE ROCKS RETREAT
PO Box 569
Cortaro, AZ 85230

The Rev. James Farrell, CSSR, Dir. Capacity 35.

FRIENDLY PINES CAMP
7400 Senator Rd.
Prescott, AZ 86301
Tel. (602) 445–2128

Secluded, rustic camp suitable for groups of 25 to 225 people.

FRANCISCAN RENEWAL CENTER
5802 E. Lincoln Drive
Scottsdale, AZ 85252

The Rev. Michael Weishaar, OFM, Dir. Capacity 64.

SPIRITUAL LIFE INSTITUTE
Star Rt. 1
Sedona, AZ 86336

Rev. Wm. McNamara, OCD, Dir. 14 rooms, private retreats only.

SANTA RITA ABBEY
Box 97
Sonita, AZ 85637
Tel. (602) 455–5595

Contact the Rev. Mother Benedict, OCSO. One room available for private retreats, for women, $10 per day.

ARKANSAS

SUNERGOS INSTITUTE, INC.
Box 342
Jasper, AR 72641
Tel. (501) 466–5201

Meditation and spiritual growth courses and retreats.

OZARK THEOSOPHICAL CAMP AND EDUCATIONAL CENTER
Box 196
Sulphur Springs, AR 72768
Contact:

Mrs. Ruth Mathews, Camp Registrar
128 Circle Dr.
Wichita, KS 67218

CALIFORNIA

SACRED HEART RETREAT HOUSE
920 East Alhambra Rd.
Alhambra, CA 91801

Sister Pius Marie, OCD, Dir. Capacity 85.

MANRESA RETREAT HOUSE
18337 E. Foothill Blvd.
Azusa, CA 91702

Rev. James J. Deasy, SJ, Dir. 65 rooms.

TATAGATAS
PO Box 216
Ben Lomond, CA 95005
Tel. (408) 336–2336

In the redwoods near Santa Cruz. Massage, isolation tank, and meditation instruction available. For small groups or individuals.

RECREATION AND PARKS DEPT.
CITY OF BERKELEY
1835 Allston Way
Berkeley, CA 94704
Tel. (415) 644–6520

The City of Berkeley runs three campgrounds. They are Cazadero Music Camp in the Russian River redwood country, Toulumne Camp near Yosemite, and Echo Lake Camp on the way to Lake Tahoe. These camps are available for rental to groups of 50 or more persons in the off season.

YMCA CAMP GUALALA
Contact:
Berkeley YMCA
2001 Allston Way
Berkeley, CA 94704

This camp has already been used for a meditation course.

IMMACULATE HEART HERMITAGE
Big Sur, CA 93920
Tel. (408) 667–2456

Father Bernard Massicotte, Retreat Master. 8 rooms for private retreats, men only, donation requested.

SATORI CONFERENCE CENTER, INC.
Rt. 1, Box 521
Boulder Creek, CA 95006
Tel. (408) 338–3917

Contact Tom and Karen Handman. They have a meditation house.

ZEN CENTER
TASSAJARA ZEN MOUNTAIN CENTER
Carmel Valley, CA 93924
Tel. Tassajara Springs #1, a toll station through
Salinas

Zen Buddhist monastery where both lay and ordained
students practice a daily schedule of zazen, services,
meals, study, and work. Open to newer students only
during the summer months (after a prior stay at the
San Francisco or Green Gulch Farm centers). Also
open as a guest resort during the summer months.

CENACLE RETREAT HOUSE
5340 Fair Oaks Blvd.
Carmichael, CA 95608

Sister Evelyn Jegen. 47 rooms.

CHRIST THE KING RETREAT CENTER
6520 Van Maren Lane
Citrus Heights, CA 95610

The Rev. Peter Berendt, CP, Dir. Capacity 48.

ANANDAJI
Rt. 1, Box 2497
Colfax, CA 95713

160 acres of land with camping facilities and a dining
room for 200 people. Run by disciples of Yogananda.

SAN DAMIANO RETREAT HOUSE
Highland Dr.
Danville, CA 94526

The Rev. David Temple, OFM, Dir. 80 rooms.

HOLY SPIRIT RETREAT HOUSE
4316 Lanai Rd.
Encino, CA 91316

Sister Barbara Geinger, SSS, Dir. Capacity 50.

GIRL SCOUT CAMP
Fairfax, CA 94930
Contact:
San Francisco Bay Girl Scout Council
1400 7th Ave.
Oakland, CA 94606

THE ISLAMIC SOCIETY OF CALIFORNIA
781 Bolinas Rd.
Fairfax, CA 94930
Tel. (415) 454–6666

Jamu Salam, The Redwood Mosque, situated on 20 acres of redwood forest, is available for the use of groups wishing to hold retreats, seminars, etc.

FOREST FARM
Forest Knolls, CA 94933
Tel. (415) 488–4457

Facilities include 13 acres of wooded land, 13 cabins, rustic meeting rooms, pool, hot baths, outdoor stage.

SIVANANDA YOGA CAMP
YOGA FARM VRINDAVAN
McCourtney Rd., Box 795
Grass Valley, CA 95945
Tel. (916) 273–9802

Founded by Swami Vishnu-Devananda. Instruction in hatha yoga and in meditation is given during the retreats. There is a teacher-training program each September under the guidance of Swami Vishnu-Devananda.

RIVERUN RETREAT
c/o Simon Jeremiah
1569 Fitch Mountain
Healdsburg, CA 95448
Tel. (707) 433–6754

Small hermitage available to individuals at no fee.

BOB MATHIAS SIERRA GIRLS CAMP
Kings Canyon National Park, CA 93633
Contact:

Bob Mathias Sierra Girls Camp
403 S. Clovis Ave.
Fresno, CA 93237

FAR HORIZONS THEOSOPHICAL CAMP
Box WW
Kings Canyon National Park, CA 93633
Tel. Lodgepole #9, through Visalia
For reservations contact:

Miss Bim Lecklider, Dir.
39 Taormina Lane
Ojai, CA 93023

EL RETIRO SAN INIGO
662 University Ave.
Los Altos, CA 94022
Tel. (415) 948-4491

Rev. John Dullea, SJ, Dir. 80 rooms.

IMMACULATE HEART RETREAT HOUSE
3431 Waverly Dr.
Los Angeles, CA 90027

Sister Mary Margaret, IHM, Dir. Capacity 31.

CALAMINGOS STAR C RANCH
Rt. 4, Box 14A
Malibu, CA 90265

SERRA RETREAT
Box 127
Malibu, CA 90265

The Rev. Tom Frost, OFM, Dir. 55 rooms.

MENDOCINO WOODLANDS CAMP
ASSOCIATION
PO Box 267
Mendocino, CA 95460

Three campgrounds in the woods, appropriate for
large groups.

VALLOMBROSA CENTER
250 Oak Grove Ave.
Menlo Park, CA 94025
Tel. (415) 325–5614

The Rev. Msgr. Warren Holleran, Dir. Capacity 100.

EARTH CAMP ONE
Montgomery Creek, CA 96065

Near Mt. Shasta; ideal for groups.

MT. BALDY ZEN CENTER
PO Box 526
Mt. Baldy, CA 91759
Tel. (714) 985–6410

This Rinzai zen center, one hour from metropolitan
Los Angeles, offers a retreat under the guidance of
Joshu Sasaki Roshi. Visitors welcome for meditation
practice and instruction Sundays 9:30 A.M. followed
by lunch at noon. Weekend stays also available at
$25 per person. Reservations required. Students
wishing to attend week-long intensive sesshins (offered monthly) under Roshi's guidance or a three-
month summer or winter training period should
contact the center in advance.

ANANDA MEDITATION RETREAT
Box 900—Alleghany Star Rt.
Nevada City, CA 95959
Tel. (916) 265–5877

A rural retreat center and spiritual community in the foothills of the Sierra Nevada Mountains founded and guided by Swami Kriyananda, a disciple of Paramahansa Yogananda. The meditation retreat is open to visitors year-round. Guests follow a daily schedule of meditation, hatha yoga, chanting, and "philosophy" classes, as well as participating in karma yoga projects with community members.

ST. CHARLES PRIORY
Benet Hill
Oceanside, CA 92054
Tel. (714) 722–3555

The Rev. Rudolph Siedling, OSB, Dir. 17 double rooms.

MARY AND JOSEPH RETREAT HOUSE
5300 Crest Rd.
Palos Verdes, CA 90274

Capacity 28 couples, married only.

EL CARMELO CHRISTIAN RENEWAL CTR.
926 E. Highland Ave.
Redlands, CA 92373

The Rev. David Costello, OCD, Dir. 51 rooms.

ST. DOMINIC SAVIO RETREAT HOUSE
8301 Arroyo Dr.
Rosemead, CA 91770

The Rev. Mario Mich, SDB, Dir. Dormitory for 25.

CHRISTIAN BROTHERS RETREAT HOUSE
2233 Sulphur Springs Rd.
St. Helena, CA 94574

Bro. Kenneth W. Biggs, FSC, Dir. 40 rooms.

UNITED CAMPS CONFERENCES AND
RETREATS
125 Mariposa Ave.
San Anselmo, CA 94960
Tel. (415) 456–5102

UCCR is a nonprofit management firm representing
six Protestant denominations in northern California.
Contact the UCCR office in order to make reservations for any of the following facilities:

1. Wesleyan Woods—in the Sierras of Sequoia National Forest. Ideal for a meditation course. Indoor
dining hall and meeting place. Tent accommodations for 70.

2. Westminster Retreat at Alamo—south of Walnut
Creek in the San Ramon Valley. The manor sleeps
37, the lodge sleeps 22.

3. Ralston L. White Conference Center on the
southern slopes of Mt. Tamalpais in Marin County.
This old mansion has space for 50–60 to meet and
sleep.

4. The Community of the Great Commission—in
Placer County overlooking the American River
Canyon. Occupies 865 acres. There are two separate
areas for group use: Claar House, a retreat center
for 15 people; and Bobbitt Area, rustic cabins accommodating 80 people. Bobbitt Hall is a large
meeting room available for use with the cabins.

5. Camp Cazadero—in the redwoods of Sonoma
County near the Russian River. 80–180 can sleep
in the cabins. A large meeting hall.

6. Valley of the Moon—in the Sonoma Mountain
Range. Capacity 85 in summer, 40 in winter (in
cabins). Not far from Petaluma.

7. Chinquapin—20 miles past Sonora on Pinecrest
Lake. 10 cabins accommodate 75–80.

8. Camp Tamarack—a rustic High Sierra camp in
Sierra National Forest. 80 people can be accommodated in 12 platform tents. Meeting hall.

9. Camp Corralitos—102 acres in the Santa Cruz Mountains. Sleeping facilities for 100. Large meeting hall.
10. Monte Toyon—near Santa Cruz. Sleeping facilities for 160. Meeting facilities for 200.
11. Seminary Conference Center—on the San Francisco Theological Seminary campus in San Anselmo. Sleeping facilities for 35. Dining and meeting facilities for 200.
12. Redwood Glen—160 acres in Pescadero Canyon adjoining San Mateo County Memorial Park. The dining hall seats 150 or can serve as a meeting hall for 200. Open-air chapel. Dorms, cabins for 125. Also 4 hogans and 12 tents for summer use.
13. Lodestar—446 acres in the Sierra Foothills above Jackson. Capacity 76 winter, 120 summer. Also a main lodge.

POVERELLO OF ASSISI RETREAT HOUSE
1519 Woodworth St.
San Fernando, CA 91340

Sister Mary Jesus, OSF, Dir. Capacity 64.

THE HERMITAGE
Contact:

Andy Alpine
461 Douglass St.
San Francisco, CA 94114
Tel. (415) 647–1120 or 652–4400

The Hermitage, on 240 acres, offers three- to five-day individual retreats. Each person has a private room and three vegetarian meals are left at the door each day. Silence is observed; eye contact is avoided. Rates based on ability to pay. Space limited.

STILLPOINT INSTITUTE
604 S. 15th St.
San Jose, CA 95112
Tel. (408) 287–5307

Stillpoint offers facilities for up to six meditators to pursue long-term retreats under the guidance of the resident teacher, Anagarika Sujata. The Theravadin Buddhist practice employed is satipatthana vipassana, insight meditation. Recommended length of retreat is one month and cost is based on ability to pay.

ST. FRANCIS RETREAT HOUSE
Box 1070
San Juan Bautista, CA 95045

The Rev. Gilbert Zlatar, OFM, Dir. Capacity 130.

OLD MISSION SAN LUIS REY RETREAT
4050 Mission Ave.
San Luis Rey, CA 92068

The Rev. Ralph Weishaar, OFM, Dir. Capacity 106.

LA CASA DE MARIA
800 El Bosque Rd.
Santa Barbara, CA 93108

Mr. and Mrs. James Rubins, Dirs. 2 dormitories with 50 beds.

ST. CLARE'S RETREAT HOUSE
2381 Laurel Glen Rd.
Santa Cruz, CA 95065

Sister Mary Joseph, OSF, Dir. Capacity 97.

VILLA MARIA DEL MAR
2–1918 E. Cliff Dr.
Santa Cruz, CA 95062

Sister Virginia Rose, SNJM. Capacity 80.

MONTECITO—SEQUOIA SEMINAR
RETREAT
Sequoia National Park, CA 93262
Contact:

Montecito
1485 Redwood Dr.
Los Altos, CA 94022

Ideal for group retreats.

MATER DOLOROSA RETREAT HOUSE
700 N. Sunnyside Ave.
Sierra Madre, CA 91024

The Rev. Joseph Gromowski, CP, Dir. Capacity 77.

ST. RAYMOND'S DOMINICAN RETREAT
1666 Hidden Valley Rd.
Thousand Oaks, CA 91630

The Rev. Edmund K. Ryan, OP, Dir. Capacity 50.

ST. ANTHONY RETREAT CENTER
43816 Sierra Dr.
Three Rivers, CA 93271

The Rev. Gregory Wooler, OFM, Dir. Capacity 50.

VALYERMO RETREAT HOUSE
St. Andrew's Priory
Valyermo, CA 93563

The Rev. Vincent Martin, OSB, Dir. Capacity 39.

WILBUR HOT SPRINGS
Williams, CA 95987
Tel. (916) 473–2306

Fine natural hot springs. An old hotel by the springs
holds 24 people. Ideal for private or small group
retreats. Large meeting room. $5 per day, $10 overnight. Call first.

CAMP MARIASTELLA
Wrightwood, CA 92397

Sister Patricia McGowan, SSS, Dir. Dormitory for 70.

COLORADO

CONVENT OF ST. WALBURGA
6717 S. Boulder Rd.
Boulder, CO 80303

Sister M. Luitgardis, OSB, Dir. Capacity 20, women
and married couples only.

BETHLEHEM CENTER
W. 128th and Zuni St.
Broomfield, CO 80220

The Rev. Anton J. Borer, SMB, Dir. Capacity 50.

ST. SCHOLASTICA ACADEMY
615 Pike Ave.
Canon City, CO 81212

Sister Kathleen MacNamara, OSB, Dir. Dormitory
for 120, women only.

EL POMAR RETREAT CENTER
1661 Mesa Ave.
Colorado Springs, CO 80906

Sister Barbara Huber, SC, Dir. Capacity 74.

THE RESTORIUM
2168 S. Lafayette St.
Denver, CO 80210
Att.: Fransister Laurel
Tel. (303) 777-9319

A retreat center in the mountains near Denver, run
by the Fransisters. Group or private retreats. Capacity 15 people overnight, 25 for a day of rest. Open
only from May to October.

ESTES PARK CENTERS—YMCA OF THE ROCKIES, YMCA ASSOCIATION CAMP
Walter G. Reusch, Exec. Dir.
Tel. (303) 586–3341

YMCA Snow Mt. Ranch
PO Box 558
Granby, CO 80446
Tel. (303) 887–3332

YMCA winter address:
25 E. 16th Ave.
Denver, CO 80202
Tel. (303) 244–4393

DORJE KHYUNG DZONG
PO Box 35
Farasita, CO 81037

240 wild, remote acres in the Green Horn Mountains used as a retreat by students of Trungpa Rinpoche. See Vajradhatu/Karma Dzong in the National Listings for more information.

POLESTAR
Box 557
Green Mountain Falls, CO 80819
Tel. (303) 684–9532

On Pike's Peak. Weekly individual rate $70 per person. Weekend groups (10 to 20 persons) $15 per person. Meditation instruction available.

ROCKY MOUNTAIN DHARMA CENTER
Rt. 1
Livermore, CO 80536

A Buddhist retreat center in the Vajradhatu organization of Trungpa Rinpoche. It is being used for short- and long-term intensive meditation sessions by his students and others interested in Buddhist meditation. For more information concerning Trungpa Rinpoche's centers, see Vajradhatu/Karma Dzong under National Listings.

SEPARATE HEART RETREAT HOUSE
Box 185
Sedalia, CO 80135

The Rev. John R. Padberg, SJ, Dir. Capacity 51.

CONNECTICUT

LENOX HILL CAMP
Bantam, CT 06750
Contact:

Lenox Hill Neighborhood Assoc.
Bantam, CT 06750
Att.: Henry Schwartz, Exec.
Tel. (203) 567–9760

Capacity 68.

YMCA CAMP BEAR ROCK LODGE
651 State St.
Bridgeport, CT. 06603
Att.: Tom Q. Moore, Camp Dir.
Tel. (203) 334–5551

CAMP HARDAR
Carter Hill Road
Clinton, CT 06413
Tel. (203) 333–0343 or 669–8312

Hal Watman, Dir. Capacity 350, heated facilities
for 225. Available March to June and September to
November.

OUR LADY OF CALVARY RETREAT HOUSE
Colton St., Box 37
Farmington, CT 06032

Sister Margaret Mary, CP, Dir. Capacity 58.

EPISCOPAL CAMP AND CONFERENCE
CENTER
Ivoryton, CT 06442
Contact:

Incarnation Camp, Inc.
209 Madison Ave.
New York, NY 10016
Att.: Andrew Katsanis, Exec.
Tel. (212) 689–3355

Available for large groups. Capacity 75.

SLOANE CAMP
Lakeville, CT 06039
Contact:

YMCA
235 Mamaroneck Ave.
White Plains, NY 10605
Att.: Lloyd Moore, Exec.
Tel. (914) 761–3628

Capacity 60.

MONTFORT MISSIONARIES RETREAT
HOUSE
PO Box 667
Litchfield, CT 06759

The Rev. Francis J. Allen, SMM, Dir. Capacity 42.

MERCY CENTER
167 Neck Rd.
Madison, CT 06433

Sister Patricia, RSM, Dir. Capacity 140.

CENACLE RETREAT HOUSE
Wadsworth St.
Middletown, CT 06457

Sister Helen Stula, RC, Dir. Capacity 42.

EDMUNDITE NOVIATE
Enders Island
Mystic, CT 06355

The Rev. Richard Myhalyk, SSE, Dir. 20 rooms, private retreats only.

HOLY GHOST FATHERS RETREAT HOUSE
705 Weed St.
New Canaan, CT 06840

The Rev. David Marshall, CSSP, Dir. Capacity 46.

VILLA MARIE RETREAT HOUSE
159 Sky Meadow Dr.
Stamford, CT 06903

Sister M. Emiliana, OSF, Dir. Capacity 71.

HOLY FAMILY RETREAT HOUSE
303 Tunxis Rd.
West Hartford, CT 06107

The Rev. Vincent D. Youngberg, CP, Dir. Capacity 195, men and married couples only.

UNIVERSAL DIVINE CENTER
5 Lockwood Circle
Westport, CT 06880
Tel. (603) 539–4997 (summer phone)

IMMACULATA RETREAT HOUSE
Windham Rd.
Willimantic, CT 06226

The Rev. James Liberty, OMI, Dir. Capacity 80.

DELAWARE

ST. FRANCIS RENEWAL CENTER
1901 Prior Rd.
Wilmington, DE 10809

The Rev. Paschal Caccavalle, OFM, Dir. Capacity 22.

DISTRICT OF COLUMBIA

WASHINGTON RETREAT HOUSE FOR WOMEN
4000 Harewood Rd., NE
Washington, D.C. 20017

Sister Walburga Reise, SA, Dir. Capacity 54.

FLORIDA

CENACLE RETREAT HOUSE
1400 S. Dixie Hwy.
Lantana, FL 33462

Sister Muriel Brown, RC, Dir. 40 rooms.

DOMINICAN RETREAT HOUSE
7275 SW 124th St.
Miami, FL 33156

Sister Carmen Aragon, OP. 40 rooms.

OUR LADY OF FLORIDA SPIRITUAL CENTER
1300 U.S. Hwy. 1
North Palm Beach, FL 33408

The Rev. Kilian McGowan, CP, Dir. Capacity 70.

ST. PHILIP NERI HOUSE OF PRAYER
Rt. 4, Box 131
Stuart, FL 33444

The Rev. Edward McCarthy, Dir. Capacity 24.

FRANCISCAN CENTER
3010 Perry Ave.
Tampa, FL 33603

Sister Theresa Collins, OSF, Dir. Capacity 40.

GEORGIA

IGNATIUS HOUSE
6700 Riverside Dr., NW
Atlanta, GA 30328

The Rev. John Hein, SJ, Dir. 49 rooms, privately
directed retreats only, $7.50 per night.

MONASTERY RETREAT HOUSE
Conyers, GA 30207

The Rev. Thomas Fidelis, OCSO, Guestmaster. 50
rooms.

CENTER FOR SPIRITUAL AWARENESS
PO Box 7
Lakemont, GA 30552

Founded and directed by Roy Eugene Davis, a disciple of Yogananda. Meditation instruction available.

ILLINOIS

BELLARMINE HALL
Box 268
Barrington, IL 60010

The Rev. Patrick J. Boyle, SJ, Dir. 62 rooms.

KING'S HOUSE OF RETREATS
North 66th St.
Belleville, IL 62223

The Rev. Pat Carroll, OMI, Dir. 65 rooms.

CENACLE RETREAT HOUSE
513 Fullerton Parkway
Chicago, IL 60614

Sister Clare Portell, Coordinator. Capacity 65.

CENACLE RETREAT HOUSE
11600 Longwood Dr.
Chicago, IL 60643

Sister Mary Sharon Riley, Coordinator. Capacity 48.

YMCA CAMP NAWAKWA
Metropolitan YMCA
19 S. LaSalle St.
Chicago, IL 60603
Att.: Roger Treloar, Camp Dir.
Tel. (312) 222–8150

CABRINI CONTACT CENTER
9430 Golf Rd.
Des Plaines, IL 60016

60 rooms.

VILLA REDEEMER RETREAT HOUSE
PO Box 6
Glenview, IL 60025

The Rev. John Andree, CSSR, Dir. 70 rooms.

KING'S HOUSE OF RETREATS
Box 313
Henry, IL 61537

The Rev. Sherman Wall, OMI, Dir. Capacity 90.

CHRISTIAN LIFE CENTER
1209 W. Ogden Ave.
LaGrange Park, IL 60525

Sister Ethel Vaca, CSJ, Coordinator. Capacity 99.

ST. MARY'S RETREAT HOUSE
1400 Main St.
Lemont, IL 60439

The Rev. Daniel Sedlar, OFM, Dir. Capacity 78.

VIATORIAN VILLA
3015 Bay View Ln.
McHenry, IL 60050

The Rev. Eugene Lutz, CSV, Dir. Capacity 45.

ST. FRANCIS RETREAT HOUSE
(MAYSLAKE)
1717 31st St.
Oak Brook, IL 60521

The Rev. Wilbert Hegener, OFM, Dir. Capacity 156.

TOLENTINE CENTER
20300 Governors Hwy.
Olympia Fields, IL 60461

The Rev. John Beretta, OSA, Dir. Capacity 110.

CHRISTIAN BROTHERS LASALLE MANOR
Rt. 1, Galena Rd.
Plano, IL 60545

Bro. Timothy McCarthy, FSC, Dir. 50 rooms.

BISHOP LANE RETREAT HOUSE
Rt. 2, Box 214 A
Rockford, IL 61102

The Rev. Lawrence M. Urbaniak, Dir. 50 rooms.

DIVINE WORD SEMINARY RETREAT HOUSE
Techny, IL 60082

Bro. Tobias, Mgr. Capacity 61.

CENACLE RETREAT HOUSE
Box 340
Warrenville, IL 60555

Sister Anne Fletcher, RC, Dir. Capacity 97.

AYLESFORD RENEWAL CENTER
Rt. 66 and Cass Ave. N.
Westmont, IL 60559

The Rev. Rene W. Hayes, O Carm, Dir. Capacity 60.

INDIANA

LOURDES RETREAT HOUSE
12915 Parrish St.
Cedar Lake, IN 46303

The Rev. Herman J. Ziemba, OFM, Dir. Capacity 57.

SARTO CENTER
4200 N. Kentucky Ave.
Evansville, IN 47711

The Rev. James J. Lex, Dir. Capacity 134.

POPE JOHN XXIII CENTER
407 W. McDonald St.
Hartford City, IN 47348

The Rev. Keith Hosey, Dir. Capacity 15.

ALVERNA RETREAT HOUSE
8140 Spring Mill Rd.
Indianapolis, IN 46260

The Rev. Anton R. Braum, OFM, Dir. Capacity 62.

OUR LADY OF FATIMA RETREAT HOUSE
5353 E. 56th St.
Indianapolis, IN 46226

The Rev. Kenny C. Sweeney, Dir. 68 rooms.

MT. ST. FRANCIS SEMINARY
Mt. St. Francis, IN 47146

The Rev. Christian Moore, OFM Conv, Dir. Dorm space for 56.

OUR LADY OF FATIMA RETREAT HOUSE
Box O
Notre Dame, IN 46556

The Rev. James Trepanier, CSC, Dir. Capacity 78.

ST. JUDE GUEST HOUSE
St. Meinrad, IN 47577

The Rev. Mel Patton, OSB, Dir. Capacity 39.

SEVEN DOLORS SHRINE
Rt. 12, Box 31
Valpariso, IN 46383

The Rev. Christopher Lynch, OFM, Dir. Capacity 40.

IOWA

AMERICAN MARTYRS RETREAT HOUSE
PO Box 605
Cedar Falls, IA 50613

The Rev. William Clark, Dir. 60 rooms.

COLFAX INTERFAITH SPIRITUAL CENTER
Colfax, IA 50054

The Rev. Sean Santos, Dir. Capacity 90.

KANSAS

ST. BENEDICT'S ABBEY
2nd & Division Sts.
Atchison, KS 66002

Capacity 20, private retreats.

SUN MOUNTAIN COMMUNITY CHURCH
RR 2, Box 155
Lawrence, KS 66044
Tel. (913) 843–7005

Rural christian meditation retreat center.

ST. AUGUSTINE'S RETREAT CENTER
3301 Parallel Pky.
Kansas City, KS 66104

The Rev. James V. Brown, OAR, Dir. 40 rooms.

VILLA CHRISTI RETREAT HOUSE
3033 W. Second St.
Wichita, KS 67203

The Rev. Paul A. Farrell, CSSR, Dir. Capacity 54.

KENTUCKY

MARYDALE RETREAT CENTER
Donaldson Rd.
Erlanger, KY 41018

The Rev. Thomas F. Middendoff, Exec. Dir. Capacity 75.

ST. MARK'S MONASTERY
South Union, KY 42283

The Rev. Thomas O'Connor, OSB, Dir. Capacity 18.

THE GUESTHOUSE
Abbey of Gethsemani
Trappist, KY 40073

The Rev. David Murphy, OCSO, Guestmaster. Capacity 20, private retreats for men.

LOUISIANA

MANRESA HOUSE OF RETREATS
PO Box 89
Convent, LA 70723

The Rev. Duval Hilbert, SJ, Dir. Capacity 89.

MARYWOOD RETREAT HOUSE
Rt. 1
Folsom, LA 70437

Sister Alvara, SCC, Sup. Dormitory for 40.

ACADEMY OF THE SACRED HEART
Grand Coteau, LA 70541

Sister M. O. Mouton, RSCJ, Dir. Capacity 50, summer retreats for women.

OUR LADY OF THE OAKS RETREAT
HOUSE
PO Box D
Grand Coteau, LA 70541

The Rev. Daniel Partridge, SJ, Dir. Capacity 61.

ST. CHARLES COLLEGE
Grand Coteau, LA 70541

The Rev. John Stack, SJ, Dir. Capacity 30, mostly private retreats.

CARMEL CENTER RETREAT HOUSE
PO Box 130
Lacombe, LA 70445

Sister Marian Louviere, Dir. Capacity 66. $15 per person per weekend for a minimum of 30 persons. Also private retreats for $6 per night.

MADONNA HALL RETREAT HOUSE
PO Box 2429
Lafayette, LA 70501

Sister M. Jeanne Guillet, MHS, Dir. Dormitory space for 35, young women only.

AVE MARIA RETREAT HOUSE
Rt. 1, Box 0368 AB
Marrero, LA 70072
Tel. (504) 689–3837 (Lafitte, LA)

The Rev. Henry Simoneaux, OMI, Dir. 50 private rooms, $15 per day.

THE CENACLE RETREAT HOUSE
5500 St. Mary St.
Metairie, LA 70004
Tel. (504) 887–1420

Sister Elizabeth Harris, Dir. 50 private rooms.

MARYHILL RETREAT HOUSE
600 Maryhill Rd.
Pineville, LA 71360

The Rev. C. Richard Nowery, CSC, Dir. 47 rooms.

ABBEY CHRISTIAN LIFE CENTER
St. Joseph Abbey
St. Benedict, LA 70457

The Rev. David Leftwich, OSB, Dir. 42 rooms.

MAINE

ST. PAUL CENTER
136 State St.
Augusta, ME 04330

The Rev. Jean Vallieres, OMI, Dir. Capacity 83.

MARYLAND

CHRISTIAN BROTHERS RETREAT HOUSE
Rt. 85 S.
Adamstown, MD 21710
Tel. (301) 874–5180

Br. Malachy J. Broderick, FSC, Dir. 40 rooms.

MANRESA-ON-SEVERN
Box 9
Annapolis, MD 21404
Tel. (301) 974–0332

The Rev. Henry Haske, SJ, Dir. Capacity 73.

PINE LAKE SPIRITUAL CENTER
Winchester Rd.
Annapolis, MD 21401
Tel. (301) 757–2336

The Very Rev. Urban Adelman, OFM Cap, Dir.
Retreat house for groups and individuals. Capacity
25.

KOINONIA
Box 5744
Baltimore, MD 21208
Tel. (301) 486–6262

A spiritual and educational community on 45 wooded acres north of Baltimore. Retreat facilities for small groups or individuals include a meditation room, hermitage, and retreat center accommodating 18 people in single and double rooms, more in sleeping bags.

ST. JOSEPH SPIRITUAL CENTER
3800 Frederick Ave.
Baltimore, MD 21229
Tel. (301) 566–3322

The Rev. Gerald Hynes, CP, Dir. 52 rooms.

LOYOLA-ON-POTOMAC
Faulkner, MD 20632

The Rev. Eugene L. Tucker, SJ, Dir. 80 rooms.

MARRIOTTSVILLE SPIRITUAL CENTER
Marriottsville, MD 21104
Tel. (301) 328–2123

Sister Dorothy Marie, Local Sup. 72 rooms.

CYO RETREAT HOUSE
15523 York Rd.
Sparks, MD 21152
Tel. (301) 472–2400

The Rev. John Zeller, Dir. 44 rooms for youths.

ST. ANTHONY'S WOOD
3938 Backwoods Rd.
Westminster, MD 21157

Ms. A. F. Fischer, Dir. Accommodations for 4, contemplative hermitage.

MASSACHUSETTS

CHRISTIAN FORMATION CENTER
475 River Rd.
Andover, MA 01810
Tel. (617) 851–6711 or 686–3941

Contact Mr. Nicholas Hapshe. 22 rooms.

LASALLETTE CENTER FOR CHRISTIAN
LIVING
947 Park St.
Attleboro, MA 02703

The Rev. Norman Lemoine, MS, Dir. 50 rooms.

YMCA CAMP SANDY ISLAND
316 Huntington Ave.
Boston, MA 02115
Att.: Bruce Taylor, Camping Dir.
Tel. (617) 536–7800

RETREAT HOUSE
near **Boston,** MA
Tel. (617) 344–9634

Country setting for groups up to 30 people.

MASTER DEI RETREAT HOUSE
Groveland Rd.
Bradford, MA 01830

The Rev. Gino Marchesani, FDP, Dir. 2 dormitories.

CENACLE RETREAT HOUSE
200 Lake St.
Brighton, MA 02135

Contact Sister Mildred Doherty. Capacity 60.

ST. GABRIEL'S MONASTERY RETREAT
159 Washington St.
Brighton, MA 02135
Tel. (617) 782–4641

The Rev. Brendan Breen, CP, Dir. 100 private rooms.

ANANDA ASHRAMA-VEDANTA CENTER
130 Beechwood St.
Cohasset, MA 02025
Tel. (617) 383–0940

Srimata Gayatri Devi, Minister. A monastic community dedicated to the teachings of Sri Ramakrisha. Reservations may be made for spending the weekend or longer at the guest cottages.

DOMINICAN RETREAT HOUSE
ST. STEPHEN PRIORY
Glen St.
Dover, MA 02030
Tel. (617) 785–0124

The Very Rev. R. J. Gardner, OP, Dir. Capacity 50.

MIRAMAR RETREAT HOUSE
Duxbury, MA 02332
Tel. (617) 585–2460

The Rev. Lawrence Poetz, Dir. Capacity 50, $30 per weekend.

EASTERN POINT RETREAT HOUSE
Gloucester, MA 01930
Tel. (617) 283–0013

The Rev. William J. Power, Administrator. Capacity 46.

DEHON RETREAT CENTER
(formerly Dehon Seminary)
Great Barrington, MA 01230
Contact:

Ed McCormick
Tel. (413) 528–0630 office or 274–6538 home

Beautiful, quiet place for large groups. 100-plus capacity.

MARIAN CENTER
1365 Northampton St.
Holyoke, MA 01040

Miriam Najimy, DHM, Dir. Capacity 35.

LORETTO RETREAT HOUSE
Jeffery's Neck Rd.
Ipswich, MA 01938

Sister Patricia O'Donnell, SND, Dir. Capacity 25.

SACRED HEART RETREAT HOUSE
PO Box 271
Ipswich, MA 01938

The Rev. Richard Mataconis, SDB, Dir. Dormitory for 30.

CENACLE RETREAT HOUSE
George Hill Rd.
Lancaster, MA 05123

Sister Angela Murphy, RC, Coordinator. Capacity 48.

SALVATORIAN CENTER
30 East St.
Methuen, MA 01844
Tel. (617) 682–2959

The Rev. Joseph Dagher, BS, Dir. Capacity 80.

MAHA YOGA ASHRAM
90 Park St.
Newton, MA 02158
Tel. (617) 965–5947

Yogiraj T. R. Khanna leads weekend retreats in meditation, hatha yoga, and chanting. Instruction available.

CAMPION HALL
1518 Great Pond Rd.
North Andover, MA 01845
Tel. (617) 685–6371 or in Boston (617) 664–5245

The Rev. John E. McCarthy, SJ, Dir. Capacity 80.

HOLY CROSS FATHERS RETREAT HOUSE
490 Washington St.
North Easton, MA 02356

The Rev. Thomas E. Lawton, CSC, Dir. Capacity 65.

ROWE CAMP
Rowe, MA 01367
Tel. (413) 339–8376

Unitarian-Universalist camp. Appropriate for groups.

CALVARY RETREAT CENTER
59 South St.
Shrewsbury, MA 01545

The Rev. Fidelis T. Connolly, CP, Dir. Capacity 70.

DON ORIONE RETREAT HOUSE
Washington St.
So. Groveland, MA 01834

Capacity 15.

ST. JOSEPH'S ABBEY
Spencer, MA 01562
Tel. (617) 885–3010

Contact the Guestmaster. Capacity 14 men, week-ends only.

ESPOUSAL RETREAT HOUSE
554 Lexington St.
Waltham, MA 02154
Tel. 893–3465

The Rev. Nicholas J. Spagnolo, CSS, Dir. Capacity 80.

MOTHER OF SORROWS RETREAT HOUSE
110 Monastery Ave.
West Springfield, MA 01089

The Rev. Leo J. Gorman, CP, Dir. Capacity 115.

MT. CARMEL CHRISTIAN LIFE CENTER
Oblong Rd.
Williamstown, MA 01267

The Rev. Pius Gagnon, O Carm, Dir. Capacity 42.

MICHIGAN

MANRESA RETREAT HOUSE
1390 Quarton Rd.
Bloomfield Hills, MI 48013

The Rev. Bernard J. Wernert, SJ, Dir. 73 rooms.

COLOMBIERE RETREAT/CONFERENCE CENTER
9075 Big Lake Rd.
Clarkson, MI 48016

The Rev. Gene Gonya, SJ, Dir. 150 rooms.

BLESSED SACRAMENT RETREAT HOUSE
U.S. 31, Box 86
Conway, MI 49722

Sister Mary Helene, OSS, Dir. Capacity 52.

MARY REPARATRIX RETREAT CENTER
17330 Quincy Ave.
Detroit, MI 48221

Sister Barbara Conklin, SMR, Coordinator. Capacity 56.

ST. PAUL RETREAT HOUSE
23333 Schoolcraft
Detroit, MI 48223

The Rev. John Devany, CP, Dir. 78 rooms.

PORTIUNCULA IN THE PINES
703 E. Main St.
De Witt, MI 48820

The Rev. Capistran Polgar, OFM, Dir. 52 rooms.

MARYGROVE CENTER
Garden, MI 49835

The Rev. Matthew Nyman, Dir. Capacity 57.

MONKS OF MT. TABOR
4326 Snook Rd.
Hadley, MI 48440

The Rev. Boniface Luykx, Dir. Capacity 8.

ST. MARY'S RETREAT HOUSE
775 W. Drahner Rd.
Oxford, MI 48051

Sister Mary Michaelene, OP, Dir. 60 rooms.

ST. BASIL'S CENTER
3990 Giddings Rd.
Pontiac, MI 48057

The Rev. Edmund Brennan, BS, Dir. 50 rooms.

QUEEN OF ANGELS RETREAT HOUSE
PO Box 2026
Saginaw, MI 48605

The Rev. Lester Bach, OFM, Dir. 56 rooms.

CHRISTIAN FRIENDSHIP HOUSE
1975 N. River Rd.
St. Clair, MI 48079

The Rev. Ben Markwell, OFM, Dir. 8 rooms.

ST. LAZARE RETREAT HOUSE
Spring Lake, MI 49456

The Rev. John J. Lawlor, CM, Dir. 50 rooms.

CAPUCHIN RETREAT
62460 Mt. Vernon Rd.
Washington, MI 48094

The Rev. Vernon Wagner, OFM, Dir. Capacity 72.

MINNESOTA

KING'S HOUSE OF RETREATS
621 S. First Ave.
Buffalo, MN 55313
Tel. (612) 682–1394 or in Twin Cities
(612) 473–5738

The Rev. Maynard Kegler, OMI, Dir. Capacity 92.

ST. JOHN'S ABBEY
Collegeville, MN 56321

The Rev. Barnabas Laubach, OSB, Dir. Summer retreats for couples in college facilities.

WELCH CENTER
605 N. Central Ave.
Duluth, MN 55807

The Rev. Noel Stretton, Dir. Capacity 48.

VILLA MARIE
Frontenac, MN 55026

Sister Eugenia Marie, OSU, Dir. Appropriate for groups.

JESUIT RETREAT HOUSE
8234 N. Demontreville Trail
Lake Elmo, MN 55042
Tel. (612) 777–1311

The Rev. Edward Sthokal, SJ, Dir. 60 single rooms. Men only.

CENTER FOR SPIRITUAL DEVELOPMENT
Good Counsel Hill
Mankato, MN 56001

Sister Margaret Picha, SSND, Dir. 150 rooms.

CHRISTIAN BROTHERS RETREAT CENTER
Rt. 1, Box 18
Marine on St. Croix, MN 55047
Tel. (612) 433–2486

Bro. Arthur Ravello, FSC, Dir.; Bro. Don Byrne, FSC, Dir. 40 rooms.

MINNEAPOLIS CATHOLIC YOUTH CENTER
2120 Park Ave.
Minneapolis, MN 55404
Tel. (612) 336–4325

The Rev. James Schuller, Dir. 65-room mansion.

FRANCISCAN RETREATS
CONVENTUAL FRANCISCAN FATHERS
AND BROTHERS
Prior Lake, MN 55372
Tel. (612) 447–2182

The Rev. Fintan Cantwell, OFM, Dir. Capacity 80.

ASSISI HEIGHTS CHRISTIAN COMMUNITY
CENTER
Box 259
Rochester, MN 55901

Sister Patricia Steffes, OSF, Co-Dir. Capacity 160.

CAMP DU NORD
Contact:
Armand Ball, Executive
475 Cedar St.
St. Paul, MN 55101
Tel. (612) 222–0771

CATHOLIC YOUTH CENTER
150 N. Smith Ave.
St. Paul, MN 55102
Tel. (612) 224–2358

The Rev. Michael Kolar, Dir. Dormitory accommodations for 80.

EPIPHANY HOUSE OF PRAYER
266 Summit Ave.
St. Paul, MN 55102
Tel. (612) 224–2235

Josephine Scrima, DHM, Dir. Capacity 7, private and directed retreats for women only.

MARYHILL RETREAT HOUSE
260 Summit Ave.
St. Paul, MN 55102
Tel. (612) 224–3615 or 224–8566

Josephine Scrima, DHM, Dir. Retreats for women and married couples, capacity 30.

THE CENACLE
1221 Wayzata Blvd.
Wayzata, MN 55391
Tel. (612) 473–7308

Contact Sr. Gloria Haagensen. 52 rooms.

FITZGERALD RETREAT CENTER
Terrace Heights
Winona, MN 55987

The Rev. Robert Brom, Dir. 33 rooms winter, 91 rooms summer.

MISSOURI

ST. ANGELA HOUSE OF RETREATS
Ursuline Academy
Arcadia, MO 63621

Women only.

OUR LADY OF THE OZARKS
PO Box 424
Carthage, MO 64836

The Rev. John A. Weissler, OMI, Dir. Capacity 39.

HOLY FAMILY RETREAT HOUSE
Conception Abbey
Conception, MO 64433

The Rev. Daniel Petsche, OSB, Guestmaster. Capacity 32.

PALLOTTINE RENEWAL CENTER
Rt. 2, 15270 Old Halls Ferry Rd.
Florissant, MO 63034

Sister Jean Valdes, SAC, Dir. Capacity 71.

MARIANIST APOSTOLIC CENTER
Marycliff
Glencoe, MO 63038

The Rev. Timothy Dwyer, SM, Dir. 40 rooms.

IMMACOLATA RETREAT HOUSE
RFD 4, Box 434
Liberty, MO 64068

The Rev. S. E. Kalamaja, SJ, Dir. Capacity 28.

FAMILY LIFE CENTER
Pevley, MO 63070
Tel. (314) 479–1500 or in St. Louis
(314) 296–7470

The Very Rev. Edwin Cole, OSB, Acting Dir. Capacity 24.

THE CENACLE
900 S. Spoede Rd.
St. Louis, MO 63131

Sister Ena Caselton, RC, Dir.

TROUT LODGE YMCA CAMP
1528 Locust St.
St. Louis, MO 63103
Att.: Leroy A. Congdon, Exec.
Tel. (314) GE 6–4100

WHITE HOUSE RETREATS
7400 Christopher Dr.
St. Louis, MO 63139

The Rev. L. Chiuminatto, SJ, Dir. 74 rooms, men only.

ST. DE CHANTAL RETREAT HOUSE
1701 S. Fort St.
Springfield, MO 65807

The Rev. Mother Margaret Mary Hogan, VHM, Dir.
Capacity 30, women only.

PASSIONIST RETREAT OF OUR LADY
Warrenton, MO 63383

The Rev. Luke Connolly, CP, Dir. 70 rooms.

MONTANA

URSULINE CENTRE
2300 Central Ave.
Great Falls, MT 59401

Sister Marietta Davis, OSU, Dir. Capacity 76.

FEATHERED PIPE RANCH
2409 Colorado Gulch
Helena, MT 59601
Tel. (406) 442–8196

AUM CENTER FOR SELF-REALIZATION
11 Meridan Road
Kalispell, MT 59901
Att.: Ken and Mona Piller

Weekends with yoga and meditation instruction available. Also a natural healing clinic.

NEBRASKA

ST. COLUMBANS RETREAT HOUSE
Bellevue, NE 68005
Tel. (402) 291–1920

The Rev. Art Friel, SSC, Dir. Capacity 70.

GOOD COUNSEL RETREAT HOUSE
Rt. 1, Box 10
Waverly, NE 68462

The Rev. Servace Ritter, OFM, Dir. Capacity 48.

NEW HAMPSHIRE

THE PLACE FARM
RD 103, Rt. 123
Greenville, NH 03048
Tel. (603) 878–9883

Ideal for large groups.

OBLATE RETREAT HOUSE
Rt. 3A, Lowell Rd.
Hudson, NH 03051

The Rev. Paul Lemiux, OMI, Dir. 58 rooms.

HUNDRED ACRES
Scobie Pond Rd.
New Boston, NH 03070

The Rev. Paul Fitzgerald, OCSO, Dir. Capacity 11, private retreats only.

THE COMMON
Peterborough, NH 03458

The Rev. Matthias Montgomery, OCD, Dir. Capacity 24.

ST. FRANCIS FRIARY
Rye Beach, NH 03871
Tel. (603) 964–5559

The Rev. Emmett Mulhern, OFM, Dir. Capacity 70.

DAVID GRAVES
Box 40
Salisbury, NH 03268

David has two fully insulated cabins standing un-
occupied on his 76-acre tract of woodlands. Available for short-term retreats.

NEW JERSEY

ALPINE CAMP
Alpine, NJ 07620
Contact:

Greater NY Council Boy Scouts
25 W. 43rd St.
New York, NY 10036
Att.: Leslie M. Loysen, Exec.
Tel. (212) 947-8400

Very large facility.

HUDSON GUILD FARM
Andover, NJ 07821
Att.: Curtis Ream, Exec.
Tel. (201) 398-2679

Capacity 125.

ST. PIUS X HOUSE OF RETREATS
(BLACKWOOD CATHOLIC CENTER)
PO Box 216
Blackwood, NJ 08012

The Rev. Msgr. C. J. Keating, Dir. Capacity 92.

DIVINE WORD SEMINAR
Bordentown, NJ 08505

The Rev. Paul Connors, SVD, Dir. Dorm space for
125.

NORTHOVER CAMP
Bound Brook, NJ 08805
Contact:

The Christodora Foundation
342 Madison Ave.
New York, NY 10017
Att.: Stephen Slobadin
Tel. (212) 682–4360

Available winters for large groups.

VACAMAS CAMP
Butler, NJ 07405
Contact:

Irving Topal
31 Union Square W.
New York, NY 10003
Tel. (212) 929–8195

Capacity 250.

STELLA MARIS RETREAT HOUSE
981 Ocean Ave.
Elberon, NJ 07740

Sister Jerome Fitzpatrick, Admin.

CENACLE CENTER FOR SPIRITUAL
RENEWAL
411 River Rd.
Highland Park, NJ 08904

Sister Joan Purvis, RC, Dir. Capacity 28.

CHRIST HOUSE
Rt. 15 at Rt. 94, Box 258
Lafayette, NJ 07848

The Rev. Eric Kyle, OFM, Dir. Capacity 90.

HARTLEY FARM
Lincoln Park, NJ 07848
Contact:

Hartley House
413 W. 46th St.
New York, NY 10036
Att.: Dan Kaplan, Exec.
Tel. (212) 246–9885

Capacity 100; very limited space in winter.

VILLA PAULINE
Hilltop Rd.
Mendham, NJ 07945

Sister Helen Claire, SCC, Dir. Capacity 40.

GOOD SHEPARD CENTER
74 Kahdena Rd.
Morristown, NJ 07960

Sister Marie Barbara, Admin. Capacity 40.

HOUSE OF PRAYER EXPERIENCE
COMMUNITY
Xavier Center, Convent Station
Morristown, NJ 07961

The Rev. James J. Ferry, Dir. 80 rooms.

LOYOLA HOUSE OF RETREATS
161 James St.
Morristown, NJ 07960

The Rev. Thomas J. O'Day, SJ, Dir. 89 rooms.

ST. MARY'S ABBEY
Morristown, NJ 07960
Att.: Retreat Coordinator
Tel. (201) 538–3231

Capacity 64, $15 per day, $50 per week.

QUEEN OF PEACE RETREAT HOUSE
St. Paul's Abbey, Box 7
Newton, NJ 07860

The Rev. Andrew O'Sullivan, OSB, Dir. Capacity 80.

YMCA CAMP LINWOOD
600 Broad St.
Newark, NJ 07102
Att.: Louis R. Briegel, Exec.
Tel. (201) 624–8900

CARMEL RETREAT HOUSE
1071 Ramapo Valley Rd.
Mahwah Box 285
Oakland, NJ 07436

The Rev. Timothy E. Moore, O. Carm., Dir. Capacity 44.

SHANTI YOGI INSTITUTE AND RETREAT
943 Central Ave.
Ocean City, NJ 08226
Tel. (609) 399–1974

Shanti Yogi teaches meditation and hatha yoga at the ocean retreat. Rooming facilities for intensive training and personal guidance.

ST. BONAVENTURE RETREAT HOUSE
174 Ramsey St.
Paterson, NJ 07501

The Rev. Jerome Gallagher, OFM, Dir. 42 rooms.

ST. JOSEPH VILLA
Peapack, NJ 07977

Sister Roberta Walsh, Admin. Women only.

BLESSED TRINITY MISS. CENACLE
1190 Long Hill Rd.
Stirling, NJ 07980

Sister Bernard Marie, MSBT, Custodian. Capacity
18.

TIBETAN BUDDHIST RETREAT HOUSE
RD 1, Box 306A
Washington, NJ 07882
Tel. (201) 689-6080

Associated with the Lamaist Buddhist Monastery of
America in Howell, NJ. Occasional classes and seminars. Tibetan Buddhist Lama Geshe Wangyal has
his residence here.

SAN ALFONSO RETREAT HOUSE
755 Ocean Ave.
West End, NJ 07740

The Rev. Wm. Heave, CSSR, Dir. 145 rooms.

NEW MEXICO

DOMINICAN RETREAT HOUSE
(OUR LADY QUEEN OF PEACE)
5825 Coors Rd., SW
Albuquerque, NM 87105

25 rooms.

JEMEZ BODHI MANDALA
Box 44
Jemez Springs, NM 87025
Tel. (505) 829-3854

A Rinzai zen meditation center. There are one-week
sessions under the guidance of Joshu Sasaki Roshi.
Visitors and resident students welcome. Groups may

use the facilities when the students are not in training during the fall and spring. Facilities include
accommodations for 40 and a large meditation hall.

THE NEXT STEP
Box 118, Rt. 2
Kingston, NM 88042

Week-long retreats guided by a staff experienced in
many new-age disciplines.

HOLY CROSS RETREAT CENTER
PO Box 158
Mesilla Park, NM 88047

The Rev. Evan Howard, OFM, Dir. 46 rooms.

BENEDICTINE ABBEY
Pecos, NM 87552

Abbot David Geraets, Dir. Capacity 70.

LAMA FOUNDATION
Box 444
San Cristobal, NM 87564

Hermitage for private retreats available at $3 per
day, subject to the acceptance of the community.

NEW YORK

JESUIT RETREAT HOUSE
Auriesville, NY 12012

The Rev. Edward F. X. Kennedy, SJ, Dir. Capacity
97.

CUMMINGS CAMPGROUND
Brewster, NY 10509
Contact:

Educational Alliance
198 E. Broadway
New York, NY 10002
Att.: Dr. Jay Sexter, Dir.
Tel. (212) 475–6061

Capacity 35.

ANDREA CLARK FACILITY
Briarcliff Manor, NY 10510
Contact:

Greater NY Council Girl Scouts
335 E. 46th St.
New York, NY 10017
Att.: Dot Nelson, Dir.
Tel. (212) 687–8383

Capacity 36.

CARDINAL SPELLMAN RETREAT HOUSE
5801 Palisade Ave.
Bronx, NY 10471

The Rev. Donatus Santorsa, CP, Dir. 105 rooms.

DIOCESAN CURSILLOS CENTER
118 Congress St.
Brooklyn, NY 11201

The Rev. Joseph M. Biosca, CM, Dir. Capacity 52.

NOTRE DAME RETREAT HOUSE
PO Box 342, Foster Rd.
Canandaigua, NY 14424

The Rev. James F. Foley, CSSR, Dir. Capacity 107.

SWEN-I-O
Canandaigua, NY 14424
Contact:

Human Dimension Institute
4380 Main St.
Buffalo, NY 14226
Tel. (716) 839–2336

Instruction in meditation is available at this rural retreat.

THE POPE JOHN XXIII CENTER
Cassadaga, NY 14718

The Rev. Roland O. Guilman, AA, Dir. Capacity 98.

IGNATIUS RETREAT HOUSE
Strickler Rd.
Clarence Center, NY 14032

The Rev. Paul J. Gampp, SJ, Dir. 64 rooms.

SURPRISE LAKE CAMP
Cold Spring, NY 10516
Contact:

Federation of Jewish Philanthropies
31 Union Sq. W.
New York, NY 10003
Att.: Jerome Mark
Tel. (212) 929–7483

Capacity 200.

OLMSTEAD CAMP
Cornwall-on-Hudson, NY 12520
Contact:

Five Points Mission
475 Riverside Dr., Room 1922
New York, NY 10027
Att.: Charles Barton
Tel. (212) 749–5717

Capacity 72.

PUMPKIN HOLLOW FARM
RR 1, Box 135
Craryville, NY 12521
Tel. (518) 325–3538
Contact:

Mrs. Dora Kunz
Hillandale Rd.
Port Chester, NY 10573

A Theosophical Society camp.

ST. COLUMBAN'S RETREAT HOUSE
Derby, NY 14047

The Rev. James X. O'Reilly, SSC, Dir. 52 rooms.

NEW YORK CITY MISSION SOCIETY
CAMPS
Dover Plains, NY 12522
Contact:

NY City Mission Society
105 E. 22nd St.
New York, NY 10010
Att.: Richard Pease
Tel. (212) 674–3500

Capacity 128.

HARRIMAN CAMP
East Jewett, NY 12424
Contact:

Boys' Club of New York
287 E. 10th St.
New York, NY 10009
Att.: George Gomes, Exec.
Tel. (212) 677–1107

Capacity 60.

BAIS YAAKOV CAMP
Ferndale, NY 12734
Contact:

National Council of Beth Jacob Schools
1415 E. 7th St.
Brooklyn, NY 11230
Att.: Rabbi Shimon Newhouse
Tel. (212) 375–3533

Capacity 250.

FRESH AIR FUND CAMPS
Fishkill, NY 12524
Contact:

Fresh Air Fund
300 W. 43rd St.
New York, NY 10036
Att.: Laurence Mickolic, Exec.
Tel. (212) 586–0200

Capacity 200.

ST. FRANCIS RETREAT HOUSE
Box 191
Garrison, NY 10524

The Rev. Terrence O'Toole, OFM, Dir. Capacity 74.

ST. JOSAPHAT RETREAT HOUSE
East Beach Rd.
Glen Cove, NY 11542

The Rev. Constantine Wysochanski, OSBM, Dir.

Capacity 58.

YOGA SEMINARY OF NEW YORK
Box 421
Harriman, NY 10926

Offers weekend and one-week retreats as well as courses by different teachers in the theory and practice of yoga.

EPWORTH METHODIST CAMP
High Falls, NY 10928
Contact:

United Methodist Church
210 Boston Post Rd.
Rye, NY 10580
Att.: Don Collier, Dir.
Tel. (914) 792–1618

Capacity 100.

HENRY KAUFMANN CAMP
Holmes, NY 12531
Contact:

Greater NY Council Girl Scouts
335 E. 46th St.
New York, NY 10017
Att.: Dot Nelson, Dir.
Tel. (212) 687–8383

Capacity 86.

WILBUR HERRLICH CAMP
Holmes, NY 12531
Contact:

Lutheran Community Service Inc.
525 Clinton Ave.
Brooklyn, NY 11238
Att.: William Borden
Tel. (212) 857–9492

Capacity 35.

YMCA CAMP GREENKILL
Huguenot, NY 12746
Contact:

YMCA of Greater New York
Big Pond Rd.
Huguenot, NY 12746
Att.: John G. Snowden, Exec.
Tel. (914) 856–8322

Capacity 80.

BISHOP MOLLOY RETREAT HOUSE
86–45 178th St.
Jamaica, NY 11432

The Rev. Lawrence Bellew, CP, Dir. 103 rooms.

CENACLE CENTER FOR SPIRITUAL
RENEWAL
Lake Ronkonkoma, NY 11779

Sister Thelma Hall, RC, Coordinator. Capacity 56.

ST. IGNATIUS RETREAT HOUSE
Inisfada
Manhasset, NY 11030

The Rev. Harvey Haberstroh, SJ, Dir. 36 rooms.

BERGAMO EAST CONFERENCE CENTER
Chaminade Rd.
Marcy, NY 13403

The Rev. Ronald L. Overman, SM, Dir. Capacity
140.

MT. TREMPER CAMP
Mt. Tremper, NY 12457
Contact:

Mt. Tremper Lutheran Camp, Inc.
585 Town Line Rd.
Hauppauge, NY 11787
Att.: Harold Haar
Tel. (516) 265–1183

SUNSHINE ACRES
Napanoch, NY 12458
Contact:

Young People's Baptists Union
3887 Hudson Ave.
Seaford, NY 11783
Att.: James Dougherty
Tel. (516) 221–2744

Capacity 80.

WEL-MET CAMPS
Narrowsburg, NY 12764
Contact:

Child Study Assn.
50 Madison Ave.
New York, NY 10010
Att.: Bernard Friedman, Exec.
Tel. (212) 889–5450

Capacity 100.

THE ABODE OF THE MESSAGE
PO Box 396
New Lebanon, NY 12125

See Sufi Order Secretariat in National Listings.

MARY REPARATRIX RETREAT HOUSE
14 E. 29th St.
New York, NY 10016

Sister Lucy Mahler, Sup. 42 rooms.

PRESBYTERIAN CHRISTIAN EDUCATION
COUNCIL
475 Riverside Dr., Room 320
New York, NY 10027
Tel. (212) 870–2111

Has the following facilities available with two or
three persons to a bedroom: Minden, **Bridgehamp-
ton,** NY; Warwick Conference Center, **Warwick,** NY;
Gilmore-Sloane House, **Stony Point,** NY; Wain-
wright House, **Rye,** NY; Seabury House, **Greenwich,**
CT; Summerfield Center, **Port Chester,** NY; Institute
of World Affairs, **Salisbury,** CT; Deer Hill Conference Center, **Wappingers Falls,** NY. In addition
there are 50 to 60 others with dorm facilities.

ST. JOSEPH'S CURSILLO CENTER
523 W. 142nd St.
New York, NY 10031

The Rev. David Arias, OAR, Dir.

HOLIDAY HILLS YMCA BRANCH
Contact:

YMCA
Pawling, NY 12564
Att.: Loyce O. McMillan, Exec.
Tel. (914) 855–7451

BETHLEHEM RETREAT HOUSE
Abbey of the Genesee
Piffard, NY 14533
Tel. (716) 243–2220

Fr. Francis Steger, Guestmaster. Capacity 15, private
retreats for men only.

REGINA MARIA RETREAT HOUSE
77 Brinkerhoff St.
Plattsburgh, NY 12901

Eleanor McCaffery, DHM, Coordinator. Women
only.

MINISINK CAMP
Port Jervis, NY 12771
Contact:

New York City Mission Society
646 Lenox Ave.
New York, NY 10037
Att.: Ted Simpkins, Dir.
Tel. (212) 368–8400

Capacity 50.

TRAIL BLAZER CAMPS
Rt. 1, Box 657
Port Jervis, NY 12771
Contact:

Lois Goodrich
56 W. 45th St.
New York, NY 10036
Tel. (212) 697–2140

Capacity 20.

METROPOLITAN BAPTIST CAMPS
Poughquag, NY 12570
Contact:

American Baptist Churches
297 Park Ave. S.
New York, NY 10010
Tel. (212) 254–0880

Capacity 98.

MADISON-FELICIA FACILITY
Putnam Valley, NY 10579
Contact:

Michael H. Friedman, Exec.
RD 1, Peekskill Hollow Rd.
Putnam Valley, NY 10579
Tel. (914) 528–8019

Capacity 100.

GODDARD-RIVERSIDE CAMP
Rifton, NY 12471
Contact:

Goddard Riverside Community Center
161 W. 87th St.
New York, NY 10024
Att.: Bernard Wohl, Exec.
Tel. (212) 873–6600

Capacity 120.

CENACLE RETREAT HOUSE
693 East Ave.
Rochester, NY 14607

Sister Marie Halligan, RC, Dir. Capacity 48.

CORMARIA RETREAT HOUSE
Sag Harbor, NY 11963

Sister Annunciation, RSHM, Dir. Capacity 114.

QUEEN OF APOSTLES RETREAT HOUSE
Sag Harbor, NY 11963

The Rev. Francis M. Gaetano, SAC, Dir. 51 rooms.

CHRIST THE KING SEMINARY
St. Bonaventure, NY 14778

The Rev. Alban A. Maguire, OFM, Rector.

DOMINICAN RETREAT HOUSE
1945 Union St.
Schenectady, NY 12309

Capacity 50.

QUINIPET CAMP
Shelter Island, NY 11964
Contact:

United Methodist Church
210 Boston Post Rd.
Rye, NY 10580
Att.: Don Collier, Exec.
Tel. (914) 792–1618

Capacity 85.

ST. GABRIEL'S RETREAT FOR YOUTH
Shelter Island Heights, NY 11965

The Rev. John McLoughlin, CP, Dir. 51 rooms.

SILVER BAY ASSOCIATION
Silver Bay, NY 12874
Winter address:

PO Box 475
Glen Falls, NY 12801
Att.: Walter H. Vanderbush, Dir.
Tel. (518) 793–4452

STELLA MARIS RETREAT HOUSE
130 E. Genesee St.
Skaneateles, NY 13152

Sister M. Edith, Admin. 39 rooms plus dorm space.

BELLE TERRE CLUBHOUSE CAMP
South Kortright, NY 13842
Att.: Mrs. Russell W. Harris
Tel. (607) 538–3701

Capacity 100.

MT. AUGUSTINE RETREAT HOUSE
144 Campus Rd.
Staten Island, NY 10301

The Rev. James F. McNulty, OSA, Dir. Capacity
140.

MOUNT MANRESA
239 Fingerboard Rd.
Staten Island, NY 10305
Att.: The Rev. Emmet Norton, SJ., Dir.
Tel. (212) 727–3844

Capacity 140.

TAGASTE MONASTERY RETREAT HOUSE
Suffern, NY 10901

The Rev. Edward Smith, OAR, Dir. 30 rooms.

CHRIST THE KING RETREAT HOUSE
500 Brookford Rd.
Syracuse, NY 13224

The Rev. Thomas G. Connolly, SJ, Dir. 60 rooms.

ST. ANDREW'S HOUSE
89A St. Andrew's Rd.
Walden, NY 12586

The Rev. Andrew Ansbro, CP, Dir. Capacity 32.

MOUNT ALVERNIA RETREAT HOUSE
Wappingers Falls, NY 12590

The Rev. Thomas Nicastro, OFM, Dir. Capacity 98.

MOUNT ALVERNO RETREAT HOUSE
20 Grand St.
Warwick, NY 10990

Paul S. McCoy, Mgr. Capacity 47.

ST. JOHN BOSCO RETREAT HOUSE
Filors Lane
West Haverstraw, NY 10992

The Rev. John Masiello, SDB, Dir. Capacity 104.

ST. MARY OF THE ANGELS
400 Mill St.
Williamsville, NY 14221

Sister M. Regina, Secy.

NORTH CAROLINA

BLUE RIDGE ASSEMBLY, INC.
PO Box 248
Black Mountain, NC 28711
Tel. (704) 669–8422

Allan G. Robertson, Dir. of Operations.

MARYHURST RETREAT HOUSE
PO Box 1390
Pinehurst, NC 28374

Sister Mary Josilda, Dir. Capacity 19.

NORTH DAKOTA

QUEEN OF PEACE RETREAT
1310 N. Broadway
Fargo, ND 58102

The Rev. Dennis Schue, Dir. Capacity 56.

CHRISTIAN LIFE CENTER
Assumption Abbey
Richardton, ND 58652
Tel. (701) 974–3315

Contact Business Manager. Capacity 92.

SACRED HEART PRIORY
Richardton, ND 58652

Sister Ruth Fox, OSB, Dir. Capacity 72.

OHIO

FRANCISCAN RENEWAL CENTER
320 West St.
Carey, OH 43316

The Rev. Michael A. Brown, OFM, Conv., Dir.
Capacity 50.

FRIARHURST RETREAT HOUSE
8136 Wooster Pike
Cincinnati, OH 45227
Tel. (513) 561–2270

The Rev. Silas Oleksinski, OFM, Dir. 35 rooms. $25
per weekend.

HOLY CROSS MONASTERY
1055 St. Paul Place
Cincinnati, OH 45202

The Rev. Conleth A. Overman, CP, Dir. Capacity 60.

MARY REPARATRIX RETREAT CENTER
3350 Ruther Ave.
Cincinatti, OH 45220
Tel. (513) 221–4624

Contact Sister M. Joan Schimian or Sister Alicia Smith. Capacity 46, $9 per day, available for women and married couples.

JESUIT RETREAT HOUSE
5629 State Rd.
Cleveland, OH 44134

The Rev. Thomas Gedeon, SJ, Dir. Capacity 115.

ST. JOSEPH CHRISTIAN LIFE CENTER
18485 Lake Shore Blvd.
Cleveland, OH 44119

The Rev. John Jacoby, Dir. Capacity 105.

LOYOLA OF THE LAKES
Jesuit Retreat Center
700 Killinger Rd.
Clinton, OH 44216

The Rev. Robert Pollauf, SJ, Dir. 39 rooms.

SHRINE CENTER FOR RENEWAL
5277 E. Broad St.
Columbus, OH 43213

A. William Bickham, Dir. 59 rooms.

BERGAMO MARIANIST CENTER
4435 E. Patterson Rd.
Dayton, OH 45430
Tel. (513) 426–2363 or 426–1325

The Rev. Philip Hoelle, SM, Dir. Capacity 160.

MARIA STEIN CATHOLIC RETREAT-
RENEWAL CENTER
Box 128
Maria Stein, OH 45860
Tel. (419) 925–4538

Sister Yvonne Voisard, CPPS, Dir. 56 private rooms,
$18 per weekend.

LOYOLA RETREAT HOUSE
Box 289
Milford, OH 45150

The Rev. Thomas Diehl, SJ, Dir. 49 rooms.

MEN OF MILFORD RETREAT HOUSE
S. Milford Rd.
Milford, OH 45150

The Rev. John Wenzel, SJ, Dir. 67 rooms.

SACRED HEART RETREAT HOUSE
3128 Logan Ave.
Youngstown, OH 44505

The Rev. Joseph Marinak, MSC, Dir. 48 rooms.

OREGON

OUR LADY OF PEACE RETREAT HOUSE
3600 SW 170th Ave.
Beaverton, OR 97005
Tel. (503) 649–7129

Sister Rose Marie Holden, OSF, Dir. Capacity 64.

ST. BENEDICT LODGE
PO Box 98
McKenzie Bridge, OR 97401

The Rev. Christopher Moschini, OP, Dir. 56 rooms.

LOYOLA RETREAT HOUSE
3320 SE 43rd Ave.
Portland, OR 97206
Tel. (503) 777–2225

The Rev. Gerald Chapdelaine, SJ, Dir. 76 rooms.

MT. ANGEL ABBEY RETREAT HOUSE
St. Benedict, OR 97373
Tel. (503) 845–2221

The Rev. Bernard Sander, OSB, Dir. Capacity 39.

PENNSYLVANIA

ST. FRANCIS RETREAT HOUSE
Monacacy Manor
Bethlehem, PA 19017

Sister M. Anita, OSF, Dir. 70 rooms.

ST. GABRIEL'S RETREAT HOUSE
631 Griffin Pond Rd.
Clarks Summit, PA 18411

Sister M. Grace, CP, Dir.

MARIAN HALL
St. Joseph Convent/Academy
Rt. 2
Columbia, PA 17512

Sister Consilia, ASC, Dir. Capacity 134.

YMCA CAMP HILLTOP
Contact:

Ellis S. Smith, Exec.
Philadelphia YMCA Camps
Box 205
Downington, PA 19335
Tel. (215) 627–4089

ST. FRANCIS RETREAT HOUSE
3918 Chipman Rd.
Easton, PA 18042

The Rev. George Jakub, OFM, Dir. Capacity 82.

ST. ANN'S RETREAT HOUSE
Carrolltown Rd.
Ebensburg, PA 15931

Sister M. Cianca, Coordinator. 30 rooms.

DOMINICAN RETREAT HOUSE
Elkins Park, PA 19117

Sister Eileen Fallon, OP, Dir. 95 rooms.

ST. MARK'S SEMINARY
429 E. Grandview Blvd.
Erie, PA 16504

The Rev. Bruce Allison, Dir. Capacity 140, men only.

THE ARK AND THE DOVE
Babcock Blvd.
Rt. 4, Box 252
Gibsonia, PA 15044

Jacinta Van Winkel, Dir. Capacity 20.

ST. EMMA RETREAT HOUSE
Rt. 4, Box 352
Greensburg, PA 15601

Mother M. Agnes Regensburger, OSB, Dir. 49 rooms.

BL. RAPHAELA MARY RETREAT HOUSE
616 Coopertown Rd.
Haverford, PA 19041

Sister Philomena Monte, ACJ, Dir. Capacity 47.

ST. FIDELIS SEMINARY
Herman, PA 15650

The Rev. Marcellus Fuller, OFM, Dir. Summer retreats.

ST. VINCENT COLLEGE
Latrobe, PA 15650

The Rev. Herman F. Ubinger, OSB, Dir. Capacity 300, men only.

ST. FRANCIS COLLEGE
Loretto, PA 15940

The Rev. Samuel Tiese, TOR, Co-Dir.; the Rev. Jonas McCarthy, TOR, Co-Dir. Capacity 280.

ST. JOSEPH-IN-THE-HILLS
Malvern, PA 19355

The Rev. Anthony W. McGuire, Dir. 330 rooms.

MARY, QUEEN OF ALL SAINTS
2850 N. Providence Rd.
Media, PA 19063

Sister Jean Marie Gustitus, OP, Coordinator. Women only.

VILLA OF OUR LADY OF THE POCONOS
Mount Pocono, PA 18344

Capacity 66.

FATIMA HOUSE
Rolling Hills Rd.
Ottsville, PA 18942

Mary C. Long, Coordinator. Capacity 15.

BYZANTINE SEMINARY RETREAT HOUSE
3605 Perryville Ave.
Pittsburgh, PA 15214

The Rev. John Opalenick, OESL, Dir. Men only.

CENCALE RETREAT HOUSE
4721 Fifth Ave.
Pittsburgh, PA 15213

Sister Mary Lou Heffernan, RC, Dir. Capacity 36.

DEER VALLEY YMCA CAMP
Contact:

Carlton C. Chopp, Exec.
YMCA Metro Board
304 Wood St.
Pittsburgh, PA 15222
Tel. (412) 261–3286

ST. PAUL OF THE CROSS RETREAT
HOUSE
148 Monastery Ave.
Pittsburgh, PA 15203

The Rev. Walter Staudohar, CP, Dir. 100 rooms.

CAMP WAYNE
Preston Park, PA 18455
Tel. (717) 798–2511 or in Woodmere, NY
(516) 295–5544

Capacity 300.

KRIPALU YOGA ASHRAM RETREAT
7 Walters Rd.
Sumneytown, PA 18084
Tel. (215) 234–4568

Yogi Amrit Desai, founder and spiritual director.
55-acre country retreat for long-term or short-term
guests and for the permanent resident disciples.

ST. ALPHONSUS OF THE POCONOS
PO Box 218
Tobyhanna, PA 18466

Rev. Leo F. Dunn, CSSR, Dir. Capacity 50, men
only.

VILLA MARIA RETREAT HOUSE
Box 218
Wernerville, PA 19565

The Rev. Walter Dean, OSFS, Dir. Capacity 76.

RHODE ISLAND

EPHPHETA HOUSE
Box 1
Manville, RI 02838

The Rev. Donald Lozier. OMI, Dir. Capacity 60.

OUR LADY OF PEACE RETREAT HOUSE
Ocean Rd.
Narragansett, RI 02882

The Rev. Msgr. Wm F. Murray, Dir. 53 rooms.

CARMEL SPIRITUAL CENTER
21 Battery St.
Newport, RI 02840

Sister Theresa, O. Carm., Dir. 45 roms.

THE ABBEY
Portsmouth, RI 02871

Contact the Guestmaster.

SOUTH CAROLINA

SPRING BANK CHRISTIAN CENTER
Rt. 2, Box 196
Kingstree, SC 29556

The Rev. John Egan, OP, Dir. Capacity 35.

CANAAN LAND
Yoga Camp Retreat
Lake Toxaway, SC 28747
Winter office:

Camp Canaan Directors
Rt. 3, Box 522
Easley, SC 29640

A daily schedule of hath yoga and meditation instruction.

MEHER-CENTER-ON-THE-LAKES
PO Box 487
Myrtle Beach, SC 29577
Att.: Elizabeth C. Patterson

This beautiful retreat was Meher Baba's home.

CAMP ST. MARY
HUMAN DEVELOPMENT CENTER
Rt. 1, Box 265
Ridgeland, SC 29936

Sister Ellen Robertson, OP, Dir. Capacity 8.

SOUTH DAKOTA

CHRISTIAN RENEWAL CENTER
Yankton, SD 57078

Sister Christine Luke, OSB, Dir. 25 rooms.

TEXAS

MT. THABOR RETREAT HOUSE
12940 Up River Rd.
Corpus Christi, TX 78410

Sister Celia Hernandez, MJMJ, Dir. Capacity 25.

CHRISTIAN HOLIDAY HOUSE
1515 Hugher Rd.
Dickinson, TX 77539

The Rev. Gerard Weber, OMI, Dir. Capacity 64.

CATHOLIC RENEWAL CENTER
4503 Bridge St.
Ft. Worth, TX 76103

Ms. Gail Smith, Dir. Capacity 40.

CENACLE CHRISTIAN LIFE CENTER
420 N. Kirkwood
Houston, TX 77024

Sister Elizabeth Mozina, RC, Dir. 48 rooms.

HOLY NAME RETREAT CENTER
430 Bunker Hill Rd.
Houston, TX 77024

The Rev. Carl Tenhundfeld, CP, Dir. 64 rooms.

MONTSERRAT RETREAT HOUSE
Box 398
Lake Dallas, TX 75065

The Rev. John Curley, SJ, Dir. 33 rooms.

OUR LADY OF THE PILLAR
CHRISTIAN RENEWAL CENTER
2507 NW 36th St.
San Antonio, TX 78228
Tel. (512) 433–1408

Sister John Marie, FMI, Dir. Capacity 75, $30 per
weekend.

ST. JOSEPH'S RETREAT HOUSE
127 Oblate Dr.
San Antonio, TX 78216
Tel. (512) 349–4173

Contact Program Director. Capacity 120.

SAN JUAN RETREAT HOUSE
PO Box 998
San Juan, TX 78589

The Rev. Ronald Duman, OMI, Dir. Capacity 40.

CORPUS CHRISTI MONASTERY RETREAT
HOUSE
Star Rt.
Box A–38–A
Sandia, TX 78383
Tel. (512) 547–3257

Contact Brother Francis. Capacity 16.

OBLATE HOUSE OF PRAYER
LaParra Ranch
Sarita, TX 78385

The Rev. Herve Marcoux, OMI, Dir. 14 rooms,
private retreats.

UTAH

ABBEY OF OUR LADY OF THE HOLY TRINITY
Huntsville, UT 84317

The Rev. Virgil Dusbabek, OCSO, Guestmaster. Capacity 23, private retreats for men.

VERMONT

MERCY RETREATS
Mt. St. Mary Convent
Burlington, VT 05401

Sister Mary de Lourdes, Dir.

VIRGINIA

PREMA DHARMSALA
Rt. 4, Box 265
Bedford, VA 24523
Tel. (703) 297–5982

Periodic retreats.

ST. ANNE'S RETREAT HOUSE
9535 Linton Hall Rd.
Bristow, VA 22013

Sister Mary Ann, OSB, Dir. Capacity 48.

HOLY FAMILY RETREAT HOUSE
1414 N. Mallory St.
Hampton, VA 23363

The Rev. John Schultz, CSSR, Dir. 60 rooms.

DOMINICAN RETREAT HOUSE
7103 Old Dominion Dr.
McLean, VA 22101

40 rooms.

SPIRITUAL RENEWAL CENTER
Rt. 2, Box 388B
Richmond, VA 23229

The Rev. William Carr, Dir. Capacity 44.

OUR LADY OF AQUIA HOUSE
MADONNA HOUSE APOSTOLATE
Rt. 3, Box 202
Stafford, VA 22554

Cottages.

FRANCISCAN CENTER FOR SPIRITUAL
RENEWAL
PO Box 825
Winchester, VA 22601

The Rev. M. Gerald Gordon, TOR, Dir. 27 rooms.

WASHINGTON

VISITATION RETREAT CENTER
3200 SW Dash Point Rd.
Auburn, WA 98002
Tel. (206) 838–9944 or 927–9359

Contact the Registrar. Retreat facility for women
only.

ST. MARY'S PROVINCIALATE
1663 Killarney Way
Bellevue, WA 98004
Tel. (206) 454–7931

Sr. Rose Ann Marti, Registrar.

ST. PETER'S RETREAT HOUSE
PO Box 86
Cowiche, WA 98923

The Rev. Perron J. Auve, Dir. Dormitory space for 60.

RAJ-YOGA MATH AND RETREAT
5984 Rutsatz Rd.
Deming, WA 98244

This semi-monastic community directed by Yogi Satchakrananda sponsors retreats for serious students of yoga.

CAMP INDRALAYA
Rt. 1, Box 86
Eastsound, WA 98245
Tel. (206) 237–4526
Contact:

Orcas Island Foundation
Att.: Mr. John Abbenhouse, Camp Mgr. at above address

A Theosophical Society camp.

PROVIDENCE HEIGHTS
4221–228th SE
Issaquah, WA 98027
Tel. (206) 392–6471

Contact Sr. Louise Gleason.

CAMP FIELD RETREAT CENTER
Leavenwort, WA 98826

The Rev. Joseph O'Grady, Dir. Private rooms and dorm space for 146.

SAINT MARTIN'S COLLEGE
Olympia, WA 98501
Tel. (206) 491–4700

Contact Business Manager's office. Capacity 200 during summer, 75 during school year.

STILL POINT HOUSE OF PRAYER
2333–13th Ave. E.
Seattle, WA 98102
Tel. (206) 322–8006

Sister Rosarii Metzgar, Registrar.

IMMACULATE HEART RETREAT HOUSE
Rt. 3, Box 653
Spokane, WA 99203

Msgr. David Rosage, Dir. Capacity 91.

PALISADES RETREAT HOUSE
PO Box 2214
Tacoma, WA 98401
Tel. (206) 927–9621 or 838–9583

The Rev. Robert C. Simon, CSSR, Dir.

ST. MARY'S CONFERENCE CENTER
Rt. 1
Toledo, WA 98591
Tel. (206) 864–6464

Contact Sister Catherine Brean.

WISCONSIN

MONTE ALVERNO RETREAT HOUSE
1000 N. Ballard Rd.
Appleton, WI 54911
Tel. (414) 733–8526

The Rev. Ellis Zimmer, OFM, Dir. Capacity 68.

ST. BENEDICT'S ABBEY
Benet Lake, WI 53102
Tel. (414) 396–4311

The Rev. Henry Nurre, OSB, Dir. Capacity 61, $30 per weekend.

ST. NORBERT ABBEY RETREAT HOUSE
1016 N. Broadway
De Pere, WI 54115

Tel. (414) 336–1321

ST. VINCENT PALLOTTI CENTER
Rt. 3, Box 47
Elkhorn, WI 53121
Tel. (414) 732–2108

The Rev. Joseph H. Zimmer, SAC, Dir. Capacity 40.

MARYNOOK—HOUSE OF THE LORD
500 S. 12th St.
Galesville, WI 54630

The Rev. Ralph Dyer, SM, Dir.

HOLY NAME RETREAT HOUSE
Box 337
Green Bay, WI 54305
Tel. (414) 435–4943

The Rev. Gary J. Crevier, Dir. Capacity 64. Located on Chambers Is. in Door County.

ST. AEMILIAN RETREAT CENTER
Friess Lake, 4905 Hwy. 167
Hubertus, WI 53033
Tel. (414) 628–2400

ST. BENEDICT CENTER
PO Box 5070
Madison, WI 53705
Tel. (608) 836–1631

Sister Mary David, OSB, Dir. Capacity 95.

ST. ANTHONY RETREAT CENTER
Marathon, WI 54448
Tel. (414) 443–2236

The Rev. Terrence Heiden, OFM, Dir. 103 rooms.

OUR LADY OF SPRING BANK RETREAT
HOUSE
34639 W. Fairview Rd.
Oconomowoc, WI 53066
Tel. (414) 567–7233

The Rev. Blaise Fuez, SO Cist., Dir. 18 rooms for
men or couples.

OUR MOTHER OF PERPETUAL HELP
RETREAT HOUSE
1800 N. Timber Trail Lane
Oconomowoc, WI 53066
Tel. (414) 567–6900

The Rev. Paul E. Schwarz, CSSR, Dir. Capacity 74.

JESUIT RETREAT HOUSE
4800 Fahrnwald Rd.
Oshkosh, WI 54901
Tel. (414) 231–9060

The Rev. Joseph T. Shinners, Dir. 45 rooms.

CAMPION HIGH SCHOOL
Prairie Duchien, WI 53821

The Rev. Benno Kornely, SJ, Dir. Capacity 164,
summer retreats.

SIENA CENTER
5635 Erie St.
Racine, WI 53402

Sister Agnes Claire Lanser, Coordinator. 40 rooms.

DOMINICAN EDUCATION CENTER
Sinsinawa, WI 53824
Tel. (608) 748–4411

SCHOENSTATT RETREAT CENTER
W. 284 N. 698 Cherry Lane
Waukesha, WI 53186
Tel. (414) 547–1885

Sister M. Ellen Hoemberg, Sup.

GEORGE WILLIAMS COLLEGE
LAKE GENEVA CAMPUS
YMCA CONFERENCE GROUNDS
CONTINUING EDUCATION CENTER
Williams Bay, WI 53191
Tel. (414) 245–5531

Mrs. Carolyn Burch, Director and Registrar.

CANADA

ALBERTA

MT. ST. FRANCIS RETREAT
Cochrane, Alta.
T0L 0W0 Canada

The Rev. Fred Williams, OFM, Dir. 42 rooms.

STAR OF THE NORTH RETREAT CENTER
Box 270
St. Albert, Alta.
T8N 1N3 Canada

The Rev. Gaston Montmigny, OMI, Dir. 55 rooms.

BRITISH COLUMBIA

INSTITUTE OF YOGA
RR 1
Enderby, BC
Canada

Summer retreats in classical astanga yoga and ashram life.

THE CENACLE
3689 Selkirk St.
Vancouver, BC
V6H 2Y9 Canada

Sister Virginia Gartland, Sup. Capacity 22.

MANITOBA

VILLA MARIA RETREAT HOUSE
PO Box 11
St. Norbert, Manitoba
Canada

Capacity 68.

NEW BRUNSWICK

VILLA MADONNA RETREAT HOUSE
Torryburn, King's County, NB
E2L 3V6 Canada

The Rev. L. G. Keleher, CSC, Dir. Capacity 54.

NOVA SCOTIA

ARUNACHALA ASHRAMA
BHAGAVAN SRI RAMANA MAHARSHI
CENTER
RR 1
Bridgetown, NS
B0S 1C0 Canada
Tel. (902) 665–2090

All are welcome 24 hours a day. A year of work at
the New York City center is required of all aspirants
wishing to live permanently at this residential ashram.
Stress is placed on hard work and the intense practice of Sri Bhagavan's teaching of Self-abidance. See
New York, NY listing for more information.

GARDINER CENTRE
Gardiner Mines, NS
Canada

The Rev. W. Regis Halloran, Dir. Capacity 50.

ONTARIO

VILLA FATIMA RETREAT HOUSE
83 St. Paul St.
Alexandria, Ont.
Canada

YOGA RETREAT
RR 2
Eganville, Ont.
Canada

Contact Franz and Helen Achatz. Capacity 16, $12
per day.

MT. CENACLE RETREAT HOUSE
88 Fennell Ave. W.
Hamilton, Ont.
L9C 1E7 Canada

Sister Mary, Dir. 44 rooms.

HOLY FAMILY RETREAT HOUSE
RR 1
Harrow, Ont.
Canada

The Rev. A. P. Jansen, Dir. 60 rooms.

MARYLAKE RETREAT HOUSE
Box 550
King City, Ont.
L0G 1K0 Canada
Tel. (416) 833–5368

The Rev. Isidor Geiss, Dir. Capacity 54.

QUEEN OF APOSTLES RENEWAL CENTRE
1617 Blythe Rd.
Mississauga, Ont.
L5H 2C3 Canada
Tel. (416) 278–5229

The Rev. M. J. Smith, OMI, Dir. 63 rooms.

MAISON NOTRE-DAME-DE-LA-PROVIDENCE
RR 1
Orleans, Ont.
K0A 2V0 Canada
Tel. (613) 824–1610

Sr. Françoise d'Alençon, SCO. Capacity 70, $10 per day.

LES FRANCISCAINES MISSIONNAIRES
DE MARIE
145 Presland Rd.
Ottawa, Ont.
K1K 2C1 Canada
Tel. (613) 749–0848

Contact Sister Anne-Marie Beaudoin. Capacity 48.

MADONNA HOUSE
101 Parent Ave.
Ottawa, Ont.
K1N 7B2 Canada
Tel. (613) 234–6930

Contact Arlene Becker. Capacity 4, no fee.

MANRESA RENEWAL CENTRE
Box 38, RR 2
Pickering, Ont.
Canada
Tel. (416) 839–2291

The Rev. James O'G. Fleming, SJ, Dir.

HOLY CROSS CENTRE
RR 1
Port Burwell, Ont.
N0J 1T0 Canada

The Rev. Stephen Dunn, CP, Dir. Capacity 18.

VILLA LOYOLA
RR 2, Site 35, Box 18
Sudbury, Ont.
Canada

The Rev. Leon Meunier, SJ, Dir. 45 rooms.

OUR LADY OF THE CENACLE
318 Lawrence Ave. E.
Toronto 12, Ont.
Tel. (416) 485–6539

Sister A. Mattle, Sup. Women only.

QUEBEC

SEMINAIRE DE ST-AUGUSTIN
Cap Rouge, Que.
G0A 1K0 Canada

INSTITUTE SECULIER, PIE X
1645 St-Chs Borromee
Charlesbourg, Que.
G1G 5C7 Canada

FITCH BAY FARM RETREAT CENTER
RR 3, Box 10
Fitch Bay, Que.
Canada
Tel. (819) 876–2526

Contact John or Tom Sargent for more information.

MAISON DES URSULINES
20 Rue des Ursulines
Loretteville, Que.
GZE ZV1 Canada

MAISON N.D. DU CENACLE
1073 St. Cyrille Ouest
Quebec, Que.
G1S 1VZ Canada

VILLA MANRESE
630 Chemin Ste-Foy
Quebec, Que.
Canada

LES PÈRES REDEMPTORISTES
10018 Ave. Royale
Ste-Anne de Beaupré (Montmorency) Que.
G0A 1C0 Canada

ABBAYE BENEDICTIN
St-Benoit-du-Lac, Cte Brome, Que.
J0B 2M0 Canada
Tel. (819) 843–4080

SOEURS DE LA PRESENTATION DE
MARIE MAISON RIVIER
999 Rue Conseil
Sherbrook, Que.
J1G 1M1 Canada

VILLA CHATEAUNEUF
C.P. 298
Sutton, Cte Brome, Que.
Canada
Tel. (514) 538–2203

SIVANANDA ASHRAM YOGA CAMP
8th Ave.
Val Morin, Que.
Canada
Tel. (819) 322–3226 or (514) 861–6002

Capacity 300. Meditation instruction available,
has skiing facilities. Directed by Swami Vishnu-
Devananda.

MAISON JESUS OUVRIER
475 Père Lelievre
Ville Vanier, Que.
Canada

SASKATCHEWAN

ST. MICHAEL'S RETREAT HOUSE
Box 220
Lumsden, Sask.
S0G 3C0 Canada

The Rev. Michael Conaghan, OFM, Dir. Capacity 55.

QUEEN'S HOUSE OF RETREATS
601 Taylor St. W.
Saskatoon, Sask.
57M 0C9 Canada

The Rev. N. M. Engel, OMI, Dir. 50 rooms.

SUGGESTED
READING

Buber, Martin. *Tales of the Hasidim—Early Masters*. New York: Schocken Books, 1947.

Byrom, Thomas, trans. *The Dhammapada*. New York: Alfred A. Knopf, 1976.

Cheng Man-Ch'ing, and Smith, Robert W. *T'ai-Chi*. Rutland, Vt.: Charles E. Tuttle Company, Inc., 1966.

Chogyam Trungpa. *The Myth of Freedom*. Berkeley, Calif.: Shambhala, 1976.

French, R. M., trans. *The Way of a Pilgrim*. New York: Seabury Press, 1970.

Goldstein, Joseph. *The Experience of Insight: A Natural Unfolding*. Santa Cruz, Calif.: Unity Press, 1976.

Goleman, Daniel. *Varieties of the Meditative Experience*. New York: E. P. Dutton, 1977.

Halevi, Z'ev Ben Shimon. *The Way of Kabbalah*. New York: Samuel Weiser, 1976.

Herrigel, Eugene. *Zen in the Art of Archery*. New York: Random House, 1974.

Kadloubovsky, E., and G. E. H. Palmer. *The Art of Prayer*. London: Faber & Faber, 1966.

Kapleau, Philip. *The Three Pillars of Zen.* Boston: Beacon Press, 1967.

Kempis, Thomas à. *The Imitation of Christ.* Garden City, N.Y.: Doubleday & Co., 1955.

Krishnamurti, J. *Commentaries on Living.* Third series. London: Victor Gollancz, 1962.

Lawrence, Brother. *Practice of the Presence of God.* Mount Vernon, N.Y. Peter Pauper Press, 1967.

Levine, Stephen. *A Gradual Awakening.* New York: Anchor-Doubleday, 1978.

Lysebeth, Andre von. *Yoga Self Taught.* New York: Harper & Row, 1968.

Mascaro, Juan, trans. *The Bhagavad Gita.* New York: Viking Penguin, Inc., 1962.

Merton, Thomas. *New Seeds of Contemplation.* New York: New Directions Publishing Corp., 1961.

Osborne, Arthur, ed. *The Teachings of Ramana Maharshi.* New York: Samuel Weiser, 1962.

Popenoe, Chris. *Books for Inner Development—The Yes! Guide.* Yes! Bookshop, Wash. D.C.: distributed by Random House, 1976. (*A comprehensive guide with detailed descriptions of books on meditation and related subjects.—eds.*)

Prabhavananda, Swami, and Christopher Isherwood, trans. *How to Know God: The Yoga Aphorisms of Patanjali.* New York: Signet, 1969.

Ram Dass. *Grist for the Mill.* Santa Cruz, Calif.: Unity Press, 1977.

Reps, Paul. *Zen Flesh, Zen Bones.* Garden City, N.Y.: Doubleday & Co., 1957.

Shah, Idries. *The Way of the Sufi.* New York: E. P. Dutton & Co., 1970.

Suzuki, Shunryu. *Zen Mind, Beginner's Mind*. New York: Weatherhill, 1970.

Tarthang Tulku. *Gesture of Balance*. Emeryville, Calif.: Dharma Pub., 1977.

Vivekananda, Swami. *Karma Yoga and Bhakti Yoga*. New York: Ramakrishna-Vivekananda Center, 1973.

Waley, Arthur, trans. *The Way and Its Power: A Study of the Tao Te Ching and Its Place in Chinese Thought*. New York: Random House, 1958.

Walker, K. *A Study of Gurdjieff's Teaching*. London: Jonathan Cape, 1969.

About the Author

RAM DASS, under his original name, Richard Alpert, first became widely known in the early sixties, when the public became aware of the experiments he and his colleague, Timothy Leary, were conducting with psychedelic drugs at Harvard University. Richard Alpert was born in Boston in 1931. He received his Ph.D. in psychology from Stanford University, then taught at Stanford, the University of California at Berkeley, and finally at Harvard until 1963. While at Harvard, he taught and researched in the fields of human motivation, Freudian theories of early social development, cognition, and clinical pathology, and served as a psychotherapist with the Harvard University Health Services. In 1961 he had his first personal experience with the effects of psychedelic drugs. The experience was a profound and unsettling one. Following it, he joined with Timothy Leary and others in a research program at Harvard concerning the altered states of consciousness created by psychedelic drugs such as LSD. In the course of many experiments, Alpert took over three hundred dosages of psychedelic drugs. Applying his training as a psychologist, as well as his experience of five years in psychoanalysis, he observed certain shifts in his own psychodynamics. He also became profoundly aware of the limitations of the drug-induced experience. In 1967 he went to India where he knew that there were spiritual traditions that dealt with occurrences which paralleled those he experienced with psychedelics. After months of searching, Alpert found his guru, Neem Karoli Baba ("Maharaj-ji"), a man who had realized in his own life the wisdom that Alpert had only glimpsed under psychedelics. Maharaj-ji named him Ram Dass and directed him to study Raja Yoga. After several months, Ram Dass returned to the United States, and through lectures and eventually the books *Be Here Now* and *Grist for the Mill,* he began sharing what he had learned. Since his first visit, Ram Dass has returned to India and the Far East from time to time to continue his studies. Now in *Journey of Awakening,* he has provided a complete guidebook to meditation, one that can be used by anyone, no matter what their experience or knowledge. Ram Dass is currently chairman of the Seva Foundation, a service organization that works in third world countries in a variety of health projects.

BANTAM NEW AGE BOOKS

Bantam New Age Books are for all those interested in reflec
ing on life today and life as it may be in the future. This im
portant new imprint features stimulating works in fields from
biology and psychology to philosophy and the new physics.

☐ 25881 **MAGICAL CHILD MATURES** Joseph C. Pearce $4.50

☐ 25388 **DON'T SHOOT THE DOG** Karen Pryor $3.9

☐ 27044 **CREATIVE VISUALIZATION** Shatki Gawain $4.50

☐ 26076 **MAGICAL CHILD** Joseph Chilton Pearce $4.5

☐ 27747 **ZEN/MOTORCYCLE MAINTENANCE** $5.50
     Robert Pirsig

☐ 25982 **THE WAY OF THE SHAMAN** Michael Hamer $4.5

☐ 27485 **TO HAVE OR TO BE** Fromm $4.9

☐ 27580 **LIVES OF A CELL** Lewis Thomas $4.50

Prices and availability subject to change without notice.

NEW AGE CLASSICS
ENDURING BOOKS FOR OUR TIME AND BEYOND

LWA

Special Offer
Buy a Bantam Book
for only 50¢.

Now you can have Bantam's catalog filled with hundreds of titles plus take advantage of our unique and exciting bonus book offer. A special offer which gives you the opportunity to purchase a Bantam book for only 50¢. Here's how!

By ordering any five books at the regular price per order, you can also choose any other single book listed (up to a $5.95 value) for just 50¢. Some restrictions do apply, but for further details why not send for Bantam's catalog of titles today!

Just send us your name and address and we will send you a catalog!